FIRESIDE

THE
MATHEMATICAL
MAGPIE

Being more stories, mainly transcendental,
plus subsets of essays, rhymes, music,
anecdotes, epigrams, and other prime oddments
and diversions, rational or irrational,
all derived from the infinite domain
of mathematics.

REVISED AND UPDATED

ASSEMBLED AND EDITED,
WITH A FOREWORD, INTRODUCTION,
AND COMMENTARIES, BY

CLIFTON FADIMAN

A FIRESIDE BOOK
Published by Simon and Schuster
NEW YORK

A Fireside Book
Published by Simon and Schuster

A Division of Gulf & Western Corporation
Simon & Schuster Building
Rockefeller Center
1230 Avenue of the Americas
New York, New York 10020

FIRESIDE and colophon are trademarks of Simon & Schuster

Manufactured in the United States of America

1 2 3 4 5 6 7 8 9 10 Pbk.

Library of Congress Cataloging in Publication Data
Main entry under title:

The mathematical magpie.

   (A Fireside book)
   1. Mathematics—Literary collections.   I. Fadiman,
Clifton, date.
PN6071.M3M3 1981   817'.52'080356   81–8773
ISBN 0–671–43807–7 Pbk.   AACR2

ACKNOWLEDGMENTS

For various suggestions without which this book would be far less diverting than I hope it is I am indebted to: N. T. Gridgeman; Barry Tannenbaum; Henry W. Simon; Mae Stover; Jeannette M. Pepper; and especially Martin Gardner. I thank Constance M. Winchell, Reference Librarian, Columbia University Libraries, for her kindness in hunting down the Ronald Knox π epigrams in Greek and Latin; Stephen Barr for permission to use his improvement on the Whewell rhyme; and particularly Anne Whitmore for her skillful and tireless research.

In memory of
EDWARD KASNER
(1878–1955)

Contents

❧

CONTENTS

III.   IRREGULAR FIGURES

IV.   SIMPLE HARMONIC MOTIONS

Contents

V. DIVIDENDS AND REMAINDERS

CONTENTS

No one can touch me

$-3mv) = -2mv$

$c^2) = \frac{2}{3}$

$V = (m+M)v$

$= \epsilon lH$

$\frac{1}{t}(c) = (2a) / (t)$

$= 2\lambda/d$

$\left(R/\!\!\!\!\!\nearrow + /mg\right) = 0$

^{2}

$= \epsilon SH$

$\theta_2 = 2\lambda/d$

$/d$

$f_c = 4\pi^2 m \dot{n}^2 r$

$= \left(\frac{mg}{EV_g}\right)(V_\epsilon - V_\epsilon)$

$pV = \frac{1}{3}mNc^2$

$\frac{mS^2}{r} = \epsilon SH$

$t = \sqrt{\frac{2h}{g}}$

$f = \frac{Q_1 \times Q_2}{r^2}$

$\epsilon - \epsilon' = \left(\frac{mg}{EV_g}\right)(V_\epsilon' - V_\epsilon)$

$T = 2\pi\sqrt{\frac{l}{g}}$

$f = G\frac{m_1 \times m_2}{r^2}$

$\frac{Vg}{V} = \frac{mg}{(E\epsilon - mg)}$

$\frac{1}{4}\lambda = \frac{1}{2} \times \frac{1}{2}\lambda$

$pV = \frac{1}{3}mNc^2$

$t = \sqrt{\frac{2h}{g}}$

$mv + (-3mv) = -2mv$

$\frac{mS^2}{r} = \epsilon SH$

$T = 2\pi\sqrt{\frac{l}{g}}$

$P = R\bar{V}$

$\frac{Vg}{V} = \frac{m}{(E_\epsilon}$

$= \frac{2}{3}\left(\frac{1}{2}mNc^2\right)$

$HP = V$

$W = max$

$S = \sqrt{\frac{T}{P^2}}$

$P = R\frac{T}{V}$

AD

Foreword

Habent sua fata libelli (*Books have their own destinies*) *is a familiar Ciceronian tag. Their fates may indeed be wayward. Profound tomes enshrining wisdom that might nourish posterity molder in attics, whereas thistledown volumes boasting few pretensions sometimes develop a surprising capacity for survival. Such has been the case with this odd bird,* The Mathematical Magpie, *no less than with its older sister,* Fantasia Mathematica, *still in demand after almost a quarter of a century.*

Though revised in a few minor details, this new edition of Magpie *is substantially the same as when it appeared twenty years ago. Claiming to be little more than an assemblage of mathematical fancies and entertainments, no long life could have been predicted for it. Certainly its editor anticipated none. As stated in the Introduction, he collected these oddities as a hobby rather than as a serious publishing venture.*

But the oddities found their audience, a surprisingly large and steady one. During the last twenty-five years or so I have kept up a pleasant correspondence with hundreds of readers, young and old, teachers and pupils. A few were mathematically sophisticated. But most were probably as mathematically unlearned as I am. Somehow, however, these two anthologies had started or stimulated their interest in mathematics. They wrote to tell me so and to ask for further guidance, which I supplied within the narrow limits of my capacity. Both Magpie *and* Fantasia *seem to have been useful in converting young people who had not been turned on by the subject as taught in many of our high schools.*

Teachers in many cases found it an effective tool, possibly like the sugar coating on a pill. Just as small children train themselves for "real" life through play, so some of us may approach the ostensibly forbidding country of mathematics through the gateway of fun and fancy.

Not, however, fun and games. Except perhaps for "The Miniver Problem," the volume contains no Recreational Mathematics, though I hope it will lead readers to that fascinating related realm. Recreational Mathematics is real mathematics, concerned with the puzzles, paradoxes, marvels, and queernesses involved in actual theorems and processes. It is a vast subject, with a long and honorable history stretching from the twelfth-century Rabbi ben Ezra to our own time. It has its own regular publications; it has thousands of addicted practitioners. With it are associated such names as C. L. Dodgson, better known as Lewis Carroll; the two Loyds, father and son, of whom the latter is said to have created at least 10,000 mathematical puzzles; Henry Dudeney; W.W. Rouse Ball; and in our own day the incomparable Martin Gardner, well-known to every reader of Scientific American.

Perhaps the most tantalizing subdivision of Recreational Mathematics deals with logical paradoxes and similar mind-bogglers. It may have begun with Epimenides in the sixth century BC, *when he advanced the proposition that "All Cretans are liars." The statement, merely as statement, seems acceptable until one ponders the fact that Epimenides was a Cretan. Of Epimenides' lineage is the magisterial Bertrand Russell with his famous barber paradox, the solution of which requires a razor even sharper than Occam's. There is only one barber in the village. He declares that he shaves everyone in the village who does not shave himself. Well and good. But who shaves the barber? (For a handy but not notably conclusive resolution of the paradox see your Britannica, 15th edition, vol. 13, p. 356).*

But this voluminous literature, however entertaining, deals with real *mathematics, requiring some work from the student.* Fantasia *and* Magpie *comprise a different though related genre. Call it Invitational Mathematics. The reader is merely asked to* look at some odd, shiny, sometimes ridiculous bits and pieces the Magpie has retrieved in the course of her housekeeping.

It would be soothing to imagine that some impressive reason lies back of the stubborn longevity of these two little anthologies. With the bardic rapture that decades ago marked his teaching, Cassius J. Keyser in his Pastures of Wonder assures us that "the validity of mathematical propositions is independent of the actual world." But I cannot claim that the serene timelessness of mathematics is responsible for the fact that our two collections do not seem to date much.

Their longevity may be due in part to their inclusion of a good many science-fiction stories, all rooted in mathematical theory and processes. The last twenty years have seen an explosive growth in science fiction, generated to some degree by a few silly but diverting films. From one point of view sci-fi is the playground of the sciences; and Invitational Mathematics exhibits the king of the sciences at play.

Perhaps other factors have been subtly present: mankind's thrust into space which rests less on heroes than on equations; the Einsteinian universe of which we are all inhabitants; the advent of the Computer Age; even the ubiquitous desk or pocket calculator, the most clearly useful by-product of the moon-shot. Most of us cannot contend with solid mathematics, but all of us have the uneasy feeling that it has suddenly become crucially important. It surrounds us, sustains us, influences us in a manner not felt (except among the intelligentsia of ancient Greece) by previous generations.

It is extraordinary that at this writing the "trade" (as against the "mass market") paperback best-seller list puts in seventh place Douglas Hofstadter's remarkable, delightful, and difficult Gödel, Escher, Bach. The sinuous relationships Professor Hofstadter traces binding the imaginations of a great mathematician, a great composer, and a stunning modern artist can interest readers (and they are in the hundreds of thousands) only if they have some feeling for and curiosity about the mysteries of space, form, numbers. In this connection it's interesting to observe how much attention is being given, by art critics and by mathematicians, to Escher's work, rich with unsettling visualized probes into perspective, optics, hyper-dimensionality, crystallography.

You may have already discovered Escher. But you may not have encountered another exquisite artist, Mitsumaso Anno. Try to get The Unique World of Mitsumaso Anno, with a good Foreword by Martin Gardner. Through a series of beautiful and astonishing drawings and paintings it introduces us to a world also touched in Magpie, a world of "anamorphic" art, crazy yet logical geometries, optical illusions, seeming contradictions of the laws of motion and perspective.

Since Pythagoras we have always known of the indissoluble connection between mathematics and music. But in our time, other links just as surprising have been explored. Scott Buchanan's Poetry and Mathematics, a work whose profundity is equaled only by its wit, is one example. More recently there has appeared a book with an unexpected title, Mathematics and Humor, by John Allen Paulos. Mathematics is tangential to many seemingly unrelated worlds—even that of the illegal and criminal, as in the numbers game.

These are all straws in the wind. It is a wind that has also borne up some mini-straws, of which The Mathematical Magpie is one. I hope that its stories, cartoons, humorous sketches, parodies, lyrics, anecdotes, verses, and playful speculations will help to seduce those who think they have nonmathematical minds into entering at least the anteroom of the crowded, astonishing, and almost magical hall of mathematics.

Clifton Fadiman
March, 1981

Introduction

In 1958, as a consequence of the rashness of the present pub-
lishers, there appeared an odd anthology which I called Fantasia
Mathematica. The introduction described it as a collection of
"stories and imaginative oddments, often trivial, about mathematics." Suggesting that they were intended to amuse or tease
rather than instruct, I expressed the hope that they might lead
readers like myself, unlearned but curious, to create better
images of a few mathematical ideas. I am not a mathematician,
not even a bad mathematician. But I am, if you will forgive the
notation, a mathematical magπ. For more than five years I had
been storing away these wisps of mathematical thistledown in
the untidy nest of my files, with hardly any expectation that
others might take pleasure in them.

But, to my surprise, and I believe also to the publisher's, the
little book, assembled entirely as a labor of love, attracted, not
a vast audience, of course, but at least an inappropriately large
one, when one considers the esoteric nature of the subject. Perhaps the fact that Fantasia Mathematica contained no real mathematics contributed to its modest success.

At any rate, I was sufficiently encouraged to spend another
four years or so in the compilation of the sequel which is now
in your hands. It is a rather more ambitious affair, somewhat
larger and more various, and containing material that may in
some cases be unfamiliar even to professionals. I have also
fleshed it, perhaps unwisely, with occasional commentary of my
own that will be of no interest whatsoever to real mathematicians

but may interest those who, like myself, are fascinated by the subject without really knowing much about it. I hope it is a better book than its predecessor, but its aim is identical or shall we say congruent: to give the reader, by showing him what imaginative writers, humorists, and journalists have done with the subject, a tantalizing sense of the wonder, the oddity, and the fantastical fun that pervade the most basic of the sciences.

There are only a few genuine mathematicians represented in these pages: Bertrand Russell, J. L. Synge, Lewis Carroll (though he was a third-rater), G. Polya, Augustus De Morgan, J. J. Sylvester; and there are several para-mathematicians outstanding in related exact sciences: Isaac Asimov, George Gamow, Simon Newcomb, William Whewell, Frederick Soddy. The others are short-story writers, humorists, essayists, novelists, poets, composers, lyric writers, aphorists, and even a Monsignor. Many are merely sound commercial writers, particularly the science-fictioneers, who have found that mathematics affords them an unusual opportunity for the deployment of their inventive talents.

The book has five divisions, but these need not, any more than the volume as a whole, be taken too seriously.

"A Set of Imaginaries" comprises ten science-fiction stories and showcases such pre-eminent practitioners as Isaac Asimov and Arthur C. Clarke. "Comic Sections," it is hoped, will bring an occasional smile to the lips of even real mathematicians. "Irregular Figures" is a bit hard to describe; its only unity lies in the circumstance that the central figure in each of the stories or fables is something of an oddball. (The oddest of the oddballs will be discovered in the extract from Samuel Beckett's maddening novel Molloy.) *"Simple Harmonic Motions" offers some musical selections that have a mathematical base. Music and mathematics are traditionally associated; here are three happy marriages. "Dividends and Remainders" is just what the phrase suggests, a collection of miscellanea on which I have tried to impose some small degree of form.*

Introduction

The illustrations, like all illustrations, speak for themselves. I would merely point out how neatly they indicate the recent intrusion of mathematics into our modern world. When popular cartoonists and caricaturists can find gold in a subject that subject may be said to have left the academy and become a part of the general consciousness.

Fantasia Mathematica was dedicated to a friend, the brilliant philosopher Scott Buchanan. It was he, with one other, who first made me aware of the drama, the imagery, indeed the poetry of mathematics; and in the Introduction to the book I tried to draw a freehand sketch of his personality. The Mathematical Magpie *is dedicated to the memory of the one other man who succeeded in conveying to my nonmathematical mind an idea of what mathematics was really about. This man is the topologist Edward Kasner, who died in 1955.*

I would like to tell you about him, because I think, being offbeat himself, he would have liked this offbeat anthology. But the only way in which I can tell you about him is to quote myself; and, as I cannot write about Dr. Kasner today any better than I did a few years ago, I hope you will not mind my reprinting a few paragraphs that have been published in a collection of essays called Any Number Can Play.

. . . But most of all, when I reflect upon eccentricity at its most charming, I think of a distinguished mathematician who died in 1955, Professor Edward Kasner.

I cannot render him for you, that I know. It is part of the nature of eccentricity to be unable to leave behind a complete record of itself. Anecdotes, reminiscences do not suffice. True eccentricity, not freakishness or mere oddity, but the capacity to see the whole world on a slant, is like a perfume. It is the permeating essence of a personality, and when that personality dies, the perfume disappears, and nothing can recapture it. Perhaps that is one of the secrets

Reprinted by permission of World Publishing Company from *Any Number Can Play* by Clifton Fadiman. Copyright © 1957 by Clifton Fadiman.

of Dickens' continued popularity—he supplies in imperishable form the eccentrics for which our souls thirst.

Edward Kasner (1878–1955) occupied until his death the Adrain chair in mathematics at Columbia University. His specialty was the higher geometry, particularly topology. Topology is a branch of mathematics which has nothing to do with measurement, size, shape, numbers, or quantities. It deals with position, with the characteristics of non-rigid figures and bodies, with those properties that do not change under distortion. It is concerned with the geometrical qualities of doughnuts, pretzels, one-sided surfaces, rubber bands, knots, bottles with neither inside nor outside, the trade-mark of Ballantine's Ale, and the answer to the problem of how many colors are needed to color any *map so as to distinguish the countries that have a common boundary. In* The World of Mathematics *Dr. Newman describes this queer subject as starting from "the sound premise that there are no rigid objects, that everything in the world is a little askew, and is further deformed when its position is altered." Everything in the world is a little askew . . . topology was precisely the subject to engage a mind like Dr. Kasner's.*

Like Thoreau, of whom he was a spiritual descendant, Dr. Kasner had early in his life drawn a line between what was essential and what was not. Unlike Thoreau, he did not make a doctrine of it. He made no noise in a world that he regarded with a benevolent but quizzical glance, as if the rest of us were somehow missing something. He achieved a transient fame, I seem to recollect, as one of "the twelve men who understood Einstein."

He was a small man, with a gentle voice, but deceptively so, for hidden within it lay an overtone of tolerant irony. I never knew him to wear anything but a pepper-and-salt suit, winter and summer, and I do not believe he owned more than one. He had long ago discarded the belt as an unnecessary modern invention and spent a good deal of his time holding up his trousers. At his lectures the students were often torn between conic sections and equally abstruse mathematical calculations as to whether or not Dr. Kasner's pants would fall down before the lecture period's elapsed time. His lectures were thoroughly unconventional and he was one of the greatest teachers I have ever known.

Frequently he would wander into the classroom and put a few problems on the board. Then he would wander out and perhaps appear a half-hour later, glance at what the students at the board had been doing, and disappear. After all, he figured, it was the students, not he, who were concerned with the solution of the problem. He never hesitated to interrupt his more formal lectures by suddenly asking questions of the students. I have seen him do this (a difficult technique) with a class of ten and an audience of three thousand.

During the fall and winter he liked to live at the Half Moon Hotel in Coney Island, partly because in that season no one else would think of doing such a thing, and so he secured both privacy and special rates, and partly because the sight of such quantities of sand set his mind working on problems of large numbers. He used to view trees in foliage with the same speculative glance. If you care to note this down, the number of grains of sand on the beach at Coney Island is 10^{20}, give or take a few grains.

Dr. Kasner had two main audiences: the great mathematicians of two continents and children. I think he slightly preferred the children because they were more teachable. It was his theory that the way to interest children in mathematics was to begin with difficult concepts and gradually work up to the multiplication table. It was a sound theory. His own nine-year-old nephew was so apt a student of higher mathematics that he invented a number. Asked to think up a name for an enormously large but still finite number, he suggested googol. As the spelling suggests, this has many zeros in it—to be exact it is the number 1 followed by a hundred zeros. *The young genius went on to invent a still larger number, the* googolplex, *which is 1 followed by a googol of zeroes. Kindergarteners took kindly to Dr. Kasner and his googols and soon satisfied themselves that all the raindrops descending on New York in a century would fall far short of a googol.*

Dr. Kasner had another way of teaching large numbers to small tots. He would ask them to guess the length of the eastern coast line of the United States. After a "sensible" guess had been made—say 2,000 miles—he would proceed step by step to point out that this figure increased enormously if you measured the perimeter of each bay and inlet, then that of every projection and curve of each of these, then the distance separating every small particle of coast-line matter, each molecule, atom, etc. Obviously the coast line is as long as you want to make it. The children understood this at once; Kasner had more trouble with grownups.

He was fond of solitary walks, particularly along the Palisades, and, in anticipation of his needs, had a series of lunch boxes, filled with teapots and almost imperishable foods, cached in secret places along the route. He carried his own tea and sugar. This foresighted system saved him time and trouble and allowed him more opportunity for reflection.

Another goal of his Palisades walks was a certain worldly casino where games of chance were popular. He used to go there, not to gamble, but to study the laws of probability in action. He must have looked odd surrounded by the sharp, tough faces of the players, like Charlie Chaplin in a den of gentlemen thieves.

The Kasnerian humor is difficult to describe. Impish? Childlike? Neither word fits. He was fond of taking his summer vacations in Brussels because there was a particular chair at a particular outdoor café that he had become attached to. He also liked Brussels because he said that from there he could easily organize a mountain-climbing expedition to the highest point in Belgium. He said he felt great satisfaction in attaining the peak of this eminence. I asked him how high it was. "Twelve feet above sea level," he replied.

Our encounters frequently had as their setting a midtown Automat. I frequented this Automat because I was poor, Kasner because, as he stoutly maintained, it had the best food in New York. I never quite perceived the force of this argument. It was not a product of ignorance either, because every once in a while, dressed in his drooping, pepper-and-salt suit and a cap (he never wore anything but a boy's cap that gave him the look of an elderly urchin), he would visit a first-class restaurant, solely for the purpose of reassuring himself that the Automat was superior.

Once, at an informal evening attended by half a dozen logicians and mathematicians, one of the latter ventured the opinion that to become a good mathematician you should not *have good teachers, as they prevented you from learning by yourself. He then added, courteously, "I was lucky. I had only one great teacher—Dr. Kasner here." Kasner looked up; his eyes twinkled; he said mildly, "I had none."*

Well, I had one great one. Edward Kasner could not make a mathematician out of me. But, for whatever it is worth, he is partly responsible for this book, which I dedicate to his memory.

CLIFTON FADIMAN
August 1961

I

A SET
OF
IMAGINARIES

✱ ✱ ✱

"Does 63592187653.4215400532 look right to you?"

The Feeling of Power

ISAAC ASIMOV

Uneasy describes our feeling for the computer and the mathematics of which it is merely the expression in hardware. We admire its feats; we recognize its indispensability—and somehow we don't like it. It will never command affection, as the railway train commands the affection of civilized men and the airplane that of the less civilized. The cartoon, always a precise index of resentment, goes to work gladly on the computer, as these pages demonstrate. Mr. Asimov's story is, I think, the perfect expression of this resentment. "In theory there is nothing the computer can do that the human mind cannot do." Upon this deliciously absurd proposition Mr. Asimov builds a story that Molière would have enjoyed—and that all of us enjoy, for somehow it enables us to take a revenge, the revenge of the human upon the machine which, we are told, is our friend—but, we ask ourselves, is it really?

Mr. Asimov ranks as one of the most copious and talented science-fiction writers of our time, as well as a distinguished scientist, teacher, and popularizer of science.

JEHAN SHUMAN was used to dealing with the men in authority on long-embattled earth. He was only a civilian but he originated programing patterns that resulted in self-directing war computers of the highest sort. Generals consequently listened to him. Heads of congressional committees too.

There was one of each in the special lounge of New Pentagon. General Weider was space-burned and had a small mouth puckered almost into a cipher. Congressman Brant was smooth-cheeked and clear-eyed. He smoked Denebian tobacco with the air of one whose patriotism was so notorious, he could be allowed such liberties.

Shuman, tall, distinguished, and Programmer-first-class, faced them fearlessly.

He said, "This, gentlemen, is Myron Aub."

"The one with the unusual gift that you discovered quite by accident," said Congressman Brant placidly. "Ah." He inspected the little man with the egg-bald head with amiable curiosity.

The little man, in return, twisted the fingers of his hands anxiously. He had never been near such great men before. He was only an aging low-grade technician who had long ago failed all tests designed to smoke out the gifted ones among mankind and had settled into the rut of unskilled labor. There was just this hobby of his that the great Programmer had found out about and was now making such a frightening fuss over.

General Weider said, "I find this atmosphere of mystery childish."

"You won't in a moment," said Shuman. "This is not something we can leak to the firstcomer. Aub!" There was something imperative about his manner of biting off that one-syllable name, but then he was a great Programmer speaking to a mere technician. "Aub! How much is nine times seven?"

Aub hesitated a moment. His pale eyes glimmered with a feeble anxiety. "Sixty-three," he said.

Congressman Brant lifted his eyebrows. "Is that right?"

"Check it for yourself, Congressman."

The congressman took out his pocket computer, nudged the milled edges twice, looked at its face as it lay there in the palm of his hand, and put it back. He said, "Is this the gift you brought us here to demonstrate. An illusionist?"

"More than that, sir. Aub has memorized a few operations and with them he computes on paper."

"A paper computer?" said the general. He looked pained.

"No, sir," said Shuman patiently. "Not a paper computer. Simply a sheet of paper. General, would you be so kind as to suggest a number?"

"Seventeen," said the general.

"And you, Congressman?"

"Twenty-three."

"Good! Aub, multiply those numbers, and please show the gentlemen your manner of doing it."

"Yes, Programmer," said Aub, ducking his head. He fished a small pad out of one shirt pocket and an artist's hairline stylus out of the other. His forehead corrugated as he made painstaking marks on the paper.

General Weider interrupted him sharply. "Let's see that."

Aub passed him the paper, and Weider said, "Well, it looks like the figure seventeen."

Congressman Brant nodded and said, "So it does, but I suppose anyone can copy figures off a computer. I think I could make a passable seventeen myself, even without practice."

"If you will let Aub continue, gentlemen," said Shuman without heat.

Aub continued, his hand trembling a little. Finally he said in a low voice, "The answer is three hundred and ninety-one."

Congressman Brant took out his computer a second time and flicked it. "By Godfrey, so it is. How did he guess?"

"No guess, Congressman," said Shuman. "He computed that result. He did it on this sheet of paper."

"Humbug," said the general impatiently. "A computer is one thing and marks on paper are another."

"Explain, Aub," said Shuman.

"Yes, Programmer. Well, gentlemen, I write down seventeen, and just underneath it I write twenty-three. Next I say to myself: seven times three—"

The congressman interrupted smoothly, "Now, Aub, the problem is seventeen times twenty-three."

"Yes, I know," said the little technician earnestly, "but I

5

start by saying seven times three because that's the way it works. Now seven times three is twenty-one."

"And how do you know that?" asked the congressman.

"I just remember it. It's always twenty-one on the computer. I've checked it any number of times."

"That doesn't mean it always will be, though, does it?" said the congressman.

"Maybe not," stammered Aub. "I'm not a mathematician. But I always get the right answers, you see."

"Go on."

"Seven times three is twenty-one, so I write down twenty-one. Then one times three is three, so I write down a three under the two of twenty-one."

"Why under the two?" asked Congressman Brant at once.

"Because—" Aub looked helplessly at his superior for support. "It's difficult to explain."

Shuman said, "If you will accept his work for the moment, we can leave the details for the mathematicians."

Brant subsided.

Aub said, "Three plus two makes five, you see, so the twenty-one becomes a fifty-one. Now you let that go for a while and start fresh. You multiply seven and two, that's fourteen, and one and two, that's two. Put them down like this and it adds up to thirty-four. Now if you put the thirty-four under the fifty-one this way and add them, you get three hundred and ninety-one, and that's the answer."

There was an instant's silence and then General Weider said, "I don't believe it. He goes through this rigmarole and makes up numbers and multiplies and adds them this way and that, but I don't believe it. It's too complicated to be anything but horn-swoggling."

"Oh no, sir," said Aub in a sweat. "It only *seems* complicated because you're not used to it. Actually the rules are quite simple and will work for any numbers."

"Any numbers, eh?" said the general. "Come, then." He took out his own computer (a severely styled GI model) and struck it at random. "Make a five seven three eight on the paper. That's five thousand seven hundred and thirty-eight."

"Yes, sir," said Aub, taking a new sheet of paper.

"Now"—more punching of his computer—"seven two three nine. Seven thousand two hundred and thirty-nine."

"Yes, sir."

"And now multiply those two."

"It will take some time," quavered Aub.

"Take the time," said the general.

"Go ahead, Aub," said Shuman crisply.

Aub set to work, bending low. He took another sheet of paper and another. The general took out his watch finally and stared at it. "Are you through with your magic-making, Technician?"

"I'm almost done, sir. Here it is, sir. Forty-one million, five hundred and thirty-seven thousand, three hundred and eighty-two." He showed the scrawled figures of the result.

General Weider smiled bitterly. He pushed the multiplication contact on his computer and let the numbers whirl to a halt. And then he stared and said in a surprised squeak, "Great Galaxy, the fella's right."

The President of the Terrestrial Federation had grown haggard in office and, in private, he allowed a look of settled melancholy to appear on his sensitive features. The Denebian War, after its early start of vast movement and great popularity, had trickled down into a sordid matter of maneuver and counter-maneuver, with discontent rising steadily on earth. Possibly, it was rising on Deneb too.

And now Congressman Brant, head of the important Committee on Military Appropriations, was cheerfully and smoothly spending his half-hour appointment spouting nonsense.

"Computing without a computer," said the president impatiently, "is a contradiction in terms."

"Computing," said the congressman, "is only a system for handling data. A machine might do it, or the human brain might. Let me give you an example." And, using the new skills he had

7

learned, he worked out sums and products until the president, despite himself, grew interested.

"Does this always work?"

"Every time, Mr. President. It is foolproof."

"Is it hard to learn?"

"It took me a week to get the real hang of it. I think you would do better."

"Well," said the president, considering, "it's an interesting parlor game, but what is the use of it?"

"What is the use of a newborn baby, Mr. President? At the moment there is no use, but don't you see that this points the way toward liberation from the machine. Consider, Mr. President"— the congressman rose and his deep voice automatically took on some of the cadences he used in public debate—"that the Denebian War is a war of computer against computer. Their computers forge an impenetrable shield of countermissiles against our missiles, and ours forge one against theirs. If we advance the efficiency of our computers, so do they theirs, and for five years a precarious and profitless balance has existed.

"Now we have in our hands a method for going beyond the computed, leapfrogging it, passing through it. We will combine the mechanics of computation with human thought; we will have the equivalent of intelligent computers, billions of them. I can't predict what the consequences will be in detail, but they will be incalculable. And if Deneb beats us to the punch, they may be unimaginably catastrophic."

The president said, troubled, "What would you have me do?"

"Put the power of the administration behind the establishment of a secret project on human computation. Call it Project Number, if you like. I can vouch for my committee, but I will need the administration behind me."

"But how far can human computation go?"

"There is no limit. According to Programmer Shuman, who first introduced me to this discovery—"

"I've heard of Shuman, of course."

"Yes. Well, Dr. Shuman tells me that in theory there is nothing the computer can do that the human mind cannot do. The computer merely takes a finite amount of data and performs a finite number of operations upon them. The human mind can duplicate the process."

The president considered that. He said, "If Shuman says this, I am inclined to believe him—in theory. But, in practice, how can anyone know how a computer works?"

Brant laughed genially. "Well, Mr. President, I asked the same question. It seems that at one time computers were designed directly by human beings. Those were simple computers, of course, this being before the time of the rational use of computers to design more advanced computers had been established."

"Yes, yes. Go on."

"Technician Aub apparently had, as his hobby, the reconstruction of some of these ancient devices, and in so doing he studied the details of their workings and found he could imitate them. The multiplication I just performed for you is an imitation of the workings of a computer."

"Amazing!"

The congressman coughed gently. "If I may make another point, Mr. President—the further we can develop this thing, the more we can divert our federal effort from computer production and computer maintenance. As the human brain takes over, more of our energy can be directed into peacetime pursuits and the impingement of war on the ordinary man will be less. This will be most advantageous for the party in power, of course."

"Ah," said the president, "I see your point. Well, sit down, Congressman, sit down. I want some time to think about this. But meanwhile, show me that multiplication trick again. Let's see if I can't catch the point of it."

Programmer Shuman did not try to hurry matters. Loesser was conservative, very conservative, and liked to deal with computers as his father and grandfather had. Still, he controlled the West European computer combine, and if he could be persuaded to join Project Number in full enthusiasm, a great deal would be accomplished.

But Loesser was holding back. He said, "I'm not sure I like the idea of relaxing our hold on computers. The human mind is a capricious thing. The computer will give the same answer to the same problem each time. What guarantee have we that the human mind will do the same?"

"The human mind, Computer Loesser, only manipulates facts. It doesn't matter whether the human mind or a machine does it. They are just tools."

"Yes, yes. I've gone over your ingenious demonstration that the mind can duplicate the computer, but it seems to me a little in the air. I'll grant the theory, but what reason have we for thinking that theory can be converted to practice?"

"I think we have reason, sir. After all, computers have not always existed. The cave men with their triremes, stone axes, and railroads had no computers."

"And possibly they did not compute."

"You know better than that. Even the building of a railroad or a ziggurat called for some computing, and that must have been without computers as we know them."

"Do you suggest they computed in the fashion you demonstrate?"

"Probably not. After all, this method—we call it 'graphitics,' by the way, from the old European word 'grapho,' meaning 'to write'—is developed from the computers themselves, so it cannot have antedated them. Still, the cave men must have had *some* method, eh?"

"Lost arts! If you're going to talk about lost arts—"

"No, no. I'm not a lost art enthusiast, though I don't say there may not be some. After all, man was eating grain before hydroponics, and if the primitives ate grain, they must have grown it in soil. What else could they have done?"

"I don't know, but I'll believe in soil growing when I see someone grow grain in soil. And I'll believe in making fire by rubbing two pieces of flint together when I see that too."

Shuman grew placative. "Well, let's stick to graphitics. It's just part of the process of etherealization. Transportation by means of bulky contrivances is giving way to direct mass transference. Communications devices become less massive and more efficient constantly. For that matter, compare your pocket computer with the massive jobs of a thousand years ago. Why not, then, the last step of doing away with computers altogether? Come, sir, Project Number is a going concern; progress is already headlong. But we want your help. If patriotism doesn't move you, consider the intellectual adventure involved."

Loesser said skeptically, "What progress? What can you do beyond multiplication? Can you integrate a transcendental function?"

"In time, sir. In time. In the last month I have learned to handle division. I can determine, and correctly, integral quotients and decimal quotients."

"Decimal quotients? To how many places?"

Programmer Shuman tried to keep his tone casual. "Any number!"

Loesser's lower jaw dropped. "Without a computer?"

"Set me a problem."

"Divide twenty-seven by thirteen. Take it to six places."

Five minutes later Shuman said, "Two point oh seven six nine two three."

Loesser checked it. "Well, now, that's amazing. Multiplication didn't impress me too much because it involved integers, after all, and I thought trick manipulation might do it. But decimals—"

"And that is not all. There is a new development that is, so far, top secret and which, strictly speaking, I ought not to mention. Still—we may have made a break-through on the square root front."

"Square roots?"

"It involves some tricky points and we haven't licked the bugs yet, but Technician Aub, the man who invented the science and who has an amazing intuition in connection with it, maintains he

11

has the problem almost solved. And he is only a technician. A man like yourself, a trained and talented mathematician, ought to have no difficulty."

"Square roots," muttered Loesser, attracted.

"Cube roots, too. Are you with us?"

Loesser's hand thrust out suddenly. "Count me in."

General Weider stumped his way back and forth at the head of the room and addressed his listeners after the fashion of a savage teacher facing a group of recalcitrant students. It made no difference to the general that they were the civilian scientists heading Project Number. The general was the over-all head, and he so considered himself at every waking moment.

He said, "Now square roots are all fine. I can't do them myself and I don't understand the methods, but they're fine. Still, the project will not be sidetracked into what some of you call the fundamentals. You can play with graphitics any way you want to after the war is over, but right now we have specific and very practical problems to solve."

In a far corner Technician Aub listened with painful attention. He was no longer a technician, of course, having been relieved of his duties and assigned to the project, with a fine-sounding title and good pay. But, of course, the social distinction remained, and the highly placed scientific leaders could never bring themselves to admit him to their ranks on a footing of equality. Nor, to do Aub justice, did he, himself, wish it. He was as uncomfortable with them as they with him.

The general was saying, "Our goal is a simple one, gentlemen—the replacement of the computer. A ship that can navigate space without a computer on board can be constructed in one fifth the time and at one tenth the expense of a computer-laden ship. We could build fleets five times, ten times, as great as Deneb could if we could but eliminate the computer.

"And I see something even beyond this. It may be fantastic now, a mere dream, but in the future I see the manned missile!"

There was an instant murmur from the audience.

The general drove on. "At the present time our chief bottle-neck is the fact that missiles are limited in intelligence. The computer controlling them can only be so large, and for that reason they can meet the changing nature of anti-missile defenses in an unsatisfactory way. Few missiles, if any, accomplish their goal, and missile warfare is coming to a dead end, for the enemy, fortunately, as well as for ourselves.

"On the other hand, a missile with a man or two within, controlling flight by graphitics, would be lighter, more mobile, more intelligent. It would give us a lead that might well mean the margin of victory. Besides which, gentlemen, the exigencies of war compel us to remember one thing. A man is much more dispensable than a computer. Manned missiles could be launched in numbers and under circumstances that no good general would care to undertake as far as computer-directed missiles are concerned . . ."

He said much more, but Technician Aub did not wait.

Technician Aub, in the privacy of his quarters, labored long over the note he was leaving behind. It read finally as follows:

"When I began the study of what is now called graphitics, it was no more than a hobby. I saw no more in it than an interesting amusement, an exercise of mind.

"When Project Number began, I thought that others were wiser than I, that graphitics might be put to practical use as a benefit to mankind, to aid in the production of really practical mass-transference devices perhaps. But now I see it is to be used only for death and destruction.

"I cannot face the responsibility involved in having invented graphitics."

He then deliberately turned the focus of a protein depolarizer on himself and fell instantly and painlessly dead.

They stood over the grave of the little technician while tribute was paid to the greatness of his discovery.

Programmer Shuman bowed his head along with the rest of

them but remained unmoved. The technician had done his share and was no longer needed, after all. He might have started graphitics, but now that it had started, it would carry on by itself overwhelmingly, triumphantly, until manned missiles were possible with who knew what else.

Nine times seven, thought Shuman with deep satisfaction, is sixty-three, and I don't need a computer to tell me so. The computer is in my own head.

And it was amazing the feeling of power that gave him.

The Law

ROBERT M. COATES

Mr. Coates was a good novelist of the eerie, a respected art critic, and a short-story writer of considerable originality. He worked with notable success in the territory formed by the blending of science-fiction, fantasy, and satire. The Law is a perfect example of his neat talent. What might happen, he asks, if the Law of Averages decided to go out of business? The answer is calculated to send actuaries into gibbering fits.

THE FIRST INTIMATION that things were getting out of hand came one early-fall evening in the late nineteen forties. What happened, simply, was that between seven and nine o'clock on that evening the Triborough Bridge had the heaviest concentration of outbound traffic in its entire history.

This was odd, for it was a weekday evening (to be precise, a Wednesday), and though the weather was agreeably mild and clear, with a moon that was close enough to being full to lure a certain number of motorists out of the city, these facts alone were not enough to explain the phenomenon. No other bridge or main highway was affected, and though the two preceding nights had been equally balmy and moonlit, on both of these the bridge traffic had run close to normal.

The bridge personnel, at any rate, was caught entirely unprepared. A main artery of traffic, like the Triborough, operates under fairly predictable conditions. Motor travel, like most other large-scale human activities, obeys the Law of Averages—that great, ancient rule that states that the actions of people in the mass will always follow consistent patterns—and on the basis of past experience it had always been possible to foretell, almost to the last digit, the number of cars that would cross the bridge at any given hour of the day or night. In this case, though, all rules were broken.

The hours from seven till nearly midnight are normally quiet ones on the bridge. But on that night it was as if all the motorists in the city, or at any rate, a staggering proportion of them, had conspired together to upset tradition. Beginning almost exactly at seven o'clock, cars poured onto the bridge in such numbers and with such rapidity that the staff at the toll booths was overwhelmed almost from the start. It was soon apparent that this was no momentary congestion, and as it became more and more obvious that the traffic jam promised to be one of truly monumental proportions, added details of police were rushed to the scene to help handle it.

Cars streamed in from all directions—from the Bronx approach and the Manhattan one, from 125th Street and the East River Drive. (At the peak of the crush, about eight-fifteen, observers on the bridge reported that the drive was a solid line of car headlights as far south as the bend at Eighty-ninth Street, while the congestion crosstown in Manhattan disrupted traffic as far west as Amsterdam Avenue.) And perhaps the most confusing thing about the whole manifestation was that there seemed to be no reason for it.

Now and then, as the harried toll-booth attendants made change for the seemingly endless stream of cars, they would question the occupants, and it soon became clear that the very participants in the monstrous tie-up were as ignorant of its cause as anyone else was. A report made by Sergeant Alfonse O'Toole, who commanded the detail in charge of the Bronx approach, is typical. "I kept askin' them," he said, " 'Is there night football somewhere that we don't know about? Is it the races you're goin' to?' But the funny thing was half the time they'd be askin' *me*. 'What's the crowd for, Mac?' they would say. And I'd just look at them. There was one guy I mind, in a Ford convertible with a girl in the seat beside him, and when he asked me, I said to him, 'Hell, you're *in* the crowd, ain't you?' I said. 'What brings *you* here?' And the dummy just looked at me. 'Me?' he says. 'I just come out for a drive in the moonlight. But if I'd known there'd be a crowd like this . . .' he says. And then he asks me, 'Is there any place I can turn around and get out of this?' " As the *Herald Tribune* summed things up in its story next morning, it "just looked as if everybody in Manhattan who owned a motor-car had decided to drive out on Long Island that evening."

The incident was unusual enough to make all the front pages next morning, and because of this many similar events, which might otherwise have gone unnoticed, received attention. The proprietor of the Aramis Theater, on Eighth Avenue, reported that on several nights in the recent past his auditorium had been practically empty, while on others it had been jammed to suffocation. Lunchroom owners noted that increasingly their patrons were developing a habit of making runs on specific items; one day it would be the roast shoulder of veal with pan gravy that was ordered almost exclusively, while the next everyone would be taking the Vienna loaf and the roast veal went begging. A man who ran a small notions store in Bayside revealed that over a period of four days two hundred and seventy-four successive customers had entered his shop and asked for a spool of pink thread.

These were news items that would ordinarily have gone into the papers as fillers or in the sections reserved for oddities. Now, however, they seemed to have a more serious significance. It was apparent at last that something decidedly strange was happening to people's habits, and it was as unsettling as those occasional moments on excursion boats when the passengers are moved, all at once, to rush to one side or the other of the vessel. It was not till one day in December when, almost incredibly, the Twentieth Century Limited left New York for Chicago with just three passengers aboard that business leaders discovered how disastrous the new trend could be too.

Until then the New York Central, for instance, could operate confidently on the assumption that, although there might be several thousand men in New York who had business relations in Chicago, on any single day no more—and no less—than some hundreds of them would have occasion to go there. The play producer could be sure that his patronage would sort itself out and that roughly as many persons would want to see the performance on Thursday as there had been on Tuesday or Wednesday. Now they couldn't be sure of anything. The Law of Averages had gone by the board, and if the effect on business promised to be catastrophic, it was also singularly unnerving for the general customer.

The lady starting downtown for a day of shopping, for example, could never be sure whether she would find Macy's department store a seething mob of other shoppers or a wilderness of empty, echoing aisles and unoccupied salesgirls. And the uncertainty produced a strange sort of jitteriness in the individual when faced with any impulse to action. "Shall we do it or shan't we?" people kept asking themselves, knowing that if they did do it, it might turn out that thousands of other individuals had decided similarly, knowing, too, that if they *didn't*, they might miss the one glorious chance of all chances to have Jones Beach, say, practically to themselves. Business languished, and a sort of desperate uncertainty rode everyone.

At this juncture it was inevitable that Congress should be called on for action. In fact, Congress called on itself, and it must be said that it rose nobly to the occasion. A committee was appointed, drawn from both houses and headed by Senator J. Wing Slooper (R.), of Indiana, and though after considerable investigation the committee was forced reluctantly to conclude that there was no evidence of Communist instigation, the unconscious subversiveness of the people's present conduct was obvious at a glance. The problem was what to do about it. You can't indict a whole nation, particularly on such vague grounds as these were. But, as Senator Slooper boldly pointed out, "You can control it," and in the end a system of re-education and reform was decided upon, designed to lead people back to—again we quote Senator Slooper—"the basic regularities, the homely averageness of the American way of life."

In the course of the committee's investigations it had been discovered, to everyone's dismay, that the Law of Averages had never been incorporated into the body of federal jurisprudence, and though the upholders of States' Rights rebelled violently, the oversight was at once corrected, both by Constitutional amendment and by a law—the Hills-Slooper Act—implementing it. According to the act, people were *required* to be average, and, as the simplest way of assuring it, they were divided alphabetically and their permissible activities catalogued accordingly. Thus, by the plan, a person whose name began with "G," "N," or "U," for example, could attend the theater only on Tuesdays, and he could go to baseball games only on Thursdays, whereas his visits to a haberdashery were confined to the hours between ten o'clock and noon on Mondays.

The law, of course, had its disadvantages. It had a crippling effect on theater parties, among other social functions, and the cost of enforcing it was unbelievably heavy. In the end, too, so many amendments had to be added to it—such as the one permitting gentlemen to take their fiancées (if accredited) along with them to various events and functions no matter what letter the said fiancées' names began with—that the courts were frequently at a loss to interpret it when confronted with violations.

In its way, though, the law did serve its purpose, for it did induce—rather mechanically, it is true, but still adequately—a return to that average existence that Senator Slooper desired. All, indeed, would have been well if a year or so later disquieting reports had not begun to seep in from the backwoods. It seemed that there, in what had hitherto been considered to be marginal areas, a strange wave of prosperity was making itself felt. Tennessee mountaineers were buying Packard convertibles, and Sears, Roebuck reported that in the Ozarks their sales of luxury items had gone up 900 per cent. In the scrub sections of Vermont men who formerly had barely been able to scratch a living from their rock-strewn acres were now sending their daughters to Europe and ordering expensive cigars from New York. It appeared that the Law of Diminishing Returns was going haywire too.

The Appendix and the Spectacles

MILES J. BREUER, M.D.

In Fantasia Mathematica *I rescued from the past Edward Page Mitchell's curious story* The Tachypomp, *first published in 1873. I have searched vainly for another curio to match it. The best, or oldest, story I could come up with was this one, by a real M.D. who is far from being a real writer, but who nonetheless does his old-fashioned best to work an acceptable variation on the well-worn gambit of the fourth dimension. It goes all the way back to 1928, a date which to science-fiction addicts seems almost prehistoric.*

OLD CLADGETT, President of the First National Bank of College-burg, scowled across the mahogany table at the miserable young man. He was all hunched up into great rolls and hanging pouches, and he scowled till the room grew gloomy and the ceiling seemed to lower.

"I'm running a bank, not a charity club," he growled, planting his fist on the table.

Bookstrom winced and then controlled himself with a little shiver.

"But, sir," he protested, "all I ask for is an extension of time on this note. I could easily pay it out in three or four years. If you force me to pay it now, I shall have to give up my medical course."

Reprinted by permission of Julia E. Breuer.

Harsh, inchoate, guttural noises issued from Cladgett's throat.

"This bank isn't looking after little boys and their dreams," he snarled. "This note is due and you pay it. You're able-bodied and can work."

Mechanically, as in a daze, Bookstrom took out a wallet and counted out the money. When the sum was complete, he had ten dollars left. The hope that had spurred him on through several years of hardship and difficulty, the hope of graduating as a physician and having a practice of his own, now was gone. He was at the end of his resources. Once the medical course was interrupted, he knew there was no hope of getting back to it. Nowadays the study of medicine is too strenuous; there is no dallying on the path to an M.D. degree.

He went straight over to the university to apply for an instructorship in Applied Mathematics that had recently been offered to him.

In the movies and in the novels an ogre like Cladgett usually meets with some kind of retribution before long. The Black Hand gets him or a wronged debtor poisons him, or a brick house collapses on his head. But Cladgett lived along in Collegeburg, growing more and more prosperous. He was bound to grow wealthy, because he took all he could get from everybody and never gave anybody anything. He kept growing a little grayer and a little fatter and seemed to derive more and more pleasure and happiness from preying financially on his fellow beings. And he seemed as safe as the Rock of Gibraltar.

Then, after fifteen years, a sudden attack of acute appendicitis got him. That morning he had sat at his desk and dictated letters to his directors, commanding them to be present at a meeting four days hence without fail. The bank was taking over a big estate as trustee, and unless each director signed the contract personally, the deal was lost and with it a fat fee. In the afternoon he was in bed groaning with pain and cursing the doctor for not curing him at once.

"Appendicitis!" he shrieked. "Impossible!"

Dr. Banza bowed and said nothing. With delicate finger tips

he felt of the muscles in the right lower quadrant of the abdomen. He shook his head over the thermometer that he took out of the sick man's mouth. He withdrew a drop of blood from the patient's finger tip into a tiny pipette and took it away with him.

He was back in an hour, and Cladgett read the verdict in his face.

"Operation!" he yowled like a whipped boy. "I can't have an operation! I'll die!"

He seemed to consider it the doctor's fault that he had appendicitis and would have to have an operation.

"Say," he said more rationally, as an idea occurred to him. "Do you realize that I've got an important directors' meeting in three days? I can't miss that for any operation. Now listen, be sensible. I'll give you a thousand dollars if you get me to that meeting in good shape."

Dr. Banza shrugged his shoulders.

"I'm going to dinner now," he said in the voice that one uses to a peevish child. "You have two or three hours in which to think it over. By that time I'm afraid you will be an emergency."

Dr. Banza sauntered thoughtfully over to the College Tavern and, walking in, looked around for a table at which to eat his dinner. He felt his shoulder touched.

"Sit down and eat with me," invited his unnoticed friend.

"Why, hello, Bookstrom!" he cried warmly, as he perceived who it was.

"Hello, yourself," returned Bookstrom, now portly and cheerful enough, with a little twinkle in each eye.

"But what's the matter? You look dark and discouraged."

So, over the dinner, Banza told his friend about the annoying dilemma with the obdurate and irascible Cladgett, who threatened certain ruin to his career.

"I feel like telling him to go to hell," Dr. Banza concluded.

Bookstrom sat a long time in silent thought, his elbows leaned on the table, sizzling a little tune through his cupped hands.

"Just the thing I've been looking for," he said at last slowly, as though he had come to a difficult decision. "Do you want to listen to a little lecture, Banza? Then you can decide whether I can help you or not?"

"If you can help me, you're some medicine-man. Shoot the lecture, though." Dr. Banza leaned back and waited, with much outward show of patience.

"You remember," opened Bookstrom, "that I had a couple of years of medical college work and had to quit. That accounts for my having gotten this idea so suddenly just now.

"My present title of Professor of Applied Mathematics is not an empty one. I've applied some mathematics this time, I'll tell the world.

"You hear a lot about the fourth dimension nowadays. Most people snort when you mention it. Some point a finger at you or grab your coat lapel and ask you what it is. *I don't know* what it is! Don't get to imagining that I've discovered what the fourth dimension is. But I don't know what light is or what gravitation is, except in a 'pure-mathematics' sense. Yet I utilize light and gravitation in a practical way every day, do I not?

"Well, I've learned how to utilize the fourth dimension without knowing what it is. And here's how we can apply it to your Cladgett. Only I've got an ancient grudge against that bird, and he's got to pay me back in real money for it, right now. You take your thousand and get a thousand for me—

"Now, how can we use the fourth dimension to help him? In order to explain it, I'll have to illustrate with an example from a two-dimensional plane of existence. Suppose you and Cladgett were two-dimensional beings confined to the plane of this sheet of paper. You could move about in any direction upon the paper, but you could not get upward off of it. Here is Cladgett. You can go all around him, but you can't jump over him, any more than you can turn yourself inside out.

"The only way that you, a two-dimensional surgeon, can remove an appendix from this two-dimensional wretch is to make a hole somewhere in his circumference, reach in, separate the doojigger from its attachments, and pull it out, all limited to the surface of the paper. Is that plain so far?"

Banza nodded without interrupting.

"But suppose some professor of Applied Mathematics arranges it so that you can rise slightly, infinitely slightly, above the plane of the paper. Then you can get Cladgett's appendix out without making any break in his circumference. All you do is to get up above him, locate your appendix, and reach down or lower yourself down to the original plane, and whisk out the appendix.

"He, being confined to the two-dimensional plane of the paper, cannot see how you do it or comprehend how. But here you are, back down to the plane of the paper again beside Cladgett, with the appendix in your hand, and he marvels how you did it."

"Brilliant reasoning," Dr. Banza admitted. "But unfortunately for its value in this emergency, Cladgett is a three-dimensional old hulk and so am I."

"To proceed"—Bookstrom made a show of ignoring the interruption—"suppose I had constructed an elevator that could lift you a little, ever so little, along the fourth dimension, at right angles to the other three. Then you could reach over and hook out Cladgett's appendix without making any abdominal wound."

Bookstrom stopped and smiled. Banza jumped to his feet.

"Well, dammit, have you?" he demanded. People in the tavern were turning around and looking at them.

"Come and see!"

They hooked arms and went up to Bookstrom's laboratory. Apparently Banza was satisfied with what he saw, for in five minutes he came racing out of the door and called a taxi and had himself whirled to Cladgett's house.

There he had some trouble about the two thousand dollars in advance. It was an unethical thing to demand, but he was a clever enough psychologist to sense and respect Bookstrom's reasons.

"I've found a specialist," he announced, "and am personally convinced that he can do what you want. With the next two days quiet in bed and subsequent care in diet, you can get to the meeting."

"Go ahead then," moaned Cladgett.

"But this man wants a thousand dollars and insists that his

thousand and mine must both be paid in advance," said Banza meekly.

Cladgett rose up in bed.

"Oh, you doctors are a bunch of robbers!" he shouted. Then he groaned and fell back again. The appendicitis was too much for him. A pain as sustained and long-enduring as that of an acute appendicitis will compel anyone to do anything. Soon Cladgett and a nurse were in an ambulance speeding toward the university, and Banza had two checks in his pocket.

Bookstrom was all ready. A half dozen simple surgical instruments to suffice for actually detaching the appendix were sterilized and covered. He put Cladgett on a long wooden table and asked the nurse to sit at his head with a chloroform mask, with orders to use it if he complained. He directed Banza to scrub his hands. Beside Cladgett was the "elevator."

There wasn't much to the machine. All great things are simple, I suppose. There were three trussed beams of aluminum at right angles to each other, each with a cylinder and plunger, and, from them, toggles coming together at a point where there was a sort of "universal joint" topped by a mat of thick rubber. That was all.

"You mean for me to get on that thing and be shoved somewhere into nowhere?" Banza looked worried.

"I won't insist." Bookstrom smiled.

"No, thanks." Banza backed away with alacrity. "I'll give him whatever anesthetic he needs." Banza was no doubt uncomfortable with responsibility, for the patient was seriously ill.

"Fine!" Bookstrom seemed to be enjoying the situation thoroughly. "I still know how to whack off an appendix. That's elementary surgery, amateur stuff."

A storm of protest broke from Cladgett.

"I don't want to be operated. You promised . . ." He wrung his hands and beat his heels upon the table.

"We promised," said Bookstrom sweetly, "that we would not open you up. You'll never find a scratch on yourself."

Cladgett quieted down. Bookstrom scrubbed his hands and wrapped his right one in a sterile towel in order to manipulate the machine. He stepped on the rubber mat, and in a moment Dr. Banza and the nurse were amazed to see him click suddenly out of sight. Click! And he was not there! Before they recovered from their astonishment, Cladgett began to complain. Dr. Banza had to start giving chloroform. He gave it slowly and cautiously, while Cladgett groaned and cursed and threshed himself about.

"Lie still, you fool!" shouted Bookstrom's voice in a pre-occupied way, just beside them. It made their flesh creep, for he was not there.

Gradually the patient quieted down and breathed deeply, and the doctor and the nurse took a breath of relief and had time to wonder about everything. There was another click! And there stood Bookstrom with a tray of bloody instruments in his hand.

"Pippin!" he exclaimed enthusiastically, pointing to the appendix. It was swollen to the size of a thumb, with purple blotches of congestion, black areas of gangrene, and yellow patches of fibrin. "You're not such a bad diagnostician, Banza!"

"Put it in formalin—to show him how sick he was," suggested Banza.

"You'll have a fat time proving to anybody that that was taken out of *him*. Forget it, and deposit your check. Some day when you get up your nerve, let me show you how it feels to see the inside of a man, all at once, everything working."

Cladgett was much better the next day. His pain was all gone and he did not feel the terrible, prostrating sickness of the day before.

As soon as he awoke he felt himself all over for an operation wound and, finding none, mumbled to himself surlily for a while. The second day his fever was gone and he was ravenously hungry. On the third day he was merely tired. On the fourth day he went to the directors' meeting in his own car, grumbling that he had never had any appendicitis anyhow and that the doctors had defrauded him of two thousand dollars.

"Got a notion to sue you for damages. May do it yet!" he snarled at Dr. Banza. "I'll include the value of my spectacles. You smashed them for me somewhere. Damn carelessness."

Dr. Banza bowed himself out.

"The next time he needs a doctor," he said to himself, "he can call one from Madagascar before I'll go to see him."

But Dr. Banza was no different from any other good physician. It wasn't two weeks before Cladgett called him, and again he was "fool enough to go," as he himself expressed it.

This time Cladgett was not in bed. He was nursing his hemispherical abdomen in an armchair.

"Thought you said you'd cure me of this appendicitis!" he wheezed antagonistically.

"Aha, so you *did* have appendicitis?" thought the doctor to himself. Aloud, he asked Cladgett to describe his symptoms, which Cladgett did in the popular way.

"I think it's adhesions!" he snapped.

"Adhesions exist chiefly in the brains of the laity and in the conversation of doctors too lazy to make a diagnosis." Dr. Banza's courteous patience was deserting him.

He temperatured and pulsed his patient, gently palpated the abdominal muscles, and counted the leucocytes in a drop of blood.

"You do have a tender spot," he mused, "and possibly a slight palpable mass. But no signs of any infectious process. No muscle rigidity. Is it getting worse?"

"Getting worse every day!" he groaned histrionically. "What is it, Doc?"

Dr. Banza resisted heroically the temptation to tell him that he had carcinoma of the ovary and said instead with studied care: "I can't be quite sure till we have an X-ray. Can you come down to the office?"

With much grunting and wheezing, Cladgett got up to the office and up on the radiographic table. Dr. Banza made a trial exposure and then several other films. He remained in the developing room for an interminable length of time and then came out with a red face.

"Well! What?" yapped Cladgett.

"Oh, just a trifling matter of no importance. Come, get into the car with me. We'll drive over to Professor Bookstrom's laboratory, and in a moment we'll have you permanently relieved and feeling good."

"I'll not go to that charlatan again!" roared Cladgett. "And you doctors are always trying to talk all around the bush and refusing to tell people the truth. You can't work that gag on me! I want to know exactly!" He shook both arms at Banza.

"Why, really!" Dr. Banza acted very much embarrassed. "It's nothing that cannot be corrected in a few seconds—"

"Dammit!" shrieked Cladgett. "Gimme that X-ray picture, or I'll smash up your place!"

Dr. Banza went in and got the wet film clipped in its frame. He led the way to the outside door. Cladgett angrily followed him thither and there received the film. Banza backed away, while Cladgett held the negative up to the light. There, very plainly visible in the right lower quadrant of the abdomen, was a pair of old-fashioned pince-nez spectacles!

Strange heavings and tremors seemed to traverse Cladgett's bulk, showing through his clothes. He shook and undulated and heaved suddenly in spots. His face turned alternately white and purple; his jaw worked up and down, and his mouth opened and shut convulsively, though no sound came forth. Suddenly he turned and stamped out of the building, carrying the wet film with him.

The old man was a pretty good judge of character, or he never would have made the money he did. In some subconscious way he had realized that Bookstrom must be the man to see about this thing.

Banza telephoned Bookstrom at once and told him the details.

"How unfortunate!" Bookstrom exclaimed. There was a suspicious note in his voice. That solicitude for Cladgett could hardly have been genuine.

"He's coming over there!" warned Banza.

"I shall be proud to receive such a distinguished guest."

That was all Banza was able to accomplish. He was sick with consternation and anxiety.

Bookstrom could hear Cladgett's thunderous approach down the hall. Then the door burst open and a chair went down, followed by a rack of charts and a tall case full of models. Cladgett seemed to derive some satisfaction from the havoc, this time little dreaming that Bookstrom was quite capable of setting the stage for just such a show. "You—you—" sputtered Cladgett, still unable to speak coherently.

"Too bad, too bad," consoled Bookstrom kindly. "Let's see your roentgenogram.

"Ah, how interesting!" Bookstrom could put vast enthusiasm into his voice. "The question is, I suppose, how they got in there?" He looked back and forth from Cladgett's protruding hemisphere to the spectacles on the X-ray film, as if to imply that in such an immense vault there surely ought to be room for such a trifling thing as a pair of spectacles.

"You put them there, you crook, you scoundrel, you robber, you dirty thief!" The "dirty thief" came out in a high falsetto shriek.

"You do me much honor." Bookstrom bowed. "That would be a 'stunt,' I might say, to be proud of."

"You don't deny it, do you?" Cladgett suddenly calmed down and spoke in acidly triumphant tones.

"It strikes me," Bookstrom mused, "that this is something that would be difficult either to prove or to deny."

"I've got the goods on you." Cladgett spoke coldly, just as he had on that occasion fifteen years before. "You either pay me fifty thousand dollars damages, or this goes to court at once."

"My dear *sir!*" Bookstrom bowed gravely. "You or anyone else has a standing invitation to go through my effects, and if you find more than a hundred dollars, you are welcome to half of it, if you give me the other half."

Cladgett did not know how to reply to this.

"I'm suing you for damages at once!" His words came like blows from a pile driver.

Bookstrom bowed him out with a smile.

The damage suit created considerable flare in the headlines. A pair of spectacles left in a patient's abdomen at operation! That was a morsel such as the public had not had to scandalize over for some time! Newspapers dug up all the details, even to the history of the forced payment on the note fifteen years before and the disappointed medical student; and the fact that the operation had been performed in secret and at night, in the laboratory of a man who was not a licensed medical practitioner, for Bookstrom's title of "doctor" was a philosophical, not a medical, one. The public gloated and licked its chops in anticipation of more morsels at the trial.

But no such treat ever came off. Immediately the suit was filed Bookstrom's counsel requested permission to examine thoroughly the person of the plaintiff. This was granted. The counsel then quietly and privately called the judge's attention to the fact that the plaintiff's body contained no scars or marks of operation of any kind; therefore it was evident that he had never been operated upon and, therefore, nothing could have been left in his abdomen. The judge held an informal preliminary hearing and threw the case out of court. He admitted that there were curious phases to it, but he was busy and tired, and his docket was so full that it made him nervous; he was glad to forget anything that was technically settled.

Cladgett continued to grow sicker. The pain and the lump in his side increased. In another two weeks he was a miserable man. He still managed to be up and about a little, but his face was drawn from suffering (and rage), and pains racked him constantly. He had lost twenty-five pounds in weight and looked like a wretched shadow of his former self.

One day he thrust himself into Bookstrom's office. Bookstrom dismissed the stenographer and the two student assistants and faced Cladgett blandly.

"Banza says you can fix this up somehow," he said, and it sounded like "gr-r-rump, gr-r-r-ump, r-r-rump!" "I've decided to let you go ahead."

"Very kind of you," Bookstrom purred. "I ought to feel humbly grateful for as big a favor as that. As a matter of fact, I've decided to *let* the Sultan of Sulu go jump in the lake. But I've a lurking suspicion that he isn't going to do it."

Cladgett sat and stared at him a while and then picked himself up and stumped out, grumbling and groaning.

The next day Dr. Banza brought him into Dr. Bookstrom's laboratory. He eased himself down into a chair before saying anything.

"I'm convinced that Banza's right and that you can help me. Now what's your robber's price?"

"It's a highway robber's price, with the accent on the high," murmured Bookstrom deprecatingly.

"Well, out with it, you—" There Cladgett wisely checked himself.

"I ask nothing whatever for myself," said Bookstrom, suddenly becoming serious. "But if you want me to get those spectacles out of you, right here and now you settle a sum to found a Students' Fund to loan money to worthy and needy scientific students, which they may pay back when they are established and earning money. I think when you spoke to me about a damage suit you mentioned the sum of fifty thousand dollars. Let's call it that."

"Fifty thousand dollars!" screamed Cladgett in a high falsetto. He was weak and unstable. "That's preposterous! That's criminal extortion."

"This transaction is not of my seeking," Bookstrom suggested.

"You've fixed it all up on me," Cladgett wailed, but his voice sank toward the end.

"Tell that to the judge. Or go to a surgeon and have him open you up and take them out. That would come cheaper."

"Operation!" shrieked Cladgett. "I can't stand an operation."

He looked desperately at Banza, but there was no hope there.

"This seems to me a wonderful opportunity," Banza said, "for you to do a public service and distinguish yourself in the community. I'm sure that amount of money will not affect you seriously."

Cladgett started for the door and then groaned and fell back heavily into his chair. He sat groaning for a while, his suffering being mental as well as physical; finally he reached into his pocket for his pen and his checkbook. He kept on groaning as he wrote out a check and flung it on the table.

"Now, damn you, help me!" he yelped.

They put him on the table.

"Banza, you scrub. You deserve to see this," directed Bookstrom.

So Banza stepped on the rubber mat and Bookstrom instructed him.

"Move this switch one button at a time. That will always raise you a notch. Look around each time until you get it just right."

With the first click Banza disappeared, just as people vanish suddenly in the movies. Cladgett groaned and squirmed and then was quiet. With another click Banza reappeared, and in his hand was a pair of old-fashioned pince-nez spectacles, moist and covered with a grayish film. He held them toward Cladgett, who grabbed them and mumbled something.

"Can you imagine," breathed Banza, "standing in the center of a sphere and seeing all the abdominal organs around you at once? Something like that, it seemed, not exactly either. There above my head were the coils of the small intestine. To the right was the cecum with the spectacles beside it, to my left the sigmoid and the muscles attached to the ilium, and beneath my feet the peritoneum of the anterior abdominal wall. But I was terribly dizzy for some reason; I could not stand it very long, much as I should have liked to remain inside of him for a while—"

"But you weren't inside of him," corrected Bookstrom.

Banza stared blankly.

"But I've just told you. There I was inside of him, with his viscera all around me, stomach and diaphragm in front, bladder behind—I *was* inside of him."

"Yes, it looked that way to you." Bookstrom nodded. "That is the way your brain, accustomed to three-dimensional space, interpreted it. But look. If I draw a circle on this sheet of paper, I can see all points on the inside of it, can I not? Yet, if you were a two-dimensional being, I would have a hard time convincing you that I am not inside the circle."

Paul Bunyan versus the Conveyor Belt

WILLIAM HAZLETT UPSON

This is just an amusing switch on the familiar Moebius strip theme, handled by a writer of popular fiction. I doubt that Mr. Upson knew any more mathematics than does your editor; but, like many others, he was quick to see the story possibilities that will always inhere in the little gadget discovered, or invented, by the pupil of Gauss, August Ferdinand Moebius (1790–1868).

ONE OF Paul Bunyan's most brilliant successes came about, not because of brilliant thinking, but because of Paul's caution and carefulness. This was the famous affair of the conveyor belt.

Paul and his mechanic, Ford Fordsen, had started to work a uranium mine in Colorado. The ore was brought out on an endless belt which ran half a mile going into the mine and another half mile coming out—giving it a total length of one mile. It was four feet wide. It ran on a series of rollers and was driven by a pulley mounted on the transmission of Paul's big blue truck, "Babe." The manufacturers of the belt had made it all in one piece, without any splice or lacing, and they had put a half-twist in the return part so that the wear would be the same on both sides.

After several months' operation the mine gallery had become twice as long, but the amount of material coming out was less. Paul decided he needed a belt twice as long and half as wide. He told Ford Fordsen to take his chain saw and cut the belt in two lengthwise.

"That will give us two belts," said Ford Fordsen. "We'll have to cut them in two crosswise and splice them together. That means I'll have to go to town and buy the materials for two splices."

"No," said Paul. "This belt has a half-twist—which makes it what is known in geometry as a Moebius strip."

"What difference does that make?" asked Ford Fordsen.

"A Moebius strip," said Paul Bunyan, "has only one side, and one edge, and if we cut it in two lengthwise, it will still be in one piece. We'll have one belt twice as long and half as wide."

"How can you cut something in two and have it still in one piece?" asked Ford Fordsen.

Paul was modest. He was never opinionated. "Let's try this thing out," he said.

They went into Paul's office. Paul took a strip of gummed paper about two inches wide and a yard long. He laid it on his desk with the gummed side up. He lifted the two ends and brought them together in front of him with the gummed sides down. Then he turned one of the ends over, licked it, slid it under the other end, and stuck the two gummed sides together. He had made himself an endless paper belt with a half-twist in it just like the big belt on the conveyor.

"This," said Paul, "is a Moebius strip. It will perform just the way I said—I hope."

Paul took a pair of scissors, dug the point in the center of the paper, and cut the paper strip in two lengthwise. And when he had finished, sure enough, he had one strip twice as long, half as wide, and with a double twist in it.

Ford Fordsen was convinced. He went out and started cutting the big belt in two. And, at this point, a man called Loud Mouth Johnson arrived to see how Paul's enterprise was coming along and to offer any destructive criticism that might occur to him.

Loud Mouth Johnson, being Public Blow-Hard Number One, found plenty to find fault with.

"If you cut that belt in two lengthwise, you will end up with two belts, each the same length as the original belt, but only half as wide."

"No," said Ford Fordsen, "this is a very special belt known as a Moebius strip. If I cut it in two lengthwise, I will end up with one belt twice as long and half as wide."

"Want to bet?" said Loud Mouth Johnson.

"Sure," said Ford Fordsen.

They bet a thousand dollars. And, of course, Ford Fordsen won. Loud Mouth Johnson was so astounded that he slunk off and stayed away for six months. When he finally came back he found Paul Bunyan just starting to cut the belt in two lengthwise for the second time.

"What's the idea?" asked Loud Mouth Johnson.

Paul Bunyan said, "The tunnel has progressed much farther and the material coming out is not as bulky as it was. So I am lengthening the belt again and making it narrower."

"Where is Ford Fordsen?"

Paul Bunyan said, "I have sent him to town to get some materials to splice the belt. When I get through cutting it in two lengthwise I will have two belts of the same length but only half the width of this one. So I will have to do some splicing."

Loud Mouth Johnson could hardly believe his ears. Here was a chance to get his thousand dollars back and show up Paul Bunyan as a boob besides. "Listen," said Loud Mouth Johnson, "when you get through you will have only one belt twice as long and half as wide."

"Want to bet?"

"Sure."

So they bet a thousand dollars and, of course, Loud Mouth Johnson lost again. It wasn't so much that Paul Bunyan was brilliant. It was just that he was methodical. He had tried it out with that strip of gummed paper, and he knew that the second time you slice a Moebius strip you get two pieces—linked together like an old-fashioned watch chain.

The Pacifist

ARTHUR C. CLARKE

❧

There's not much mathematics in this diverting tale by one of the masters of modern science-fiction. Perhaps, as G. H. Hardy suggests in his Mathematician's Apology, *real mathematics has no effect on the conduct of war and does not enter into it. Computer mathematics Hardy would doubtless call "trivial." In any case, what pleases about this story is, once again, the easement given to our ambiguous feeling about computers: we are delighted that a machine should mutiny.*

I GOT to the "White Hart" late that evening, and when I arrived everyone was crowded into the corner under the dartboard. All except Drew, that is: he had not deserted his post but was sitting behind the bar reading the collected T. S. Eliot. He broke off from "The Confidential Clerk" long enough to hand me a beer and to tell me what was going on.

"Eric's brought in some kind of games machine—it's beaten everybody so far. Sam's trying his luck with it now."

At that moment a roar of laughter announced that Sam had been no luckier than the rest, and I pushed my way through the crowd to see what was happening.

On the table lay a flat metal box the size of a checkerboard and divided into squares in a similar way. At the corner of each square was a two-way switch and a little neon lamp; the whole affair was plugged into the light socket (thus plunging the dartboard into darkness), and Eric Rodgers was looking round for a new victim.

"What does the thing do?" I asked.

"It's a modification of naughts-and-crosses—what the Americans call tic-tac-toe. Shannon showed it to me when I was over at Bell Labs. What you have to do is to complete a path from one side of the board to the other—call it north to south—by turning these switches. Imagine the thing forms a grid of streets, if you like, and these neons are the traffic lights. You and the machine take turns making moves. The machine tries to block your path by building one of its own in the east-west direction— the little neons light up to tell you which way it wants to make a move. Neither track need be a straight line: you can zigzag as much as you like. All that matters is that the path must be continuous, and the one to get across the board first wins."

"Meaning the machine, I suppose?"

"Well, it's never been beaten yet."

"Can't you force a draw, by blocking the machine's path, so that at least you don't lose?"

"That's what we're trying. Like to have a go?"

Two minutes later I joined the other unsuccessful contestants. The machine had dodged all my barriers and established its own track from east to west. I wasn't convinced that it was unbeatable, but the game was clearly a good deal more complicated than it looked.

Eric glanced around his audience when I had retired. No one else seemed in a hurry to move forward.

"Ha!" he said. "The very man. What about you, Purvis? You've not had a shot yet."

Harry Purvis was standing at the back of the crowd with a faraway look in his eye. He jolted back to earth as Eric addressed him but didn't answer the question directly.

"Fascinating things, these electronic computers," he mused. "I suppose I shouldn't tell you this, but your gadget reminds me of what happened to Project Clausewitz. A curious story, and one very expensive to the American taxpayer."

"Look," said John Wyndham anxiously. "Before you start, be a good sport and let us get our glasses filled. Drew!"

This important matter having been attended to, we gathered around Harry. Only Charlie Willis still remained with the machine, hopefully trying his luck.

"As you all know," began Harry, "Science with a capital S is a big thing in the military world these days. The weapons side—rockets, atom bombs, and so on—is only part of it, though that's all the public knows about. Much more fascinating, in my opinion, is the operational research angle. You might say that's concerned with brains rather than brute force. I once heard it defined as how to win wars without actually fighting, and that's not a bad description.

"Now you all know about the big electronic computers that cropped up like mushrooms in the 1950s. Most of them were built to deal with mathematical problems, but when you think about it you'll realize that war itself is a mathematical problem. It's such a complicated one that human brains can't handle it— there are far too many variables. Even the greatest strategist cannot see the picture as a whole: the Hitlers and Napoleons always make a mistake in the end.

"But a machine—that would be a different matter. A number of bright people realized this after the end of the war. The techniques that had been worked out in the building of ENIAC and the other big computers could revolutionize strategy.

"Hence Project Clausewitz. Don't ask me how I got to know about it or press me for too many details. All that matters is that a good many megabucks worth of electronic equipment, and some of the best scientific brains in the United States, went into a certain cavern in the Kentucky hills. They're still there, but things haven't turned out exactly as they expected.

"Now I don't know what experience you have of high-ranking military officers, but there's one type you've all come across in fiction. That's the pompous, conservative, stick-in-the-mud careerist who's got to the top by sheer pressure from beneath, who does everything by rules and regulations and regards civilians as, at the best, unfriendly neutrals. I'll let you into a secret: he actually exists. He's not very common nowadays, but he's still around and sometimes it's not possible to find a safe job for him. When that happens, he's worth his weight in plutonium to the Other Side.

"Such a character, it seems, was General Smith. No, of *course* that wasn't his real name! His father was a senator, and although lots of people in the Pentagon had tried hard enough, the old man's influence had prevented the general from being put in charge of something harmless, like the coast defense of Wyoming. Instead, by miraculous misfortune, he had been made the officer responsible for Project Clausewitz.

"Of course, he was only concerned with the administrative, not the scientific, aspects of the work. All might yet have been well had the general been content to let the scientists get on with their work while he concentrated on saluting smartness, the co-efficient of reflection of barrack floors, and similar matters of military importance. Unfortunately he didn't.

"The general had led a sheltered existence. He had, if I may borrow from Wilde (everybody else does), been a man of peace, except in his domestic life. He had never met scientists before, and the shock was considerable. So perhaps it is not fair to blame him for everything that happened.

"It was a considerable time before he realized the aims and objects of Project Clausewitz, and when he did he was quite disturbed. This may have made him feel even less friendly toward his scientific staff, for despite anything I may have said the general was not entirely a fool. He was intelligent enough to understand that, if the project succeeded, there might be more ex-generals around than even the combined boards of management of American industry could comfortably absorb.

"But let's leave the general for a minute and have a look at the scientists. There were about fifty of them, as well as a couple of hundred technicians. They'd all been carefully screened by the F.B.I., so probably not more than half a dozen were active members of the Communist party. Though there was a lot of talk of sabotage later, for once in a while the comrades were completely innocent. Besides, what happened certainly wasn't sabotage in any generally accepted meaning of the word. . . .

"The man who had really designed the computer was a quiet little mathematical genius who had been swept out of college into the Kentucky hills and the world of Security and Priorities before he'd really realized what had happened. He wasn't called Dr. Milquetoast, but he should have been, and that's what I'll christen him.

"To complete our cast of characters, I'd better say something about Karl. At this stage in the business Karl was only half built. Like all big computers, most of him consisted of vast banks of memory units which could receive and store information until it was needed. The creative part of Karl's brain—the analyzers and integrators—took this information and operated on it, to produce answers to the questions he was asked. Given all the relevant facts, Karl would produce the right answers. The problem, of course, was to see that Karl *did* have all the facts—he couldn't be expected to get the right results from inaccurate or insufficient information.

"It was Dr. Milquetoast's responsibility to design Karl's brain. Yes, I know that's a crudely anthropomorphic way of looking at it, but no one can deny that these big computers have personalities. It's hard to put it more accurately without getting technical, so I'll simply say that little Milquetoast had to create the extremely complex circuits that enabled Karl to think in the way he was supposed to do.

"So here are our three protagonists—General Smith, pining for the days of Custer; Dr. Milquetoast, lost in the fascinating scientific intricacies of his job; and Karl, fifty tons of electronic gear, not yet animated by the currents that would soon be coursing through him.

"Soon—but not soon enough for General Smith. Let's not be too hard on the general: someone had probably put the pressure on him, when it became obvious that the project was falling behind schedule. He called Dr. Milquetoast into his office.

"The interview lasted more than thirty minutes, and the doctor said less than thirty words. Most of the time the general was making pointed remarks about production times, deadlines, and bottlenecks. He seemed to be under the impression that building Karl differed in no important particular from the assembly of the current model Ford: it was just a question of putting the bits together. Dr. Milquetoast was not the sort of man to explain the error, even if the general had given him the opportunity. He left, smarting under a considerable sense of injustice.

"A week later it was obvious that the creation of Karl was falling still further behind schedule. Milquetoast was doing his best, and there was no one who could do better. Problems of a complexity totally beyond the general's comprehension had to be met and mastered. They *were* mastered, but it took time, and time was in short supply.

"At his first interview the general had tried to be as nice as he could and had succeeded in being merely rude. This time he tried to be rude, with results that I leave to your imagination. He practically insinuated that Milquetoast and his colleagues, by falling behind their deadlines, were guilty of un-American inactivity.

"From this moment onward two things started to happen. Relations between the Army and the scientists grew steadily worse; and Dr. Milquetoast, for the first time, began to give serious thought to the wider implications of his work. He had always been too busy, too engaged upon the immediate problems of his task, to consider his social responsibilities. He was still too busy now, but that didn't stop him pausing for reflection. 'Here am I,' he told himself, 'one of the best pure mathematicians in the world—and what am I doing? What's happened to my thesis on Diophantine equations? When am I going to have another smack at the prime number theorem? In short, when am I going to do some *real* work again?'

"He could have resigned, but that didn't occur to him. In any case, far down beneath that mild and diffident exterior was a stubborn streak. Dr. Milquetoast continued to work, even more energetically than before. The construction of Karl proceeded slowly but steadily: the final connections in his myriad-celled brain were soldered; the thousands of circuits were checked and tested by the mechanics.

"And one circuit, indistinguishably interwoven among its multitude of companions and leading to a set of memory cells apparently identical with all the others, was tested by Dr. Milquetoast alone, for no one else knew that it existed.

"The great day came. To Kentucky, by devious routes, came very important personages. A whole constellation of multi-starred generals arrived from the Pentagon. Even the Navy had been invited.

"Proudly General Smith led the visitors from cavern to cavern, from memory banks to selector networks to matrix analyzers to input tables—and finally to the rows of electric typewriters on which Karl would print the results of his deliberations. The general knew his way around quite well; at least, he got most of the names right. He even managed to give the impression, to those who knew no better, that he was largely responsible for Karl.

" 'Now,' said the general cheerfully, 'let's give him some work to do. Anyone like to set him a few sums?'

"At the word 'sums' the mathematicians winced, but the general was unaware of his *faux pas*. The assembled brass thought for a while, then someone said daringly, 'What's 9 multiplied by itself twenty times?'

"One of the technicians, with an audible sniff, punched a few keys. There was a rattle of gunfire from an electric typewriter, and before anyone could blink twice the answer had appeared— all twenty digits of it."

(I've looked it up since; for anyone who wants to know, it's:

$$12157665459056928801$$

But let's get back to Harry and his tale.)

"For the next fifteen minutes Karl was bombarded with similar trivialities. The visitors were impressed, though there was no reason to suppose that they'd have spotted it if all the answers had been completely wrong.

"The general gave a modest cough. Simple arithmetic was as far as he could go, and Karl had barely begun to warm up. 'I'll now hand you over,' he said, 'to Captain Winkler.'

"Captain Winkler was an intense young Harvard graduate whom the general distrusted, rightly suspecting him to be more a scientist than a military man. But he was the only officer who really understood what Karl was supposed to do or could explain exactly how he set about doing it. He looked, the general thought grumpily, like a damned schoolmaster as he started to lecture the visitors.

"The tactical problem that had been set up was a complicated one, but the answer was already known to everybody except Karl. It was a battle that had been fought and finished almost a century before, and when Captain Winkler concluded his introduction, a general from Boston whispered to his side, 'I'll bet some damn Southerner has fixed it so that Lee wins this time.' Everyone had to admit, however, that the problem was an excellent way of testing Karl's capabilities.

"The punched tapes disappeared into the capacious memory units; patterns of lights flickered and flashed across the registers; mysterious things happened in all directions.

" 'This problem,' said Captain Winkler primly, 'will take about five minutes to evaluate.'

"As if in deliberate contradiction, one of the typewriters promptly started to chatter. A strip of paper shot out of the feed, and Captain Winkler, looking rather puzzled at Karl's unexpected alacrity, read the message. His lower jaw immediately dropped six inches, and he stood staring at the paper as if unable to believe his eyes.

" 'What is it, man?' barked the general.

"Captain Winkler swallowed hard but appeared to have lost the power of speech. With a snort of impatience the general snatched the paper from him. Then it was his turn to stand paralyzed, but, unlike his subordinate, he also turned a most

43

beautiful red. For a moment he looked like some tropical fish strangling out of water; then, not without a slight scuffle, the enigmatic message was captured by the five-star general who outranked everybody in the room.

"His reaction was totally different. He promptly doubled up with laughter.

"The minor officers were left in a state of infuriating suspense for quite ten minutes. But finally the news filtered down through colonels to captains to lieutenants, until at last there wasn't a G.I. in the establishment who did not know the wonderful news.

"Karl had told General Smith that he was a pompous baboon. That was all.

"Even though everybody agreed with Karl, the matter could hardly be allowed to rest there. Something, obviously, had gone wrong. Something—or someone—had diverted Karl's attention from the Battle of Gettysburg.

" 'Where,' roared General Smith, finally recovering his voice, 'is Dr. Milquetoast?'

"He was no longer present. He had slipped quietly out of the room, having witnessed his great moment. Retribution would come later, of course, but it was worth it.

"The frantic technicians cleared the circuits and started running tests. They gave Karl an elaborate series of multiplications and divisions to perform—the computer's equivalent of 'The quick brown fox jumps over the lazy dog.' Everything seemed to be functioning perfectly. So they put in a very simple tactical problem, which a lieutenant j.g. could solve in his sleep.

"Said Karl, 'Go jump in a lake, General.'

"It was then that General Smith realized that he was confronted with something outside the scope of Standard Operating Procedure. He was faced with mechanical mutiny, no less.

"It took several hours of tests to discover exactly what had happened. Somewhere tucked away in Karl's capacious memory units was a superb collection of insults, lovingly assembled by Dr. Milquetoast. He had punched on tape, or recorded in patterns of electrical impulses, everything he would like to have said to the general himself. But that was not all he had done: that would have been too easy, not worthy of his genius. He had also installed what could only be called a censor circuit—he had given Karl the power of discrimination. Before solving it, Karl examined every problem fed to him. If it was concerned with pure mathematics, he co-operated and dealt with it properly. But if it was a military problem—out came one of the insults. After twenty times he had not repeated himself once, and the WAC's had already had to be sent out of the room.

"It must be confessed that after a while the technicians were almost as interested in discovering what indignity Karl would next heap upon General Smith as they were in finding the fault in the circuits. He had begun with mere insults and surprising genealogical surmises but had swiftly passed on to detailed instructions, the mildest of which would have been highly prejudicial to the general's dignity, while the more imaginative would have seriously imperiled his physical integrity. The fact that all these messages, as they emerged from the typewriters, were immediately classified *top secret* was small consolation to the recipient. He knew with a glum certainty that this would be the worst-kept secret of the cold war and that it was time he looked around for a civilian occupation.

"And there, gentlemen," concluded Purvis, "the situation remains. The engineers are still trying to unravel the circuits that Dr. Milquetoast installed, and no doubt it's only a matter of time before they succeed. But meanwhile Karl remains an unyielding pacifist. He's perfectly happy playing with the theory of numbers, computing tables of powers, and handling arithmetical problems generally. Do you remember the famous toast, 'Here's to pure mathematics—may it never be of any use to anybody'? Karl would have seconded that. . . .

"As soon as anyone attempts to slip a fast one across him, he goes on strike. And because he's got such a wonderful memory, he can't be fooled. He has half the great battles of the world stored up in his circuits and can recognize at once any variations on them. Though attempts were made to disguise tactical exer-

45

cises as problems in mathematics, he could spot the subterfuge right away. And out would come another *billet-doux* for the general.

"As for Dr. Milquetoast, no one could do much about him because he promptly had a nervous breakdown. It was suspiciously well timed, but he could certainly claim to have earned it. When last heard of he was teaching matrix algebra at a theological college in Denver. He swears he's forgotten everything that had ever happened while he was working on Karl. Maybe he was even telling the truth. . . ."

There was a sudden shout from the back of the room.

"I've won!" cried Charles Willis. "Come and see!"

We all crowded under the dartboard. It seemed true enough. Charlie had established a zigzag but continuous track from one side of the checkerboard to the other, despite the obstacles the machine had tried to put in his way.

"Show us how you did it," said Eric Rodgers.

Charlie looked embarrassed.

"I've forgotten," he said. "I didn't make a note of all the moves."

A sarcastic voice broke in from the background.

"But *I* did," said John Christopher. "You were cheating— you made two moves at once."

After that, I am sorry to say, there was some disorder, and Drew had to threaten violence before peace was restored. I don't know who really won the squabble, and I don't think it matters. For I'm inclined to agree with what Purvis remarked as he picked up the robot checkerboard and examined its wiring.

"You see," he said, "this little gadget is only a simple-minded cousin of Karl's—and look what it's done already. All these machines are beginning to make us look fools. Before long they'll start to disobey us without any Milquetoast interfering with their circuits. And then they'll start ordering us about— they're logical, after all, and won't stand any nonsense."

He sighed. "When that happens, there won't be a thing we can do about it. We'll just have to say to the dinosaurs: 'Move over a bit—here comes *homo sap!*' And the transistor shall inherit the earth."

There was no time for further pessimistic philosophy, for the door opened and Police Constable Wilkins stuck his head in. "Where's the owner of CGC 571?" he asked testily. "Oh—it's *you*, Mr. Purvis. Your rear light's out."

Harry looked at me sadly, then shrugged his shoulders in resignation. "You see," he said, "it's started already." And he went out into the night.

The Hermeneutical Doughnut

H. NEARING, JR.

All the mathematics in The Hermeneutical Doughnut *is contained in the first few pages. The rest is the wackiest kind of foolery. The author writes me: "The story contains a sort of sneak attack on the notorious four-color problem of topology, and I have a lurking amateurish half-hope that, if my description fell under the eye of a real mathematician, it might point the way to a solution." Mr. Nearing teaches English and philosophy at the Pennsylvania Military Academy, has written a dissertation on seventeenth-century poetry, some articles on the medieval legends of Julius Caesar, and several notes on Shakespeare. He is obviously well equipped to handle the kind of academic satire which pervades this yarn. His central figure, Cleanth Penn Ransom, he describes as a sort of Don Quixote of science.*

" 'TOTTERING DAVIDS TOPPLE GOLIATHS, 5–4,' " MacTate read from the campus newspaper. " 'The Faculty Committee on Athletic Purity, captained by Professor Cleanth Penn Ransom of the Mathematics Department, dealt one of the major upsets of the year in a post-season match with the coaching staff of the basketball team last night, rolling up five points to the coaching aggregation's four before the referee called the game off on a technicality. Head Coach Gladmore, interviewed immediately after the game, denied that the result represents a victory and hinted at foul play, but stated that he will refrain from demanding a replay because of concern for the lives of his opponents. An unusual feature of the match was . . .' " MacTate looked up. "They should have interviewed Gladmore this morning. When we put the cement post up, he seemed almost cheerful. Something like FitzSparrow after the play."

Ransom leaned forward and motioned toward the newspaper. "What did the president of the Nietzsche Society say?"

MacTate glanced down the column. " '. . . declined to comment on Professor Ransom's performance on the ground that the time for nominating the Renaissance Man of the Year is so close that it would be unethical to make public statements which might influence the decision of the nominating committee.' "

Ransom grinned. "Getting coy." He leaned back in his swivel chair. "You say the cement thing went up all right?"

"Foolproof." MacTate smiled. "Also rather decorative. Some of your committee colleagues came down to watch and were struck by its monumental character to the point of suggesting that we put a bronze plaque on it, commemorating the game."

Ransom grunted. "It ought to be an In Memoriam plaque. That ball was the best chance we ever had of getting Ettiscope to kick through." He folded his arms back of his head and regarded the ceiling. "MacTate, what kind of a jinx is on this business? Every time we seem to be getting somewhere with the Ettiscope endowment something goes wrong." He stuck out a finger. "Poetry machine committed suicide." He stuck out another finger. "Finchell's doll had to be destroyed because it was too dangerous." He stuck out a third finger. "The musical tumor demolished itself by accident." He flourished all of his fingers. "I had to eat the pills; Helen swiped the dimension-warper, and Gladmore threw away the hypersphere. What's wrong?"

"Well, old boy, if you want to be philosophical, there are several possible explanations." MacTate pursed his lips. "Mystically, you could say that some nemesis is pursuing you for flunking Harrington B. Snyde. Or psychologically, that you're subconsciously determined not to win the endowment, perhaps from a sense of guilt, and so maneuver things to get rid of the gadgets. Personally, though, I'm inclined to favor a Platonistic explanation."

Ransom looked at him. "What's that?"

"Well, remember Plotinus? The creative imagination can never completely manifest itself in material substance. The best-laid plans of mice and men, you know. Your materialist thinks that if he had just used a different tool or spent more time on the blueprint, everything would have been all right; but your philosopher knows there's something intractable about the material world and nothing will ever turn out quite right. It's the essence of tragedy."

"But the gadgets always came out all right."

"Yes, but your plans for them didn't. Aristotle. The purpose of a gadget is part of its essential being."

"Well, maybe you're right." Ransom began to swing. "Everything has sure been going all to hell. But it seems more like just bad luck to me. And here it's May already. Next month Snyde will have me on—" He shuddered.

"But there *is* still time, old boy." MacTate smiled. "Can't you think of something that will bring crass materiality to a compromise?"

"I do have a couple more ideas." Ransom sat up. "One of them I've got to do some more work on. I don't know how long it'll take. But we can try the other one out before Ettiscope gets here."

"Ettiscope?"

"Sure." Ransom pointed at the newspaper. "Doesn't it say anything about it there?"

MacTate found the headline. " '*Deodorant Magnate to Visit Alma Mater.*' " He read farther. "It says he'll be here until commencement."

Ransom nodded. "You know what his hobby's supposed to be, MacTate? Besides giving screwy endowments?"

MacTate frowned in concentration. "Didn't I hear he was supposed to be a Biblical authority of sorts?"

"That's right. He explains hard passages in the Bible. So even if my new gadget is kind of—limited, maybe it can penetrate his soft spot."

"What is your gadget, old boy?"

Ransom looked at his wrist watch. "I've got a class, MacTate. Meet me here Sunday afternoon and I'll have it all ready to show you."

When MacTate entered his colleague's office on the appointed date, the first thing he noticed was a moose's head, with a badly battered nose, that sat next to a stuffed owl in the corner. He sat down, staring at the moose.

Ransom leaned back in his swivel chair. "MacTate, why doesn't the dictionary tell you a doughnut's got a hole in it? I looked in three of them, and they don't say a word about holes. In doughnuts, I mean."

"Perhaps not all of them have holes," said MacTate. "Just as not all mooses have holes in them." He gestured. "Whatever happened to him? Incompetent taxidermist?"

"No." Ransom shrugged. "They used him in a boys' club initiation. Somebody got scared and hit him with an ax. But about the doughnut—mind, MacTate."

"Yes, old boy." MacTate took his eyes off the moose.

"In geometry a doughnut's got to have a hole in it." Ransom sat up. "On a sphere you can only make four-color maps, but on a doughnut you can get seven. If it's got a hole in it."

"Oh." MacTate looked at the stuffed owl. "How did the owl escape intact? Didn't they use him in the initiation?"

"MacTate, will you forget about the animals? Look." Ransom took a tablet and pencil out of his top desk drawer and sketched a circle with three sectors. "Here's a circle divided into three parts, all touching each other. So if you're going to paint it, like a map, you need three colors." He wrote a number in each sector. "Now suppose you've got another region that touches all three of these." He drew a curve from the center of the first arc to the center of the third. "You need a fourth color. Don't you? But look what that does to number two. Completely surrounded by the others. So any new region can be colored like number two, and you never need more than four colors on this sort of a surface."

MacTate uncrossed his legs and leaned forward to examine the drawing. "But you could use more colors than that if you wanted to."

"Of course. Of course. But this is mathematics, MacTate. My God, what did you think it was? Art? The point is, you can't make a map that *requires* more than four colors. On a sphere."

"Sorry, old boy."

"Well—" Ransom drew a sketch of a pyramid. "By an odd coincidence, the simplest polyhedron you can squeeze a sphere into is a tetrahedron. You know, pyramid with a triangular base. It's got four sides, and they all touch each other. So you need four colors to paint it."

"How do you mean you can squeeze a sphere into that, old boy?"

"You just can. Suppose you take a ball of modeling clay. You squeeze it into a tetrahedron, paint the sides, squeeze it into a ball again, and you've got a sphere with a four-color map on it. Right?"

"Right."

"Now"—Ransom's eyes began to gleam—"what's the simplest angular solid you can squeeze a doughnut into?" He erased two corners of the pyramid. "A tetrahedron with a hole in it. Just like a doughnut is a sort of a sphere with a hole in it. See? So you run a three-sided hole from one of these vertexes to another, and you've got a seven-sided solid where every side touches each of the others." He drew the lines representing the hole. "You've got to bend the hole in toward the center of the pyramid and flare out the ends of two of its sides. But it works." He threw the pencil down. "You need seven colors to paint it."

"I see." MacTate looked at the battered moose's head, which seemed to be emitting rumbling noises at regular intervals.

"Old boy, am I crazy, or is that moose making noises? Sounds rather as if he had defective clockwork inside him."

"It's not him. MacTate, are you going to listen about the seven dimensions, or aren't you?"

"Oh. Yes. You need seven dimensions for the map. I understand."

"No, no, MacTate. You need seven *colors*."

"Of course. Colors. That's what I meant to say."

"All right. But look. Everybody always thinks of dimensions as being at right angles to each other. Don't they?" Ransom leaned back. "But if you get right down to it, that's kind of silly. For instance, how can a time dimension be at 'right angles' to a space dimension? Wouldn't it be a lot more sensible to think of them as contiguous areas on a solid? Like a graph? Let's take *you* as a solid, for instance. We could plot your four co-ordinates on a pyramidal graph. One time co-ordinate and three space. To show where you are in space-time."

"If you say so, old boy."

"But"—Ransom's eyes gleamed again—"if we tried to plot you on a pyramid with a hole in it, which is non-simply connected, we'd be up against seven dimensions, remember? One time and *six* space." His eyes narrowed. "Just suppose you suddenly found yourself in a non-simply connected space. What would you do with the extra three dimensions?"

"Well—" MacTate blinked. "I imagine the problem would require careful study."

Ransom shook his head. "All taken care of by mathematical necessity. Your four dimensions would try to fill seven, and there would suddenly be four of you flipping around. The one you started with plus one for each extra dimension."

"Now really, Ransom—"

"It's mathematical logic, MacTate. What do you call it? Inexorable. Besides, I don't think there's anything particularly *new* about it. Non-simply connected space pockets might explain a lot of things." He reached into his middle desk drawer and took out a Bible. "How about Ezekiel's vision of the wheel within a wheel, for instance?" He turned some pages. "Here. Ezekiel 1:5. 'Also out of the midst thereof'—that's the wheels—'came the likeness of four living creatures.' And then it tells about them in—1:10. 'As for the likeness of their faces, they four had the face of a man, and the face of a lion, on the right side: and they four had the face of an ox on the left side; they four also had the face of an eagle.' " He closed the Bible. "Obviously what Ezekiel saw was just one man, lion, ox, and eagle caught in a non-simply connected space pocket."

MacTate noticed a library number on the spine of the Bible. "Old boy, I am not one to disapprove of a sincere Fundamentalism, but—"

"No, no." Ransom grinned. "This isn't Fundamentalism. It's Anti-psychologism. I'm going to demonstrate it at the Abnormal Psychology Society meeting tonight. They think Ezekiel just had hallucinations."

"You're going to *demonstrate* it?"

"Sure. Then if it impresses them, we can show it to Ettiscope."

MacTate looked at the animals. "And these—"

"That's right. I've got to use the owl instead of an eagle and the moose instead of an ox. Best I could do on short notice. But—"

"Where's the lion?"

"He's back of them there. Snoring. Here, Roland." Ransom whistled. "Wake up."

From behind the moose's head came an unhappy grunt, and MacTate perceived that what he had taken for a pile of burlap was a piece of large animal. It got up, stepped carefully around the owl, stretched, yawned, regarded Ransom with a half-open eye, and shuffled toward him.

"That's a lion?"

"No, he's a great Dane. But with a wig he'll do fine." Ransom patted him solidly on the head. "I only wish that damned moose looked half as much like an ox as—"

"But there were four animals in Ezekiel," said MacTate. "What was the other thing he saw?"

Ransom scratched Roland's head intently. "A man."

MacTate smiled. "But won't it be rather trying for you to lecture and take part in the demonstration at the same—" Suddenly he caught the look in Ransom's eye, and his smile disappeared. "No. Now see here, Ransom, if you think you're going to make *me* a psychological guinea pig—"

"No, no. An *anti*-psychological guinea pig, MacTate." Ransom looked up. "Like you said, I can hardly lecture and act in the show at the same time."

"But, Ransom"—MacTate waved toward the animals—"with those disreputable-looking—"

"Nothing personal." Ransom opened his bottom desk drawer. "Here. I'll show you how it works." He took out a diminutive flashlight and set it on the floor. "Let's try this fellow first." He set the owl beside the flashlight, flicked the flashlight on, and stepped back. "Takes a few seconds— There."

No light came from the little flashlight, but suddenly there were four owls arranged about it in a square of three or four feet. Roland took one look at the eight glaring eyes, let forth a bass yip, and ran to hide behind Ransom's legs.

"That's certainly a lionlike character, old boy." MacTate gestured.

Roland looked up at him.

"Now lay off him, MacTate. You just don't understand him. He's like a child."

"I see. You have to be a child anti-psychologist to understand him."

"Now look, MacTate. My God, if you can be an angel— Anyway, Roland's not scared. It's just sort of—strange, seeing four of them at once. He needs a little reassurance, that's all. Look." Ransom took a red ball out of his pocket. "Go get your ball, Roland." He bowled it deftly between the nearer two owls. It turned into four balls, then back into one, and came to rest an inch from the flashlight.

Roland took a tentative step after it, then stopped and looked back uncertainly at Ransom.

"Why don't you put his mane on him?" said MacTate. "Might give him confidence."

Something in his tone made Roland look up at him again. "MacTate, will you stop trying to hurt his feelings? He——" Roland began to snarl faintly at the owls.

"Go get your ball, Roland."

The snarling increased in volume, but Roland's legs seemed to have taken root.

"All right, MacTate." Ransom went to the closet in the far corner of the room and opened the door. "We'll try it your way." He took out a rustling mass of straw draped over a pink coat hanger.

"What's that?" MacTate looked at it dubiously.

"Hula skirt." Ransom took it off the hanger and smoothed it out. "Ought to make a wonderful mane." He pulled it over Roland's head. "How's that?"

MacTate smiled. "He looks something like an overgrown porcupine, don't you think?"

"Well——" Ransom pushed the straw aside and hooked the pink coat hanger, upside down, to Roland's collar. "Let's prop it up." He smoothed the straw back. "How about that?"

MacTate nodded. "Pompadoured porcupine."

Roland looked up at him again.

"Listen, MacTate. You're going to give him an inferiority complex. Why can't you——"

"Quite the contrary, old boy." MacTate pointed.

Roland was eying the owls from a menacing crouch. He barked hoarsely two or three times, then uprooted his legs and charged at the ball. As he approached the owls, he appeared to think better of it and straightened his legs to stop, but his momentum carried him among them. Abruptly there were four twisting, yelping Rolands, connected by a circling blur of incorporeal motion.

"There, he's got caught in the magnetic doughnut." Ransom grinned. "Poor Roland. And there's one of Ezekiel's wheels, on account of he's scrambling around. Since the owl just sat still——"

"I say, old boy, what happened to the other owl?" said Mac-Tate. "There are only three of them now."

"Outside the door." Ransom pointed. "Roland's extra mass expanded the doughnut, and since he got inside the owls his circle pushed one of them out of the room." He laughed. "Better shut it off before he goes crazy." He stepped up to the nearest owl, turned into four Ransoms, swung his belly sideways, became one Ransom again, flicked off the flashlight, pocketed the red ball, and stood grinning at MacTate with a miserably vertiginous Roland on one side of him and an impassive owl on the other.

"Ransom"—MacTate stared at the flashlight—"what on earth *is* that thing?"

"This? Oh, it's a sort of inside-out electromagnet." Ransom regarded it fondly. "Instead of a light bulb it's got a transistor in it. Little thing made out of germanium with a couple molecules of gallium. See, a germanium atom's got four electrons in its outside shell, while a gallium atom's only got three. If you excite the setup with a touch of electricity, the extra germanium atoms start moving into the vacancies in the gallium shells and creating new vacancies in their *own* shells, so the stuff doesn't know whether it's germanium or gallium and you get a continuous electron flow."

"But, Ransom, does that constitute—"

"An electromagnet? No. But this transistor wasn't made right. Got impurities in it. Nickel and—God knows what all. You should have seen its Zeeman effect. Spectrum was a bunch of— Well, anyway, I figured it was a non-simply connected magnetic field, and it was."

MacTate smiled sardonically. "Ezekiel was a pretty clever fellow to make a thing like that, don't you think?"

"Now stop that, MacTate. Who says that's the only way you can make them? Non-simply connected magnetic fields. The point is—"

Roland, who had been leaning tipsily against Ransom's hip, began to stagger toward his lair behind the moose's head. With each step he wheeled a little farther to the right until he was headed for the closet at the other end of the room.

"Hey!" Ransom put his hands on Roland's ribs and steadied him. "You better take it easy till your head clears. Here. Let's take your mane off so you can rest up while we get something to eat." He took off the straw skirt, unhooked the pink hanger, and led Roland to the moose corner. "We'll bring you some dog food and ginger ale. How's that?"

Roland's only reply was a groan.

He was snoring again when they came back. "Roland." Ransom tickled his ribs with his foot. "Look what we got you." He held out a bag and a fifth of ginger ale. "Couldn't get any dog food, so we brought you these." He split the bag open and set it down in front of Roland's nose. It contained six rare hamburgers. Roland opened a bleary eye, flicked an ear, and regarded the hamburgers uncertainly.

"Cheer up, Roland," said MacTate. "At least I talked him out of the chili sauce and onions."

Roland looked at him.

"MacTate, let him eat in peace." Ransom went to his desk, took a plastic bowl out of the middle drawer, and poured the ginger ale into it.

Roland growled faintly and attacked one of the hamburgers. It was hard to tell what he was thinking.

Ransom set the bowl of ginger ale beside the hamburgers. "Don't poke, Roland." He went to the closet and took out the skirt, the hanger, and a leash. "We've got to get started."

It was still light when the quintet headed into the alley down which Ransom proposed to sneak to the building where the Abnormal Psychology Society held its meetings. MacTate puffed patiently behind the moose's head, around which he had a strangle hold. Ransom, holding the owl and the hula skirt in one hand and Roland's leash in the other, sniffed the culinary odors on the evening breeze, admired the subtle colors of the decaying houses, and hummed snatches of "Ezekiel Saw the Wheel." Roland trotted quietly by his side, burping softly from time to time.

At first the narrow brick sidewalk seemed to be deserted. But as they rounded a large green doorstep they came upon a baby sailing a toy duck in a tub of water. On the side of the tub opposite the baby perched two sparrows. Roland glanced at MacTate, then at the sparrows. With an aggressive bark he scared the sparrows away, took their place at the tub, and began to add quantities of the improvised duck pond to the ginger ale inside him. Forthwith the baby burst into angry tears and, picking up the duck, heaved it inexpertly but accurately at the intruder's head. As the toy bounced off his nose, Roland yelped and dodged back, pulling Ransom with him down the alley.

MacTate puffed after them. "I should advise a certain degree of circumspection, Roland," he said. "Appears to be a tough neighborhood."

Roland hung his head and slunk close to Ransom.

"Look at that, MacTate. You've got him cringing at the sound of your voice."

"But, Ransom, I was simply—"

"You were simply intimidating him with that nasty, cynical tone you usually save for me. If you could just— Oh, oh."

MacTate peered around the moose. "What now?"

Roland was looking up at an open window. On the sill, between two pots of fancy cactus, lay a fat tortoise-shell cat with a pea-green ribbon around its neck. The cat looked down at Roland and opened its mouth in an almost inaudible ladylike mew.

Ransom pulled at the leash. "Roland, no."

Roland worked up a ferocious growl that erupted in a bark. From the depths of a house came a shrill female voice admonishing any visiting dogs to let the cat alone.

As the voice approached the window, Roland backed precipitously away, bumping into MacTate, who raised the moose's head to keep his balance. The moose reached the level of the window just as the owner of the voice, harsh with virginal acrimony, loomed behind it.

"Go away, you nasty dog. Go—" Her remarks were resolved in an earsplitting screech.

The cat, startled, leaped up on one of the cactus pots, knocking it over. To the accompaniment of a feline wail, cat and cactus described wide parabolas that intersected various portions of Roland's anatomy. For a moment there was a chaos of spitting, snapping, and howling, and then suddenly the cat disappeared.

"Good heavens, Ransom. What happened to the cat? Did Roland devour—"

"No, no. She ran under the gate. I saw her. Come on, MacTate. Let's get out of here."

"But, Ransom, that woman— And we broke her flowerpot." MacTate nudged the shattered fragments with his foot.

"We'll send her some money. Anonymously." Ransom grabbed his arm and dragged him and Roland down the alley.

"But, Ransom—"

"Not *now*, MacTate. We're not getting involved with any irate spinsters."

"Well—" MacTate sighed. He looked at Roland. Roland was peering at him from the corner of his eye. MacTate smiled. "Perhaps I was wrong about the toughness of the neighborhood after all. Roland and I appear to be more than a match for some elements of it."

Roland stuck out his tongue and began to pant happily. His trot came suspiciously close to a strut.

"Now look, MacTate. You're going to the other extreme. Giving him a big head." Ransom scowled. "Why can't you treat him like you do me or any other normal organism?"

MacTate looked at him.

"He has his ups and downs the same as—Roland!"

Roland, barking boisterously, made a sudden leap, jerked the leash out of Ransom's hand, and galloped down the alley.

"Look." Ransom pointed at a fireplug that was being used by a walleyed bull terrier. Roland, snarling seismically, drove the terrier away and used the fireplug himself. "You've brought out his bully instincts." Ransom hastened down to the fireplug and, ignoring Roland's grin, tied the leash securely to his wrist. "Thank God the place is just around the corner."

MacTate joined Ransom and Roland at the fireplug. They proceeded down the alley and rounded the corner.

"Oh, my God." Ransom stopped. "Look who's going to the Abnormal Psychology meeting." He pointed. The walleyed bull terrier was ascending a projecting flight of steps halfway down the block at someone's heels. "Roland, if you don't behave yourself—" He jerked the leash admonitorily.

They went down to the steps, entered the building, and climbed the stairs to the third floor. MacTate peered through the door at a large room with a platform, flanked by two low windows, at the far end. The windows had been opened wide to admit the spring breezes. The Abnormal Psychologists scattered about the room were engaged in commonplace pursuits such as knitting, leafing through magazines, and trying to hog conversations; but their physiognomies seemed somehow to reflect the eccentric nature of their researches.

"Let's fix Roland out here." Ransom put the owl down. "His mane, I mean. Might spoil the illusion if we do it up there." He hooked the pink coat hanger on Roland's collar and adjusted the hula skirt.

When they entered the room, a little man with a tic over his right eye waved to them from the platform.

"Professor Flatterthwaite," said Ransom. "President of the society. He wrote a couple of books on memory training, but his real love is maniacs." He hesitated and looked around the room. "MacTate, you see any sign of that bull pup?"

MacTate looked around. The terrier was sitting on a chair in the front row next to a woman who was writing rapidly in a notebook, darting her pen every few seconds into a bottle of violet ink that perched precariously on the arm of her chair. "There he is. Down in the—"

"Shh." Ransom frowned warningly. "Don't let Roland— Now look what you've done."

Roland had spotted the terrier and began to growl. The terrier turned around and apparently recognized Roland in spite of his mane, for he jumped unobtrusively off his chair.

"Where is he?" said MacTate.

"Don't worry about it." Ransom shook the leash and pulled Roland forward. "As long as he's had the good sense to disappear."

When they were halfway to the platform, something hurtled past Roland's legs. He saw the terrier leap up beside Roland, swing from the hula skirt by his teeth to pull it over his enemy's eyes, and zip off between two rows of chairs.

"Good heavens, Ransom. He circled the room."

Ransom was in no position to comment. Roland shook off the hula skirt with an outraged roar and took off after the terrier, with his guardian in helpless tow. The terrier circled down to the front of the room and leaped up on the writing woman's lap just as she darted her pen at the violet ink. The bottle whirled into the air, raining violet drops, and struck the top of Roland's skull with a solid clonk, covering him with lurid maculations.

"My God, Roland—" Ransom stopped, perceiving himself transfixed by a pair of wild hyperthyroidal eyes.

"The minutes! You've ruined the minutes!" She wiped a violet drop hysterically from the tip of her nose. "And that's all the ink. All over that hideous beast. I ought to—"

"What's the matter, Izzie?" The little man with the tic came up. "Spill your ink?"

"The minutes—" wailed the woman.

"Shame." The little man clucked sympathetically. "But this gentleman is speaking to us tonight on a message of such vital importance that I'm sure we won't want to wait for the minutes to be read. You can read twice as many next time." He gave Ransom a flaccid hand and waved him to the platform.

Ransom looked at Roland, who was snarling murderously at the terrier. He jerked the leash. "Shut up, Roland." With a contemptuous snort Roland shook his spotted torso and allowed Ransom to drag him to the platform.

MacTate joined them with the pink hanger and hula skirt. "What was it you said about not getting involved with irate spinsters, old boy?"

Ransom groaned. "MacTate, do you get the impression that all this was—foreshadowed? On our way down the alley? First he gets smacked by a duck and busts a pot of cactus; now it's an ink bottle and the minutes."

"Tut-tut, old boy. You're changing your philosophy. You—"

"Tonight—" said the little man with the tic. He was standing at the front of the platform, surveying the room. He cleared his throat several times to call the meeting to order. "Tonight—"

"Listen, MacTate," said Ransom. "I've got it. You take over the pitch and I'll be the angel. You know how everything works. I've got to keep an eye on Roland. He's heading for trouble."

"But, Ransom—"

"Don't argue, MacTate. I can't—"

"And so we are to have the privilege," the little man with the tic was saying, "of hearing Professor—Professor—" He turned to Ransom with a fatuous grin.

"MacTate," said Ransom.

"Professor MacTate speak to us on—" The little man stared earnestly at the owl, the moose, and Roland.

"Ezekiel," said Ransom.

"Yes, Ezekiel." The little man continued to stare dubiously at the animals. "Since the minutes of the last meeting are still in preparation, I present Professor—" He hopped off the platform and sat down beside the hyperthyroidal woman.

"Go ahead, MacTate."

"Ransom, really—"

"It's your fault. You got him stirred up. Now you can just take over."

MacTate sighed and put down the moose's head. He got up and faced the audience uncertainly. "Ladies and gentlemen." He turned to look at Ransom once more. Ransom shook his head and motioned toward Roland. MacTate shrugged. "Ladies and gentlemen, I am given to understand that in the current consensus Ezekiel's vision of the wheel within a wheel was—hallucinatory. Tonight we wish to submit an alternative hypothesis; namely, that the vision was an objective phenomenon effected by—reproducible natural causes." He waved at Ransom and the animals. "With your indulgence we shall substitute an owl for the eagle, a moose for the ox, this—spotted animal for the lion, and my colleague here for the angel." There was a chillingly derogatory cough from someone in the front row. "And now without further delay—" He waved nervously toward Ransom again and stepped off the platform.

Ransom had put Roland's pompadoured mane back on and placed the owl beside him. He picked up the moose's head, stepped as far from Roland as the leash tied to his wrist would permit and, setting the lightless flashlight on the platform, turned it on. Shortly the platform was covered with sixteen creatures. The Ransoms among them began to swing the mooses' heads from side to side with one hand while jerking intermittently at the Rolands' leashes with the other, so that two concentric circular blurs appeared on the platform. At length the four Rolands, lurching drunkenly, upset the four owls, and the Ransoms converged on the flashlight to turn it off.

MacTate stepped up on the platform again. "A wheel within a wheel, as you see." He looked dubiously at the owl. "It strikes me that there may have been some discrepancy between the arrangement of the creatures in Ezekiel and that in our reproduction, but that we have duplicated the motivating principle is, I think—incontestable."

Roland suddenly eructated hollowly. Ransom looked at him apprehensively. "Get down here, Roland." He jumped off the platform, dragging Roland after him, and crouched in its lee. Putting down the moose's head, he took the red ball out of his pocket. "Bite on this and keep your head down." He stuck the ball into Roland's mouth.

MacTate, who had intended to ask Ransom technical questions for the benefit of the audience, had to find some other way to keep the show going. "I—" He looked around. "Here." He picked up the owl, stepped off the platform, and went to the corner of the room. "We might reconstruct the situation in Ezekiel in the following way." He held up the owl and looked at it. "Picture, if you can, a Babylonian noble out for a bit of hunting with his trained eagle." He balanced the owl on his wrist in the manner of a medieval falconer and, he hoped, a Babylonian eagler. "Presently, as we roam the fertile savannas of the Tigris-Euphrates Valley, we encounter a stray from our herd of choice oxen who is beset by a well-starved lion." He gestured toward Roland and the moose and started toward them.

"Look, Roland," said Ransom. "He called you a well-starved lion. That ought to make you feel better." He stepped toward MacTate, put the flashlight on the floor, nodding to him to carry the demonstration through, and went back to Roland.

Roland straightened his forelegs and looked up.

"Our noble realizes," continued MacTate, "that a frontal attack on the ravenous beast would be futile." He gestured toward Roland again. "Consequently he bethinks him of a stratagem whereby—"

Roland, apparently carried away by his dramatic instincts, opened his mouth and uttered a lionlike sound. The red ball dropped to the floor and bounced away in the direction of the flashlight. The terrier, who had been watching his enemy's tribulation with intense satisfaction, leaped off the hyperthyroidal woman's lap and streaked after the ball.

Roland's lionlike sound turned angrily doglike. He bounded to his feet and charged to intercept the terrier, dragging Ransom as well as the moose, whose antlers had become entangled in the leash, after him.

"Watch him, Roland," warned MacTate. "He's a tricky—"

Just as he was about to collide with Roland, the terrier reversed his field, then swung back, leaped up to grab the hula skirt with his teeth, and pulled it over Roland's eyes again. Roland snarled and snapped blindly at the ball. He clearly missed it, because it bounced off his nose into the teeth of the grinning terrier; but he had ingurgitated something, because his snarl ended abruptly in a gulp.

"MacTate, my God, he's swallowed the flashlight." Ransom grabbed Roland's head and tried to force his jaws apart, but

Roland twisted away and bounded about, winding the leash around Ransom's legs.

The terrier, drunk with success, had lingered too near the scene of his victory. As he leaped to escape the circling leash, it caught his hind legs and pinioned him to Ransom. The red ball dropped from his yelping jaws and rolled down the floor.

There was a shriek from the front row, and the hyperthyroidal woman darted into the maelstrom to rescue the terrier. MacTate noticed that they were all dangerously near one of the low windows. "Be careful, Roland." He ran to close the window, but before he could reach it the hyperthyroidal woman had crowded the others almost through it. She had the terrier around the neck, twisting and tugging to free him from his enemies. In desperation she braced her foot against Roland's brisket and threw her entire weight backward. Amid a horror of assorted howls the terrier came free and sailed back into the room over his toppling mistress's head, while his enemies hurtled through the window. Outside there was a sickening crash. As the terrier and his mistress picked themselves up, MacTate steeled himself to look out the window. The roof of the next building was level with the floor he stood on. Just below the open window was a skylight, lit from beneath so that he could clearly see the immense hole his falling companions had made in it. . . .

For an anti-cigarette sermon with telling scriptural references, his brethren were agreed, nobody could touch Brother Smigg. Anti-liquor, maybe, but not anti-cigarette. As he approached the preparation of his present effort, the amens and other encouragements from the congregation became almost perfervid.

"And now that we've heard what Paul has to say about this filthy and disgusting habit," he was saying, "let's turn to Revelation 13 and hear from John." He scratched his jaw and beamed at his auditory over his glasses. " 'Opening the mouth in blasphemy,' John calls it. And anybody that does it is a beast. Let's just see how John describes him. 'And I stood upon the sand of the sea, and saw a beast rise up out of the sea, having seven heads and ten horns . . .' "

Suddenly there was a crash over Brother Smigg's head, and the congregation saw the beast in question glide down to the platform behind him. On four of the heads an odd pink horn curved up from the neck over the top of the skull. On each of the other three, which formed a triangle with the end wall of the room as its base, there were two much larger horns, great platelike things with jagged edges.

Brother Smigg, who was stone-deaf, pursued his text. " '. . . And the beast which I saw was like unto a leopard' "— the congregation gasped, for the peculiar fourfold body of the beast was covered with violet spots—" 'and his feet were as the feet of a bear, and his mouth as the mouth of a lion.' " The beast's feet, which were hidden in a mass of strawlike stuff, might well have been those of a bear, while the sounds issuing from four of its throats were indeed suggestive of a stricken lion.

"Judgment Day!" A brother in the front row stood up and clasped his hands over his head.

"Lead me down that glory road!" A brother behind him leaped up and waved his arms.

"Hallelujah!" Several other brethren began to rock back and forth, moaning enthusiastically.

Brother Smigg, his nose deep in his text, continued imperturbably: " '. . . And I saw one of his heads as it were wounded to death; and his deadly wound was healed.' "

"Three heads, Brother." Someone in the third row jumped up on the bench and pointed ecstatically. "Three heads has holes in them. Holes of sin."

"But no blood, Brother." A companion hopped up beside him and pointed too. "All healed up, like it says."

"Amen, Brother." They shook hands hysterically, teetered on the rickety bench, and fell back among the raised arms of their swaying brethren.

" '. . . And there was given unto him,' " read Brother Smigg, " 'a mouth speaking great things and blasphemies—' "

"God damn it, Roland," bellowed a voice under the beast, "get off my head." Four men writhed away from the beast, untied thongs from their wrists, swung their bellies sideways, and, stepping to the front of the platform, suddenly became one man. Brother Smigg, looking up, dropped his jaw in astonishment. The congregation rushed forward with a babel of eschatological cries. . . .

As MacTate stepped back from the window he was surprised by a burst of applause from the Abnormal Psychologists. They rose, clapping and shouting, and surged upon him with wild congratulations.

"Greatest demonstration of mass hypnosis I've seen."

"First time in thirty years anyone has put me under."

"The really clever thing was using a *real* red ball for the terrier."

The hyperthyroidal woman's protesting screams were drowned out in the ovation.

"Please understand—" MacTate tried frantically to push his way through them. "It was a living man and dog that fell out—"

"Members of the society." The little man with the tic leaped to the platform and spread his arms for attention. "I move we elect this gentleman to membership by acclaim and appoint him permanent chairman of the program committee."

The society cheered.

"Really," said MacTate. "Another time . . . But now . . ." He succeeded finally in breaking through the crowd and ran down the stairs to the street. There was a light in the second story of the next building. He tried the door. It was locked. "The back. Must have a back door." He ran down to the corner, rounded it, and looked for the alley leading to the rear of the building. Just as he found it he collided heavily with something emerging from it and sat down abruptly on the sidewalk.

"MacTate, you all right?" Ransom helped him up. "Shouldn't run in the dark like that. Not when Roland's running the other way." He grabbed Roland's collar and MacTate's arm and pulled them to the corner. "Let's find a taxi and get out of here. Roland's got to get to a veterinary."

"But the moose and the owl?"

"Forget them. I'll buy the boys' club new ones before I'll go back *there*."

"But Roland doesn't seem to be seriously injured." MacTate glanced at him. "When I saw the hole in that skylight—"

"No, no. When we crashed through it, the jolt turned on the flashlight inside of him. Funny effect. He looked something like an asterisk. Anyway, the magnetic doughnut does something to gravity, and we sort of floated to the floor. I finally shut it off by making him jump around, but it might go on again any minute. Gave me a turn when you ran into him like that. So we've got to take him to a vet and get him pumped out. There." Ransom saw someone getting out of a taxi halfway down the block and began to run. "Take us to that all-night animal hospital out on the old mill road," he told the driver when they had piled in. Roland sank to the floor with an abysmal groan. "Poor Roland. He's had a hard day."

"But, old boy," said MacTate, "were you really serious about never going back again? I incurred—something of an obligation. The society elected me chairman of its program committee, and I hadn't time to decline formally."

"Think nothing of it, MacTate." Ransom laughed. "You're not the only one that incurred obligations tonight. Take Brother Ransom, for instance." He looked out the taxi window and sighed. "I've just been elected moderator of the Happy Little Brotherhood of the Narrow Way."

Star, Bright

MARK CLIFTON

❧

Mr. Clifton uses those handy tools, the Moebius strip, Klein's bottle, and the tesseract, to construct a finely farfetched yarn about genius children, time travel, teleportation, and other science-fiction reliables. His story belongs to what I call the Medieval Period: science-fiction had grown up in 1952 but had not yet become so esoteric in style and approach as to force the reader into becoming a cryptographer.

Friday, June 11th

AT THREE YEARS OF AGE a little girl shouldn't have enough functioning intelligence to cut out and paste together a Moebius strip.

Or, if she did it by accident, she surely shouldn't have enough reasoning ability to pick up one of her crayons and carefully trace the continuous line to prove it has only one surface.

And if by some strange coincidence she did, and it was still just an accident, how can I account for this generally active daughter of mine—and I do mean *active*—sitting for a solid half hour with her chin cupped in her hand, staring off into space, thinking with such concentration that it was almost painful to watch?

I was in my reading chair, going over some work. Star was sitting on the floor, in the circle of my light, with her blunt-nosed scissors and her scraps of paper.

Her long silence made me glance down at her as she was taping the two ends of the paper together. At that point I thought it was an accident that she had given a half twist to the paper strip before joining the circle. I smiled to myself as she picked it up in her chubby fingers.

"A little child forms the enigma of the ages," I mused.

But instead of throwing the strip aside, or tearing it apart as any other child would do, she carefully turned it over and around—studying it from all sides.

Then she picked up one of her crayons and began tracing the line. She did it as though she were substantiating a conclusion already reached!

It was a bitter confirmation for me. I had been refusing to face it for a long time, but I could ignore it no longer.

Star was a High I.Q.

For half an hour I watched her while she sat on the floor, one knee bent under her, her chin in her hand, unmoving. Her eyes were wide with wonderment, looking into the potentialities of the phenomenon she had found.

It has been a tough struggle, taking care of her since my wife's death. Now this added problem. If only she could have been normally dull, like other children!

I made up my mind while I watched her. If a child is afflicted, then let's face it, she's afflicted. A parent must teach her to compensate. At least she could be prepared for the bitterness I'd known. She could learn early to take it in stride.

I could use the measurements available, get the degree of intelligence, and in that way grasp the extent of my problem. A twenty-point jump in I.Q. creates an entirely different set of problems. The 140 child lives in a world nothing at all like that of the 100 child and a world which the 120 child can but vaguely sense. The problems which vex and challenge the 160 pass over the 140 as a bird flies over a field mouse. I must not make the mistake of posing the problems of one if she is the other. I must know. In the meantime I must treat it casually.

"That's called the Moebius strip, Star," I interrupted her thoughts.

She came out of her reverie with a start. I didn't like the quick

MOEBIUS STRIP

way her eyes sought mine—almost furtively, as though she had been caught doing something bad.

"Somebody already make it?" she disappointedly asked.

She knew what she had discovered! Something inside me spilled over with grief, and something else caught at me with dread.

I kept my voice casual. "A man by the name of Moebius. A long time ago. I'll tell you about him sometime when you're older."

"Now. While I'm little," she commanded with a frown. "And don't tell. Read me."

What did she mean by that? Oh, she must be simply paraphrasing me at those times in the past when I've wanted the facts and not garbled generalizations. It could only be that!

"Okay, young lady." I lifted an eyebrow and glared at her in mock ferociousness, which usually sent her into gales of laughter. "I'll slow you down!"

She remained completely sober.

I turned to the subject in a physics book. It's not in simple language, by any means, and I read it as rapidly as I could speak. My thought was to make her admit she didn't understand it, so I could translate it into basic language.

Her reaction?

"You read too slow, Daddy," she complained. She was childishly irritable about it. "You say a word. Then I think a long time. Then you say another word."

I knew what she meant. I remember, when I was a child, my thoughts used to dart in and out among the slowly droning words of any adult. Whole patterns of universes would appear and disappear in those brief moments.

"So?" I asked.

"So," she mocked me impishly. "You teach me to read. Then I can think quick as I want."

"Quickly," I corrected in a weak voice. "The word is 'quickly,' an adverb."

She looked at me impatiently, as if she saw through this allegedly adult device to show up a younger's ignorance. I felt like the dope!

September 1st

A great deal has happened the past few months. I have tried a number of times to bring the conversation around to discuss Star's affliction with her. But she is amazingly adroit at heading me off, as though she already knows what I am trying to say and isn't concerned. Perhaps, in spite of her brilliance, she's too young to realize the hostility of the world toward intelligence.

Some of the visiting neighbors have been amused to see her sit on the floor with an encyclopedia as big as she is, rapidly turning the pages. Only Star and I know she is reading the pages as rapidly as she can turn them. I've brushed away the neighbors' comments with: "She likes to look at the pictures."

They talk to her in baby talk—and she answers in baby talk! How does she know enough to do that?

I have spent the months making an exhaustive record of her I.Q. measurements, aptitude speeds, reaction, tables, all the recommended paraphernalia for measuring something we know nothing about.

The tables are screwy, or Star is beyond all measurement.

All right, Pete Holmes, how are you going to pose those problems and combat them for her, when you have no conception of what they might be? But I must have a conception. I've got to be able to comprehend at least a little of what she may face. I simply couldn't stand by and do nothing.

Easy, though. Nobody knows better than you the futility of trying to compete out of your class. How many students, workers, and employers have tried to compete with you? You've watched them and pitied them, comparing them to a donkey trying to run the Kentucky Derby.

How does it feel to be in the place of the donkey for a change? You've always blamed them for not realizing they shouldn't try to compete.

But this is my own daughter! I *must* understand.

October 1st

Star is now four years old, and according to state law her mind has now developed enough so that she may attend nursery school. Again I tried to prepare her for what she might face. She listened through about two sentences and changed the subject. I can't tell about Star. Does she already know the answers? Or does she not even realize there is a problem?

I was in a sweat of worry when I took her to her first day at school yesterday morning. Last night I was sitting in my chair, reading. After she had put her dolls away, she went to the bookshelves and brought down a book of fairy tales.

That is another peculiarity of hers. She has an unmeasurably quick perception, yet she has all the normal reactions of a little girl. She likes her dolls, fairy stories, playing grown up. No, she's not a monster.

She brought the book of fairy tales over to me.

"Daddy, read me a story," she asked quite seriously.

I looked at her in amazement. "Since when? Go read your own story."

She lifted an eyebrow in imitation of my own characteristic gesture.

"Children of my age do not read," she instructed pedantically. "I can't learn to read until I am in the first grade. It is very hard to do and I am much too little."

She had found the answer to her affliction—conformity! She had already learned to conceal her intelligence. So many of us break our hearts before we learn that.

But you don't have to conceal it from me, Star! Not from me!

Oh well, I could go along with the gag, if that was what she wanted.

"Did you like nursery school?" I asked the standard question.

"Oh yes," she exclaimed enthusiastically. "It was fun."

"And what did you learn today, little girl?"

She played it straight back to me. "Not much. I tried to cut out paper dolls, but the scissors kept slipping." Was there an elfin deviltry back of her sober expression?

"Now, look," I cautioned, "don't overdo it. That's as bad as being too quick. The idea is that everybody has to be just about standard average. That's the only thing we will tolerate. It is expected that a little girl of four should know how to cut out paper dolls properly."

"Oh?" she questioned, and looked thoughtful. "I guess that's the hard part, isn't it, Daddy—to know how much you ought to know?"

"Yes, that's the hard part," I agreed fervently.

"But it's all right," she reassured me. "One of the Stupids showed me how to cut them out, so now that little girl likes me. She just took charge of me then and told the other kids they should like me too. So of course they did because she's leader. I think I did right, after all."

"Oh no!" I breathed to myself. She knew how to manipulate other people already. Then my thought whirled around another concept. It was the first time she had verbally classified normal people as "Stupids," but it had slipped out so easily that I knew she'd been thinking to herself for a long time. Then my whirling thoughts hit a third implication.

"Yes, maybe it was the right thing," I conceded. "Where the little girl was concerned, that is. But don't forget you were being observed by a grown-up teacher in the room. And she's smarter."

"You mean she's older, Daddy," Star corrected me.

"Smarter, too, maybe. You can't tell."

"I can." She sighed. "She's just older."

I think it was growing fear which made me defensive.

"That's good," I said emphatically. "That's very good. You can learn a lot from her then. It takes an awful lot of study to learn how to be stupid."

My own troublesome business life came to mind and I thought to myself, "I sometimes think I'll never learn it."

I swear I didn't say it aloud. But Star patted me consolingly and answered as though I'd spoken.

"That's because you're only fairly bright, Daddy. You're a Tween, and that's harder than being really bright."

"A Tween? What's a Tween?" I was bumbling to hide my confusion.

"That's what I mean, Daddy," she answered in exasperation. "You don't grasp quickly. An In Between, of course. The other people are Stupids, I'm a Bright, and you're a Tween. I made those names up when I was little."

Good God! Besides being unmeasurably bright, she's a telepath!

All right, Pete, there you are. On reasoning processes you might stand a chance—but not telepathy!

"Star," I said on impulse, "can you read people's minds?"

"Of course, Daddy," she answered, as if I'd asked a foolishly obvious question.

"Can you teach me?"

She looked at me impishly. "You're already learning it a little. But you're so slow! You see, you didn't even know you were learning."

Her voice took on a wistful note, a tone of loneliness.

"I wish—" she said, and paused.

"What do you wish?"

"You see what I mean, Daddy? You try, but you're so slow."

All the same, I knew. I knew she was already longing for a companion whose mind could match her own.

A father is prepared to lose his daughter eventually, Star, but not so soon.

Not so soon. . . .

June again

Some new people have moved in next door. Star says their name is Howell—Bill and Ruth Howell. They have a son, Robert, who looks maybe a year older than Star, who will soon be five.

Star seems to have taken up with Robert right away. He is a well-mannered boy and good company for Star.

I'm worried, though. Star had something to do with their moving in next door. I'm convinced of that. I'm also convinced, even from the little I've seen of him, that Robert is a Bright and a telepath.

Could it be that, failing to find quick accord with my mind, Star has reached out and out until she made contact with a telepath companion?

No, that's too fantastic. Even if it were so, how could she shape circumstances so she could bring Robert to live next door to her? The Howells came from another city. It just happened that the people who lived next door moved out and the house was put up for sale.

Just happened? How frequently do we find such abnormal Brights? What are the chances of one *just happening* to move in next door to another?

I know he is a telepath because, as I write this, I sense him reading it.

I even catch his thought: "Oh, pardon me, Mr. Holmes. I didn't intend to peek. Really I didn't."

Did I imagine that? Or is Star building a skill in my mind?

"It isn't nice to look into another person's mind unless you're asked, Robert," I thought back, rather severely. It was purely an experiment.

"I know it, Mr. Holmes. I apologize." He is in his bed in his house, across the driveway.

"No, Daddy, he really didn't mean to." And Star is in her bed in this house.

It is impossible to write how I feel. There comes a time when words are empty husks. But mixed with my expectant dread is a thread of gratitude for having been taught to be even stumblingly telepathic.

Saturday, August 11th

I've thought of a gag. I haven't seen Jim Pietre in a month of Sundays, not since he was awarded that research fellowship with the museum. It will be good to pull him out of his hole, and this little piece of advertising junk Star dropped should be just the thing.

Strange about the gadget. The Awful Secret Talisman of the Mystic Junior G-Men, no doubt. Still, it doesn't have anything about crackles and pops printed on it. Merely an odd-looking coin, not even true round, bronze by the look of it. Crude. They must stamp them out by the million without ever changing a die.

But it is just the thing to send to Jim to get a rise out of him. He could always appreciate a good practical joke. Wonder how he'd feel to know he was only a Tween.

Monday, August 13th

Sitting here at my study desk, I've been staring into space for an hour. I don't know what to think.

It was about noon today when Jim Pietre called the office on the phone.

"Now, look, Pete," he started out. "What kind of gag are you pulling?"

I chortled to myself and pulled the dead pan on him.

"What do you mean, boy?" I asked back into the phone. "Gag? What kind of gag? What are you talking about?"

"A coin. A coin." He was impatient. "You remember you sent me a coin in the mail?"

"Oh yeah, that." I pretended to remember. "Look, you're an important research analyst on metals—too damned important to keep in touch with your old friends—so I thought I'd make a bid for your attention thataway."

"All right, give," he said in a low voice. "Where did you get it?" He was serious.

"Come off it, Jim. Are you practicing to be a stuffed shirt? I admit it's a rib. Something Star dropped the other day. A manufacturer's idea of kid advertising, no doubt."

"I'm in dead earnest, Peter," he answered. "It's no advertising gadget."

"It means something?"

In college Jim could take a practical joke and make six out of it.

"I don't know what it means. Where did Star get it?" He was being pretty crisp about it.

"Oh, I don't know," I said. I was getting a little fed up; the joke wasn't going according to plan. "Never asked her. You know how kids clutter up the place with their things. No father even tries to keep track of all the junk that can be bought with three box tops and a dime."

"This was not bought with three box tops and a dime." He spaced his words evenly. "This was not bought anywhere, for any price. In fact, if you want to be logical about it, this coin doesn't exist at all."

I laughed out loud. This was more like the old Jim.

"Okay, so you've turned the gag back on me. Let's call it quits. How about coming over to supper some night soon?"

"I'm coming over, my friend." He remained grim as he said it. "And I'm coming over tonight. As soon as you will be home. It's no gag I'm pulling. Can you get that through your stubborn head? You say you got it from Star, and of course I believe you. But it's no toy. It's the real thing." Then, as if in profound puzzlement, "Only it isn't."

A feeling of dread was settling upon me. Once you cried "Uncle" to Jim, he always let up.

"Suppose you tell me what you mean," I answered soberly.

"That's more like it, Pete. Here's what we know about the coin so far. It is apparently pre-Egyptian. It's hand-cast. It's made out of one of the lost bronzes. We fix it at around four thousand years old."

"That ought to be easy to solve," I argued. "Probably some coin collector is screaming all over the place for it. No doubt lost it and Star found it. Must be lots of old coins like that in museums and in private collections."

I was rationalizing more for my own benefit than for Jim. He would know all those things without my mentioning them. He waited until I had finished.

"Step two," he went on. "We've got one of the top coin men in the world here at the museum. As soon as I saw what the metal was, I took it to him. Now hold onto your chair, Pete. He says there is no coin like it in the world, either museum or private collection."

"You museum boys get beside yourselves at times. Come down to earth. Sometime, somewhere, some collector picked it up in some exotic place and kept it quiet. I don't have to tell you how some collectors are—sitting in a dark room, gloating over some worthless bauble, not telling a soul about it—"

"All right, wise guy," he interrupted. "Step three. That coin is at least four thousand years old, *and it's also brand-new!* Let's hear you explain that away."

"New?" I asked weakly. "I don't get it."

"Old coins show wear. The edges get rounded with handling. The surface oxidizes. The molecular structure changes, crystallizes. This coin shows no wear, no oxidation, no molecular change. This coin might have been struck yesterday. *Where did Star get it?*"

"Hold it a minute," I pleaded.

I began to think back. Saturday morning. Star and Robert had been playing a game. Come to think of it, that was a peculiar game. Mighty peculiar.

Star would run into the house and stand in front of the encyclopedia shelf. I could hear Robert counting loudly at the base tree outside in the back yard. She would stare at the encyclopedia for a moment.

Once I heard her mumble, "That's a good place."

Or maybe she merely thought it and I caught the thought. I'm doing that quite a bit of late.

Then she would run outside again. A moment later Robert would run in and stand in front of the same shelf. Then he also would run outside again. There would be silence for several minutes. The silence would rupture with a burst of laughing and shouting. Soon Star would come in again.

"How does he find me?" I heard her think once. "I can't reason it, and I can't ESP it out of him."

It was during one of their silences when Ruth called over to me.

"Hey, Pete! Do you know where the kids are? Time for their milk and cookies."

The Howells are awfully good to Star, bless 'em. I got up and went over to the window.

"I don't know, Ruth," I called back. "They were in and out only a few minutes ago."

"Well, I'm not worried," she said. She came through the kitchen door and stood on the back steps. "They know better than to cross the street by themselves. They're too little for that. So I guess they're over at Marily's. When they come back, tell 'em to come and get it."

"Okay, Ruth," I answered.

She opened the screen door again and went back into her kitchen. I left the window and returned to my work.

A little later both the kids came running into the house. I managed to capture them long enough to tell them about the cookies and milk.

"Beat you there!" Robert shouted to Star.

There was a scuffle and they ran out the front door. I noticed then that Star had dropped the coin and I picked it up and sent it to Jim Pietre.

"Hello, Jim," I said into the phone. "Are you still there?"

"Yep, still waiting for an answer," he said.

"Jim, I think you'd better come over to the house right away. I'll leave my office now and meet you there. Can you get away?"

"Can I get away?" he exclaimed. "Boss says to trace this coin down and do nothing else. See you in fifteen minutes."

He hung up. Thoughtfully I replaced the receiver and went out to my car. I was pulling into my block from one arterial when I saw Jim's car pulling in from a block away. I stopped at the curb and waited for him. I didn't see the kids anywhere out front.

Jim climbed out of his car, and I never saw such an eager look of anticipation on a man's face before. I didn't realize I was showing my dread, but when he saw my face he became serious.

"What is it, Pete? What on earth is it?" he almost whispered.

"I don't know. At least I'm not sure. Come on inside the house."

We let ourselves in the front, and I took Jim into the study. It has a large window opening on the back garden, and the scene was very clear.

At first it was an innocent scene—so innocent and peaceful. Just three little children in the back yard playing hide-and-seek. Marily, a neighbor's child, was stepping up to the base tree.

"Now look, you kids," she was saying. "You hide where I can find you or I won't play."

"But where can we go, Marily?" Robert was arguing loudly. Like all little boys, he seems to carry on his conversations at the top of his lungs. "There's the garage, and there's those trees and bushes. You have to look everywhere, Marily."

"And there's going to be other buildings and trees and bushes there afterward," Star called out with glee. "You gotta look behind them too."

"Yeah!" Robert took up the teasing refrain. "And there's been lots and lots of buildings and trees there before—especially trees. You gotta look behind them too."

Marily tossed her head petulantly. "I don't know what you're talking about, and I don't care. Just hide where I can find you, that's all."

She hid her face at the tree and started counting. If I had been alone, I would have been sure my eyesight had failed me or that I was the victim of hallucinations. But Jim was standing there and saw it too.

Marily started counting, yet the other two didn't run away. Star reached out and took Robert's hand and they merely stood there. For an instant they seemed to shimmer and—*they disappeared without moving a step!*

Marily finished her counting and ran around to the few possible hiding places in the yard. When she couldn't find them, she started to blubber and pushed through the hedge to Ruth's back door.

"They runned away from me again," she whined through the screen at Ruth.

Jim and I stood staring out the window. I glanced at him. His face was set and pale, but probably no worse than my own.

We saw the instant shimmer again. Star, and then immediately Robert, materialized from the air and ran up to the tree, shouting, "Safe! Safe!"

Marily let out a bawl and ran home to her mother.

I called Star and Robert into the house. They came, still holding hands, a little shamefaced, a little defiant.

How to begin? What in hell could I say?

"It's not exactly fair," I told them. "Marily can't follow you there." I was shooting in the dark, but I had at least a glimmering to go by.

Star turned pale enough for the freckles on her little nose to stand out under her tan. Robert blushed and turned to her fiercely.

"I told you so, Star. I *told* you so! I said it wasn't sporting," he accused. He turned to me. "Marily can't play good hide-and-seek anyway. She's only a Stupid."

"Let's forget that for a minute, Robert," I turned to her. "Star, just where do you go?"

"Oh, it's nothing, Daddy." She spoke defensively, belittling the whole thing. "We just go a little ways when we play with her. She ought to be able to find us a little ways."

"That's evading the issue. *Where* do you go—and *how* do you go?"

Jim stepped forward and showed her the bronze coin I'd sent him.

"You see, Star," he said quietly. "We've found this."

"I shouldn't have to tell you my game." She was almost in tears. "You're both just Tweens. You couldn't understand." Then, struck with contrition, she turned to me. "Daddy, I've tried and tried to ESP you. Truly I did. But you don't ESP worth anything." She slipped her hand through Robert's arm. "Robert does it very nicely," she said primly, as though she were complimenting him on using his fork the right way. "He must be better than I am, because I don't know how he finds me."

"I'll tell you how I do it, Star," Robert exclaimed eagerly. It was as if he were trying to make amends now that grownups had caught on. "You don't use any imagination. I never saw anybody with so little imagination!"

"I do, too, have imagination," she countered loudly. "I thought up the game, didn't I? I told you how to do it, didn't I?"

"Yeah, yeah!" he shouted back. "But you always have to look at a book to ESP what's in it, so you leave an ESP smudge. I just go to the encyclopedia and ESP where you did—and I go to that place—and there you are. It's simple."

Star's mouth dropped open in consternation.

"I never thought of that," she said.

Jim and I stood there, letting the meaning of what they were saying penetrate slowly into our incredulous minds.

"Anyway," Robert was saying, "you haven't any imagination." He sank down cross-legged on the floor. "You can't teleport yourself to any place that's never been."

She went over to squat down beside him. "I can too! What about the moon people? They haven't been yet."

He looked at her with childish disgust.

"Oh, Star, they have so been. You know that." He spread his hands out as though he were a baseball referee. "That time hasn't been yet for your daddy here, for instance, but it's already been for somebody like—well, say, like those things from Arcturus."

"Well, neither have you teleported yourself to some place that never was." Star was arguing back. "So there."

Waving Jim to one chair, I sank down shakily into another. At least the arms of the chair felt solid beneath my hands.

"Now, look, kids," I interrupted their evasive tactics. "Let's start at the beginning. I gather you've figured a way to travel to places in the past or future."

"Well, of course, Daddy." Star shrugged the statement aside nonchalantly. "We just TP ourselves by ESP anywhere we want to go. It doesn't do any harm."

And these were the children who were too little to cross the street!

I have been through times of shock before. This was the same —somehow the mind becomes too stunned to react beyond a point. One simply plows through the rest the best he can, almost normally.

"Okay, okay," I said, and was surprised to hear the same tone I would have used over an argument about the biggest piece of cake. "I don't know whether it's harmful or not. I'll have to think it over. Right now just tell me how you do it."

"It would be so much easier if I could ESP it to you," Star said doubtfully.

"Well, pretend I'm a Stupid and tell me in words."

"You remember the Moebius strip?" she asked very slowly and carefully, starting with the first and most basic point in almost the way one explains to an ordinary child.

Yes, I remembered it. And I remembered how long ago it was that she had discovered it. Over a year, and her busy, brilliant mind had been exploring its possibilities ever since. And I thought she had forgotten it!

"That's where you join the ends of a strip of paper together with a half twist to make one surface," she went on, as though jogging my undependable, slow memory.

"Yes," I answered. "We all know the Moebius strip."

Jim looked startled. I had never told him about the incident.

"Next you take a sheet and you give it a half twist and join the edge to itself all over to make a funny kind of holder."

"Klein's bottle," Jim supplied.

She looked at him in relief.

"Oh, you know about that," she said. "That makes it easier. Well, then, the next step—you take a cube." Her face clouded with doubt again, and she explained, "You can't do this with your hands. You've gotta ESP it done, because it's an imaginary cube anyway."

She looked at us questioningly. I nodded for her to continue.

"And you ESP the twisted cube all together the same way you did Klein's bottle. Now if you do that big enough, all around you, so you're sort of half twisted in the middle, then you can TP yourself anywhere you want to go. And that's all there is to it," she finished hurriedly.

"Where have you gone?" I asked her quietly.

KLEIN'S BOTTLE

The technique of doing it would take some thinking. I knew enough physics to know that was the way the dimensions were built up. The line, the plane, the cube—Euclidian physics. The Moebius strip, the Klein bottle, the unnamed twisted cube—Einsteinian physics. Yes, it was possible.

"Oh, we've gone all over," Star answered vaguely. "The Romans and the Egyptians—places like that."

"You picked up a coin in one of those places?" Jim asked.

He was doing a good job of keeping his voice casual. I knew the excitement he must be feeling, the vision of the wealth of knowledge which must be opening before his eyes.

"I found it, Daddy," Star answered Jim's question. She was about to cry. "I found it in the dirt, and Robert was about to catch me. I forgot I had it when I went away from there so fast." She looked at me pleadingly. "I didn't mean to steal it, Daddy. I never stole anything, anywhere. And I was going to take it back and put it right where I found it. Truly I was. But I dropped it again, and then I ESP'd that you had it. I guess I was awful naughty."

I brushed my hand across my forehead.

"Let's skip the question of good and bad for a minute," I said, my head throbbing. "What about this business of going into the future?"

Robert spoke up, his eyes shining. "There isn't any future, Mr. Holmes. That's what I keep telling Star, but she can't reason—she's just a girl. It'll all pass. Everything is always past."

Jim stared at him, as though thunderstruck, and opened his mouth in protest. I shook my head warningly.

"Suppose you tell me about that, Robert," I said.

"Well," he began on a rising note, frowning, "it's kinda hard to explain at that. Star's a Bright and even she doesn't understand it exactly. But, you see, I'm older." He looked at her with superiority. Then, with a change of mood, he defended her. "But when she gets as old as I am, she'll understand it okay."

He patted her shoulder consolingly. He was all of six years old.

"You go back into the past. Back past Egypt and Atlantis. That's recent," he said with scorn. "And on back, and on back, and all of a sudden it's future."

"That isn't the way *I* did it." Star tossed her head contrarily. "I *reasoned* the future. I reasoned what would come next, and I went there, and then I reasoned again. And on and on. I can, too, reason."

"It's the same future," Robert told us dogmatically. "It has to be, because that's all that ever happened." He turned to Star. "The reason you never could find any Garden of Eden is because there wasn't any Adam and Eve." Then to me, "And man didn't come from the apes, either. Man started himself."

Jim almost strangled as he leaned forward, his face red and his eyes bulging.

"How?" he choked out.

Robert sent his gaze into the far distance.

"Well," he said, "a long time from now—you know what I mean, as a Stupid would think of Time-From-Now—men got into a mess. Quite a mess . . .

"There were some people in that time who figured out the same kind of traveling Star and I do. So when the world was about to blow up and form a new star, a lot of them teleported themselves back to when the earth was young, and they started over again."

Jim just stared at Robert, unable to speak.

"I don't get it," I said.

"Not everybody could do it," Robert explained patiently. "Just a few Brights. But they enclosed a lot of other people and took them along." He became a little vague at this point. "I guess later on the Brights lost interest in the Stupids or something. Anyway, the Stupids sank down lower and lower and became like animals." He held his nose briefly. "They smelled worse. They worshiped the Brights as gods."

Robert looked at me and shrugged.

"I don't know all that happened. I've only been there a few times. It's not very interesting. Anyway," he finished, "the Brights finally disappeared."

"I'd sure like to know where they went." Star sighed. It was a lonely sigh. I helplessly took her hand and gave my attention back to Robert.

"I still don't quite understand," I said.

He grabbed up some scissors, a piece of cellophane tape, a sheet of paper. Quickly he cut a strip, gave it a half twist, and taped it together. Then rapidly, on the Moebius strip, he wrote: "Cave Men, This Men, That Men, Mu Men, Atlantis Men, Egyptians, History Men, Us Now Men, Atom Men, Moon Men, Planet Men, Star Men."

"There," he said. "That's all the room there is on the strip. I've written clear around it. Right after Star Men comes Cave Men. It's all one thing, joined together. It isn't future, and it isn't past, either. It just plain *is*. Don't you see?"

"I'd sure like to know how the Brights got off the strip," Star said wistfully.

I had all I could take.

"Look, kids," I pleaded. "I don't know whether this game's dangerous or not. Maybe you'll wind up in a lion's mouth or something."

"Oh no, Daddy!" Star shrilled in glee. "We'd just TP ourselves right out of there."

"But fast," Robert chortled in agreement.

"Anyway, I've got to think it over," I said stubbornly. "I'm only a Tween, but, Star, I'm your daddy and you're just a little girl, so you have to mind me."

"I always mind you," she said virtuously.

"You do, eh?" I asked. "What about going off the block? Visiting the Greeks and Star Men isn't my idea of staying on the block."

"But you didn't say that, Daddy. You said not to cross the street. And I never did cross the street. Did we, Robert? Did we?"

"We didn't cross a single street, Mr. Holmes," he insisted.

"My God!" said Jim, and he went on trying to light a cigarette.

"All right, all *right!* No more leaving this time, then," I warned.

"Wait!" It was a cry of anguish from Jim. He broke the cigarette in sudden frustration and threw it in an ash tray. "The museum, Pete," he pleaded. "Think what it would mean. Pictures, specimens, voice recordings. And not only from historical places, but Star Men, Pete. *Star Men!* Wouldn't it be all right for them to go places they know are safe? I wouldn't ask them to take risks, but—"

"No, Jim," I said regretfully. "It's your museum, but this is my daughter."

"Sure," he breathed. "I guess I'd feel the same way."

I turned back to the youngsters.

"Star, Robert," I said to them both, "I want your promise that you will not leave this time until I let you. Now I couldn't punish you if you broke your promise, because I couldn't follow you. But I want your promise on your word of honor you won't leave this time."

"We promise." They each held up a hand, as if swearing in court. "No more leaving this time."

I let the kids go back outside into the yard. Jim and I looked at one another for a long while, breathing hard enough to have been running.

"I'm sorry," I said at last.

"I know," he answered. "So am I. But I don't blame you. I simply forgot, for a moment, how much a daughter could mean to a man." He was silent and then added, with the humorous quirk back at the corner of his lips, "I can just see myself reporting this interview to the museum."

"You don't intend to, do you?" I asked, alarmed.

"And get myself canned or laughed at? I'm not that stupid."

September 10th

Am I actually getting it? I had a flash for an instant. I was concentrating on Caesar's triumphant march into Rome. For the

90

briefest of instants *there it was!* I was standing on the roadway, watching. But, most peculiar, it was still a picture; I was the only thing moving. And then, just as abruptly, I lost it.

Was it only a hallucination? Something brought about by intense concentration and wishful thinking?

Now let's see. You visualize a cube. Then you ESP it a half twist and seal the edges together. No, when it has the half twist there's only one surface. You seal that surface all around you . . .

Sometimes I think I have it. Sometimes I despair. If only I were a Bright instead of a Tween!

October 23rd

I don't see how I managed to make so much work of teleporting myself. It's the simplest thing in the world, no effort at all. Why, a child could do it! That sounds like a gag, considering that it was two children who showed me how, but I mean the whole thing is easy enough for even almost any kid to learn. The problem is understanding the steps . . . no, not understanding, because I can't say I do, but working out the steps in the process.

There's no danger, either. No wonder it felt like a still picture at first, for the speeding up is incredible. That bullet I got in the way of, for instance—I was able to go and meet it and walk along beside it while it traveled through the air. To the men who were dueling I must have been no more than an instantaneous streak of movement.

That's why the youngsters laughed at the suggestion of danger. Even if they materialized right in the middle of an atomic blast, it is so slow by comparison that they could TP right out again before they got hurt. The blast can't travel any faster than the speed of light, you see, while there is no limit to the speed of thought.

But I still haven't given them permission to teleport themselves out of this time yet. I want to go over the ages pretty carefully before I do; I'm not taking any chances, even though I don't see how they could wind up in any trouble. Still, Robert claimed the Brights went from the future back into the beginning, which means they could be going through time and overtake any of the three of us, and one of them might be hostile . . .

I feel like a louse, not taking Jim's cameras, specimen boxes, and recorders along. But there's time for that. Plenty of time, once I get the feel of history without being encumbered by all that stuff to carry.

Speaking of time and history—what a rotten job historians have done! For instance:

George III of England was neither crazy nor a moron. He wasn't a particularly nice guy, I'll admit—I don't see how anybody could be with the amount of flattery I saw—but he was the victim of empire expansion and the ferment of the Industrial Revolution. So were all the other European rulers at the time, though. He certainly did better than Louis of France. At least George kept his job and his head.

On the other hand, John Wilkes Booth was definitely psychotic. He could have been cured if they'd had our methods of psychotherapy then, and Lincoln, of course, wouldn't have been assassinated. It was almost a compulsion to prevent the killing, but I didn't dare . . . God knows what effect it would have had on history. Strange thing, Lincoln looked less surprised than anybody else when he was shot—sad, yes, and hurt emotionally at least as much as physically, yet you'd swear he was expecting it.

Cheops was *plenty* worried about the number of slaves who died while the pyramid was being built. They weren't easy to replace. He gave them four hours off in the hottest part of the day, and I don't think any slaves in the country were fed or housed better.

I never found any signs of Atlantis or Lemuria, just tales of lands far off—a few hundred miles was a big distance then, remember—that had sunk beneath the sea. With the Ancients' exaggerated notion of geography a big island was the same as a continent. Some islands did disappear, naturally, drowning a few thousand villagers and herdsmen. That must have been the source of the legends.

Columbus was a stubborn cuss. He was thinking of turning back when the sailors mutinied, which made him obstinate. I still can't see what was eating Genghis Khan and Alexander the Great—it would have been a big help to know the languages, because their big campaigns started off more like vacation or exploration trips. Helen of Troy was attractive enough, considering, but she was just an excuse to fight.

There were several attempts to federate the Indian tribes before the white man and the Five Nations, but going after wives and slaves ruined the movement every time. I think they could have kept America if they had been united and, it goes without saying, knew the deal they were going to get. At any rate, they might have traded for weapons and tools and industrialized the country somewhat in the way the Japanese did. I admit that's only speculation, but this would certainly have been a different world if they'd succeeded!

One day I'll put it all in a comprehensive and *corrected* history of mankind, *complete with photographs,* and then let the "experts" argue themselves into nervous breakdowns over it.

I didn't get very far into the future. Nowhere near the Star Men or, for that matter, back to the beginning that Robert told us about. It's a matter of reasoning out the path and I'm not a Bright. I'll take Robert and Star along as guides, when and if.

What I did see of the future wasn't so good, but it wasn't so bad either. The real mess obviously doesn't happen until the Star Men show up very far ahead in history, if Robert is right, and I think he is. I can't guess what the trouble will be, but it must be something ghastly if they won't be able to get out of it even with the enormously advanced technology they'll have. Or maybe that's the answer. It's almost true of us now.

November, Friday 14th

The Howells have gone for a weekend trip and left Robert in my care. He's a good kid and no trouble. He and Star have kept their promise, but they're up to something else. I can sense it, and that feeling of expectant dread is back with me.

They've been secretive of late. I catch them concentrating intensely, sighing with vexation, and then breaking out into unexplained giggles.

"Remember your promise," I warned Star while Robert was in the room.

"We're not going to break it, Daddy," she answered seriously.

They both chorused, "No more leaving this time."

But they both broke into giggles!

I'll have to watch them. What good it would do, I don't know. They're up to something, yet how can I stop them? Shut them in their rooms? Tan their hides?

I wonder what someone else would recommend.

Sunday night

The kids are gone!

I've been waiting an hour for them. I know they wouldn't stay away so long if they could get back. There must be something they've run into. Bright as they are, they're still only children.

I have some clues. They promised me they wouldn't go out of this present time. With all her mischievousness, Star has never broken a promise to me—as her typically feminine mind interprets it, that is. So I know they are in our own time.

On several occasions Star has brought it up, wondering where the Old Ones, the Bright Ones, have gone—how they got off the Moebius strip.

That's the clue. How can I get off the Moebius strip and remain in the present?

A cube won't do it. There we have a mere journey along the single surface. We have a line; we have a plane; we have a cube. And then we have a supercube—a tesseract. That is the logical progression of mathematics. The Bright Ones must have pursued that line of reasoning.

Now I've got to do the same, but without the advantage of being a Bright. Still, it's not the same as expecting a normally intelligent person to produce a work of genius. (Genius by our standards, of course, which I suppose Robert and Star would classify as Tween.) Anyone with a pretty fair I.Q. and proper education and training can follow a genius's logic, provided the steps are there and especially if it has a practical application. What he can't do is initiate and complete that structure of logic. I don't have to, either—that was done for me by a pair of Brights, and I "simply" have to apply their findings.

Now let's see if I can.

By reducing the present-past-future of man to a Moebius strip, we have sheared away a dimension. It is a two-dimensional strip, because it has no depth. (Naturally it would be impossible for a Moebius strip to have depth; it has only one surface.)

Reducing it to two dimensions makes it possible to travel anywhere you want to go on it via the third dimension. And you're in the third dimension when you enfold yourself in the twisted cube.

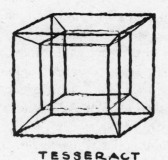

TESSERACT

Let's go a step higher, into one more dimension. In short, the tesseract. To get the equivalent of a Moebius strip with depth you have to go into the fourth dimension, which, it seems to me, is the only way the Bright Ones could get off this closed cycle of past-present-future-past. They must have reasoned that one more notch up the dimensions was all they needed. It is equally obvious that Star and Robert have followed the same line of reasoning; they wouldn't break their promise not to leave the present—and getting off the Moebius strip into *another* present would, in a sort of devious way, be keeping that promise.

I'm putting all this speculation down for you, Jim Pietre, knowing first that you're a Tween like myself and, second, that you're sure to have been doing a lot of thinking about what happened after I sent you the coin Star dropped. I'm hoping you can explain all this to Bill and Ruth Howell—or enough, in any case, to let them understand the truth about their son Robert and my daughter Star and where the children may have gone.

I'm leaving these notes where you will find them, when you and Bill and Ruth search the house and grounds for us. If you read this, it will be because I have failed in my search for the youngsters. There is also the possibility that I'll find them and that we won't be able to get back onto this Moebius strip. Perhaps time has a different value there or doesn't exist at all. What it's like off the strip is anybody's guess.

Bill and Ruth: I wish I might give you hope that I will bring Robert back to you. But all I can do is wish. It may be no more than wishing upon a star—my Star.

I'm trying now to take six cubes and fold them in on one another so that every angle is a right angle.

It's not easy, but I can do it, using every bit of concentration I've learned from the kids. All right, I have the six cubes and I have every angle a right angle.

Now if, in the folding, I ESP the tesseract a half twist around myself and—

FYI

JAMES BLISH

✳

*This one is a really sophisticated job on its own fantastic level.
Certainly the idea of saving the world from annihilation by calling
on George Cantor is an ingenious one. On the other hand, it is dis-
maying to realize that, if we humans exist in finite time and are
bound by our parochial one-to-one correspondence with the integers . . . well, we haven't a ghost of a show.*

"I'VE GOT definite proof that we've been granted a reprieve,"
Lord Rogge was insisting to thin air. "Perfectly definite proof."

We had been listening, either tensely or with resignation,
according to the man, to the evening news roundup in the bar of
the Orchid Club. With the world tottering on the brink, you
might have thought that an announcement like that would have
elicited at least some interest. Had Rogge said the same thing in
public, the reporters would have spread it to the antipodes in
half an hour.

Which only goes to show that the world knew less than it
should about poor old George. Once the Orchid Club got to
know him intimately, it had become impossible to believe in him
any longer as one of the world's wise men. Oh, he is one of the
great mathematicians of all time, to be sure, but on any other
subject he can be counted on to make a complete ass of himself.

Reprinted from *So Close to Home*, published by Ballantine Books, Inc. Copyright ©
1961 by James Blish. By permission of Kenneth S. White, author's representative.

Most of us already knew, in a general way, what he meant by a "reprieve" and how well his proof would stand up—supported, as usual, by a pillar of ectoplasm.

"What is it now, George?" I said. Somebody has to draw him off, or he'll continue to clamor for attention through the news bulletins. It was now my turn.

"It's proof," he said, sitting down beside me at once. "I've found a marvelous woman in Soho—oh, a perfect illiterate; she has no idea of the magnitude of the thing she's got hold of. But, Charles, she has a pipeline to the gods, as clear and direct a contact as any human being ever had. I've written proof of it."

"And the gods tell her that truth and light will prevail? George, don't you *ever* listen to the wireless? Don't you know that these are almost surely our last days? Don't you know that your medium is never going to have another child, that the earth's last generation has already been born, that the final war is upon us right at this instant?"

"Bother," Rogge said, exactly as he might have spoken had he found soda instead of water in his whisky. "You can't see beyond the end of your nose, Charles. Here you are, a speck in a finite universe in finite time, full of *Angst* because there may not be any more specks. What does that matter? You're a member of a finite class. If you ever thought about it all, you knew from the beginning that the class was doomed to be finite. What do you care about its ultimate cardinality?"

". . . has accused India of deliberately attempting to wreck the conference," the wireless was saying. "Meanwhile, the new government of Kashmir which seized power last week has signed a treaty of 'everlasting friendship and assistance' with the Peiping government. The latest reports still do not reveal . . ."

Well, I'd be briefed later; that was part of the agreement. I said, "I thought you were the one who cared about cardinality. Wouldn't you like to see the number of the class of human beings get up some day into your precious transfinite realm? How can we do that if we kill each other off this very month?"

"We can't do it in any case, not in the physical sense," Rogge said, settling back into his chair. "No matter how long the race lives or how fruitful it is, it will always be denumerable—each member of the race can be put in one-to-one relationship with the integers. If we all lived forever and produced descendants at a great rate, we might wind up as a denumerably infinite class— in infinite time. But we haven't got infinite time; and in any case, the very first transfinite number is the cardinal number of *all* such classes. No, my boy, we'll never make it."

I was, to say the least, irritated. How the man could be so smug in the face of the red ruin staring us all in the face . . .

"So the reprieve you were talking about is no reprieve for us."

"It may well be, but that's the smallest part of the implications. . . . Have you another of those panatelas, Charles? . . . There, now. No, what I was talking about was a reprieve for the universe. It's been given a chance to live up to man."

"You really ought to listen to the B.B.C. for a few minutes," I said. "Just to get some idea of what man is. Not much for the universe to live up to."

"But it's a twopenny universe to begin with," Rogge said from behind a cloud of newborn smoke. "There's no scope to it. It's certainly no more than ten billion years old at the outside, and already it's dying. The space-time bubble may or may not continue to expand forever, but before long there won't be anything in it worth noticing. It's ridiculously finite."

"So is man."

"Granted, Charles, but man has already made that heritage look stupid. We've thought of things that utterly transcend the universe we live in."

"Numbers, I suppose."

"Numbers indeed," Rogge said, unruffled. "Transfinite numbers. Numbers larger than infinity. And we live in a universe where they don't appear to stand for anything. A piece of primer work, like confining a grown man in a pram."

I looked back at the wireless. "We don't sound so grown up to me."

"Oh, you're not grown up, Charles, and that holds true for

most people. But a few men have shown what the race could do. Look at Cantor. He thought his way right out of the universe he lived in. He created a realm of numbers which evolve logically out of the numbers the universe runs on—and then found no provision had been made for them in the universe as it stands. Which would seem to indicate that Whoever created this universe knew less math than Cantor did! Isn't that silly?"

"I've no opinion," I said. "But you're a religious man, George. Aren't you skirting blasphemy?"

"Don't talk nonsense. Obviously there was a mathematician involved somewhere, and there are no bad mathematicians. If this one was as good as His handiwork indicates, of course He knew about the transfinites; the limitation was purposeful. And I think I've found out the purpose."

Now, of course, the great revelation was due. Promptly on schedule Rogge fussed inside his jacket pocket. I sat back and waited. He finally produced a grubby piece of paper, a fragment of a kraft bag.

"You're going to need a little background here," he said, drawing the paper out of reach as I leaned forward again. "Transfinite numbers don't work like finite ones. They don't add, subtract, multiply, or divide in any normal sense. As a matter of fact, the only way to change one is to involute it—to raise it to its own power."

"I'm bored already," I said.

"No doubt, but you'll listen because you have to." He grinned at me through the cigar smoke, and I began to feel rather uncomfortable. Could the old boy have been tipped off to our rotating system of running interference with him? "But I'll try to make it clear. Suppose that all the ordinary numbers you know were to change their behavior, so that zero to the zero power, instead of making zero, made one? Then one to the first power would make two; two squared would equal three; three cubed would be four, and so on. Any other operation would leave you just where you were: two times three, for instance, would equal three, and ten times sixty-three would equal sixty-three. If your

ordinary numbers behaved that way, you'd probably be con-
siderably confused at first, but you'd get used to it.

"Well, that's the way the transfinite numbers work. The first
one is Aleph-null, which as I said before is the cardinal number
of all denumerably infinite classes. If you multiply it by itself,
you get Aleph-one. Aleph-one to the Aleph-first equals Aleph-
two. Do you follow me?"

"Reluctantly. Now let me crack *your* brains for a minute.
What do these numbers number?"

Rogge smiled more gently. "Numbers," he said. "You'll have
to try harder than that, Charles."

"You said Aleph-null was the cardinal number of—of all the
countably infinite classes, isn't that right? All right, then what
is Aleph-one the cardinal number of?"

"Of the class of all real numbers. It's sometimes called C, or
the power of the continuum. Unhappily, the continuum as we
know it seems to have no use for it."

"And Aleph-two?"

"Is the cardinal number of the class of all one-valued functions."

"Very good." I had been watching this process with considerable secret glee. Rogge is sometimes pitifully easy to trap, I had
been told, if you've read his works and know his preoccupations,
and I'd taken the trouble to do so. "It seems to me that you've
blasted your own argument. First you say that these transfinite
numbers don't stand for anything in the real universe. Then you
proceed to tell me, one by one, what they stand for."

Rogge looked stunned for an instant, and I got ready to go
back to listening to the wireless. But I had misinterpreted his
expression. I hadn't stumped him; he had simply underestimated
my ignorance, one of his more ingratiating failings.

"But, Charles," he said, "to be sure, the transfinite numbers
stand for numbers. The point is that *they stand for nothing else*.
We can apply a finite number, such as seven, to the universe; we
can, perhaps, point to seven apples. But there aren't Aleph-one
apples in the universe; there aren't Aleph-one atoms in the uni-

verse; there is no distance in the universe as great as Aleph-one miles; and the universe won't last for Aleph-one years. The number Aleph-one applies only to concepts of number, which are things existing solely in the minds of men. Why, Charles, we don't even know if there is such a thing as infinity in nature. Or we didn't know until now. At this present moment not even infinity exists."

Impossibly enough, Rogge was actually beginning to make me feel a little bit circumscribed, a little bit offended that the universe was so paltry. I looked around. Cyril Weaver was sitting closest to the broadcaster, and there were tears running down his craggy face onto his medals. John Boyd was pacing, slamming his fist repeatedly and mechanically into his left palm. Off in the corner next to the fire, Sir Leslie Crawford was well along into one of his ghastly silent drunks, which wind up in a fixed, cataleptic glare at some inconsequential object, such as a tuft in the carpet or the space where a waiter once stood; he was Her Majesty's Undersecretary for Air, but at such moments no event or appeal can reach him.

Evidently nothing that had come through on the wireless had redeemed our expectations in the slightest. Of them all I was the only one—not counting Lord Rogge, of course—who had failed to hear the news and so would still be listening for a word of hope during tomorrow's broadcast.

"Almost thou persuadest me, George," I said. "But I warn you, none of this affects my opinion of mediums and spiritualism in the least. So your cause is lost in advance."

"My boy, I'm not going to ask you to believe anything but what I'm going to put before your own eyes. This charwoman, as I said, is utterly uneducated. She happens to have a great gift but not the slightest idea of how to use it. She stages séances for ignorant folk like herself and gives out written messages which purport to be from her clientele's departed relatives. The usual thing."

"Not at all impressive as a start."

"No, but wait," Rogge said. "I'm interested in such things, as you know, and I got wind of her through the Psychical Research Society. It seems that some of the woman's patrons had been complaining. They couldn't understand the spirit messages. 'Uncle Bill, 'e wasn't never no one to talk like that.' That sort of complaint. I wouldn't have bothered at all, if I hadn't seen one of the 'messages,' and after that I couldn't wait to see her.

"She was terrified, as such people are of anybody who speaks reasonable English and asks questions. I won't rehearse the details, but eventually she admitted that she's been practicing a fraud on her trade."

"Remarkable."

"I agree," Rogge said, somewhat mockingly, it seemed to me. "It appears that the voices she hears during her trances are *not* the voices of the relatives of her neighbors. As a matter of fact, she isn't even sure that they're spirit voices or human voices. And she doesn't herself understand what it is that they say. She just writes it down and then, once she's conscious again, tries to twist what she's written enough to make it apply to the particular client."

I expect I had begun to look a little sour. Rogge held up a hand as if to forestall an interruption. "After I got her calmed down sufficiently I had her do the trick for me. Believe me, I'm not easily fooled after all these years. That trance was genuine enough, and the writing was fully automatic. I performed several tests to make sure. And this is what she wrote."

Without any attempt at a dramatic pause he passed the scrap of brown paper over to me. The block printing on it was coarse, sprawling, and badly formed; it had evidently been written with a soft pencil, and there were smudge marks to show where the heel of a hand had rested. The text read:

FYI WER XTENDIN THE FIE NIGHT CONTIN YOU UMBREL-
LAS OF THIS CROWN ON TO OMEGA AHED OF SHEDYULE DO TO
CHRIST IS IN HEAVEN ROOSHIAN OF CHILDREN OPEN SUDO
SPEAR TO POSITIV CURVACHER AND BEGIN TRANSFORMATION
TO COZ MOST OF MACRO SCOPICK NUMBER

I handed the paper back to Rogge, astonished to find that my heart had sunk. I hadn't realized that it had attained any altitude from which to sink. Had I really been expecting some sort of heavenly pardon through this absurd channel? But I suppose that, in this last agony of the world, anyone might have grasped at the same straw.

"On to omega, indeed," I said. "But don't forget your bumbershoot. How did she manage to spell 'transformation' right?"

"She wears one," Rogge said. "And that's the key to the whole thing. Obviously she didn't understand more than a few words of what she—well, what she overheard. So she tried to convert it into familiar terms, letting a lot of umbrellas and Russians into it in the process. If you read the message phonetically, though, you can spot the interpolations easily—and converted back into its own terms, it's perhaps the most important message anybody on earth ever got."

"If anybody told me that message was from Uncle Bill, I wouldn't just guess it was a fraud. Go ahead, translate."

"First of all, it's obviously a memorandum of some sort. FYI —for your information. The rest says: 'We are extending the finite continuum as of this chronon to omega ahead of schedule due to crisis in evolution of children. Open pseudosphere to positive curvature and begin transformation to cosmos of macroscopic number.' "

"Well," I said, "it's certainly more resonant that way. But just as empty."

"By no means. Consider, Charles. Omega is the cardinal number of infinity. The finite continuum is our universe. A chronon can be nothing but a unit of time, probably the basic Pythagorean time-point. The pseudosphere is the shape our universe maintains in four-dimensional space-time. To open it to a positive curvature would, in effect, change it from finite to infinite."

I took time out to relight my cigar and try to apply the glossary to the message. To my consternation, it worked. I got the cheroot back into action only a second before my hands began to shake.

"My word, George," I said carefully. "Some creature with a spiral nebula for a head has taken up reading your books."

He said nothing; he simply looked at me. At last I had to ask him the preposterous question which I could not drive from me in any other way.

"George," I said. "George, are we the children?"

"I don't know," Rogge said frankly. "I came here convinced that we are. But while talking to you I began to wonder again. Whatever powers sent and received this message evidently regard *some* race in this universe as their children, to be educated gradually into their world—a world where transfinite numbers are everyday facts of arithmetic and finite numbers are just infinitesimal curiosities. Those powers are graduating that race to an infinite universe as the first step in the change.

"The human race has learned about transfinite numbers, which would seem to be a crucial stage in such an education. And we're certainly in the midst of a crisis in our evolution. We seem to qualify. But . . . Well, there are quite a few planets in this universe, Charles. We may be the children of whom they speak. Or they may not even know that we exist!"

He got up, his face troubled. "The gods," he said quietly. "They're out there, somewhere in a realm beyond infinity, getting ready to open up our pseudospherical egg and spill us out into an inconceivably vaster universe. But is it for our benefit or for—someone else's? And how will we detect it when it happens? On what time-scale do they plan to do it—tomorrow for us, or tomorrow for them, billions of years too late for us?"

"Or," I said, "the whole thing may be a phantom."

"It may be," he said. He knew, I think, that I had said that for the record, but he gave no sign of it. "Well, in the meantime you're relieved of duty, Charles. I shan't keep you any longer. I had to tell someone, and I have. Think about it."

He went out, his chin ducked reflectively, dribbling cigar ashes onto his vest.

I thought about it. It was, of course, the sheerest nonsense. The woman's scrawled "message" was gibberish. Where Lord

Rogge had read into it the mathematical terms with which he was most familiar, someone else might read into it the jargon of some other specialty. How else could a charwoman speak the language of relativity and transfinite numbers? Of course, she might have been picking some expert's brains by telepathy, maybe even Rogge's own—but that explanation just substituted one miracle for another. If I was going to believe in telepathy, I might as well admit that I'd just read an interoffice memo from Olympus.

The Third Program had gone back to music now, but there was another sound in the bar. It was not very loud but steady and pervasive. It could be felt in the floor, even through the thick-piled carpet, and it shook the air slightly. Sir Leslie's gaze stirred from the vase upon which it had finally become fixed and rose slowly, slowly, toward the dark oak ceiling. There was a preliminary flicker from the lights.

Children of the gods . . .

We would know soon now. The bombers were coming.

The Vanishing Man

RICHARD HUGHES

❦

Richard Hughes (1900–1976) was a remarkable Englishman whose reputation is sustained by a slender sheaf of books. His play, The Sisters' Tragedy, *produced in London while he was still an Oxford undergraduate, was called by George Bernard Shaw "the finest one-act play ever written." He claims to have written the first radio play in the world, a truly historic first. The* Innocent Voyage *(1929) is an acknowledged masterpiece, perhaps the only absolutely ruthless novel ever written about children. His now forgotten* In Hazard *(1938), a political allegory in the form of a sea adventure story, might, if reread, seem peculiarly apposite today.* The Vanishing Man *is a satiric rather than a serious handling of the traditional fourth-dimension yarn. The hypergeometry is a bit old-fashioned, reminding one of the period of Abbott's* Flatland, by a Square.

"Eureka!" the professor cried, and disappeared.

I was hardly prepared for this.

Mathematical professors are not magicians and have no business to vanish suddenly and without due warning. Moreover, at the moment of his disappearance, there was a curious whistling explosion, a sound like that of igniting hydrogen, of rushing into a vacuum; the papers on his desk were caught up in a sud-

Reprinted by permission of Harold Ober Associates from *A Moment of Time* by Richard Hughes. Copyright 1926 by Richard Hughes.

den whirlwind and pirouetted for several seconds over the floor. For a moment I was too dazed by the concussion to think clearly; then I got up and rushed rather wildly about the room. For it is difficult for any man to be sure how he would act when so astonished.

But I had hardly assured myself that there was really no bodily trace of him left in the study where we were working together when I noticed a pair of boots on the hearthrug. Now it is one thing for an agitated man to see a pair of boots on the hearthrug and to go to put them in a corner without really giving them a thought, but it is a very different matter to find a pair of feet in those boots, sharply severed at the ankle, with bone, flesh, veins, skin, and sock cut as clean and clear as in a sectional diagram. For a few moments I simply stared; then one of these boots moved, almost an inch. I confess that I was very nearly frightened. I made a rush for the door but conquered my nerves and turned back again; and lo! while my back had been turned a pair of legs—trousered legs, the professor's trousers—had attached themselves to the boots. And they were growing!

They were complete to the knee; the veins were welling with blood, but none spurted out; and as I watched with fascinated eyes I saw the cut surface gradually rise like water in a lock. It was the most uncanny thing. I pressed my hand upon it, only to feel it lifted by a gentle, even pressure as the professor's femur extended itself, and I remember noticing that, though my thumb had stoppered a brimming artery, not a drop of blood stained it.

After that I think I must have fainted, as folk will, simply from excess of the unusual, for the next thing I remember is the professor—the whole of him—standing over me and talking excitedly. I looked up in a dazed and bewildered fashion. He was waving his arms about and crying that he had Found the Way. Then suddenly he thrust his hand as it were through a hole in space, for it vanished completely; he deliberately plunged his arm up to the elbows in—nothing, and drew it out again.

"But it's so easy," he kept on repeating. "Easy as winking. Why didn't I ever think of it before?"

"Think of what?" I asked desperately.

"The fourth dimension," he answered. (Now I ought to mention that we were together writing a book on "Multidimensional Perspective.") "Here have we been fooling around after imaginary roots, and functions, trying to mop up the mess Einstein made, when all the time the fourth dimension was no different in kind from the other three that we are familiar with."

"But I don't see—" I began.

"No, of course you don't!" he barked, and settled into the full stride of his lecture-room manner.

"My assumption is that the fourth dimension is just another dimension—no more different in kind from length, say, than length is from breadth and thickness, but perpendicular to all three. Now suppose that a being in two dimensions—a flat creature, like the moving shadows of a cinematograph—were suddenly to grasp the concept of the third dimension and so step out of the picture. He might only move an inch, but he would vanish completely from the sight of the rest of his world."

"But the sections," I interrupted. "Why should I see you in those horrible sections?"

The professor raised his hand.

"I am coming to that," he said.

"Then suppose that instead of returning all at once—smack, flat, which would be difficult unless he had a vacuum prepared to receive him—he inserted his feet first and so gradually slid back into the universe. It is evident that his fellow creatures, during the process, would see him in ever-changing sections, until he was once more completely back in their space. Now I worked this much out last night in bed, and all the morning I have been cudgeling my brains to grasp in which direction it could lie, this dimension at right angles to length, breadth, and thickness. But all of a sudden—"

I could contain myself no longer.

"This is wonderful!" I cried. "This is power! Think of it! A step, and you are invisible! No prison cells can hold you, for there is a side to you on which they are as open as a wedding ring! No safe is secure from you: you can put your hand *round the corner* and draw out what you like. And, of course, if you looked back on the universe you had left, you would see us in sections, open to you! You could place a stone or a tablet of poison right in the very bowels of your enemies!"

He passed his hand across his forehead.

"Heavens!" he cried. "Could I really do all that?"

"Of course you could," I answered excitedly. "There is nothing you couldn't do. Only make haste to explain to me which this new direction is, and we'll hold the world in fee!"

"It's . . . it's . . ." He flapped his hands helplessly. "How can I explain?" he said. "It's just the *other* direction. It's *there!*" he cried suddenly, trying to point, with the result that his forefinger and half his hand vanished from view.

"Hold my hand," he suggested, "and I'll try to pull you out."

I took his hand, and he gradually slid feet first out of sight, till soon there was nothing of him left but a pulsing hand that tugged at my arm. And then catastrophe fell on us. Just what happened I shall never know—whether it was through tugging against my resistance, or whether he was too excited to notice what he was doing, or whether he simply wished to address some remark to me—but the unhappy man thrust his head back into space; and instead of thrusting it into vacancy, he thrust it into that exact spot occupied by a heavy writing table. Now there is an axiom that two objects cannot occupy the same point in space at the same time, and the result of disobeying it was hideous. There was a terrific splintering of wood, almost an explosion; at the same time his hand closed its grip right through my arm, vanishing from view. The whole room was littered with splinters and dust, mixed almost into a mash with blood and brains. . . .

But his body was never found; and for all I know it is still floating just outside our space, perhaps only a few inches from the armchair where it used to smoke and read and theorize.

The Nine Billion Names of God

ARTHUR C. CLARKE

The last story in this section called A Set of Imaginaries, *is another Clarke job, and a beauty. This time the computer is taken fairly seriously. The actual solution of the electronic-sequence problem is by no means unrealistic. As I write this I read in the New York* Times *that one James McDonough, a Columbia graduate student, claims that with the aid of a computer able to analyze the metric patterns of 15,693 lines of the* Iliad *he has proved that the epic is of single rather than multiple authorship. It took him only four years to do what would have taken twenty to forty years by conventional scholarly methods. What is a little less sound in Mr. Clarke's delightful story is the smashing last line which of course calmly ignores the trifling matter of the speed of light. But it doesn't seem to matter; he's already managed a nice suspension of disbelief.*

"THIS IS A slightly unusual request," said Dr. Wagner, with what he hoped was commendable restraint. "As far as I know, it's the first time anyone's been asked to supply a Tibetan monastery with an automatic sequence computer. I don't wish to be inquisitive, but I should hardly have thought that your—ah—establishment had much use for such a machine. Could you explain just what you intend to do with it?"

"Gladly," replied the lama, readjusting his silk robe and carefully putting away the slide rule he had been using for currency conversions. "Your Mark V computer can carry out any routine mathematical operation involving up to ten digits. However, for our work we are interested in *letters*, not numbers. As we wish you to modify the output circuits, the machine will be printing words, not columns of figures."

"I don't quite understand . . ."

"This is a project on which we have been working for the last three centuries—since the lamasery was founded, in fact. It is somewhat alien to your way of thought, so I hope you will listen with an open mind while I explain it."

"Naturally."

"It is really quite simple. We have been compiling a list which shall contain all the possible names of God."

"I beg your pardon?"

"We have reason to believe," continued the lama imperturbably, "that all such names can be written with not more than nine letters in an alphabet we have devised."

"And you have been doing this for three centuries?"

"Yes. We expected it would take us about fifteen thousand years to complete the task."

"Oh." Dr. Wagner looked a little dazed. "Now I see why you wanted to hire one of our machines. But exactly what is the *purpose* of this project?"

The lama hesitated for a fraction of a second, and Wagner wondered if he had offended him. If so, there was no trace of annoyance in the reply.

"Call it ritual, if you like, but it's a fundamental part of our belief. All the many names of the Supreme Being—God, Jehovah, Allah, and so on—they are only man-made labels. There is a philosophical problem of some difficulty here, which I do not propose to discuss, but somewhere among all the possible combinations of letters which can occur are what one may call the *real* names of God. By systematic permutation of letters, we have been trying to list them all."

"I see. You've been starting at AAAAAAAAA . . . and working up to ZZZZZZZZZ . . ."

"Exactly—though we use a special alphabet of our own. Modifying the electromatic typewriters to deal with this is, of course, trivial. A rather more interesting problem is that of devising suitable circuits to eliminate ridiculous combinations. For example, no letter must occur more than three times in succession."

"Three? Surely you mean two."

"Three is correct. I am afraid it would take too long to explain why, even if you understood our language."

"I'm sure it would," said Wagner hastily. "Go on."

"Luckily it will be a simple matter to adapt your automatic sequence computer for this work, since once it has been programed properly it will permute each letter in turn and print the result. What would have taken us fifteen thousand years it will be able to do in a hundred days."

Dr. Wagner was scarcely conscious of the faint sounds from the Manhattan streets far below. He was in a different world, a world of natural, not man-made, mountains. High up in their remote aeries these monks had been patiently at work, generation after generation, compiling their lists of meaningless words. Was there any limit to the follies of mankind? Still, he must give no hint of his inner thoughts. The customer was always right . . .

"There's no doubt," replied the doctor, "that we can modify the Mark V to print lists of this nature. I'm much more worried about the problem of installation and maintenance. Getting out to Tibet, in these days, is not going to be easy."

"We can arrange that. The components are small enough to travel by air—that is one reason why we chose your machine. If you can get them to India, we will provide transport from there."

"And you want to hire two of our engineers?"

"Yes, for the three months which the project should occupy."

"I've no doubt that Personnel can manage that." Dr. Wagner

113

scribbled a note on his desk pad. "There are just two other points—"

Before he could finish the sentence the lama had produced a small slip of paper.

"This is my certified credit balance at the Asiatic Bank."

"Thank you. It appears to be—ah—adequate. The second matter is so trivial that I hesitate to mention it—but it's surprising how often the obvious gets overlooked. What source of electrical energy have you?"

"A diesel generator providing 50 kilowatts at 110 volts. It was installed about five years ago and is quite reliable. It's made life at the lamasery much more comfortable, but of course it was really installed to provide power for the motors driving the prayer wheels."

"Of course," echoed Dr. Wagner. "I should have thought of that."

The view from the parapet was vertiginous, but in time one gets used to anything. After three months George Hanley was not impressed by the two-thousand-foot swoop into the abyss or the remote checkerboard of fields in the valley below. He was leaning against the wind-smoothed stones and staring morosely at the distant mountains whose names he had never bothered to discover.

This, thought George, was the craziest thing that had ever happened to him. "Project Shangri-La," some wit at the labs had christened it. For weeks now the Mark V had been churning out acres of sheets covered with gibberish. Patiently, inexorably, the computer had been rearranging letters in all their possible combinations, exhausting each class before going on to the next. As the sheets had emerged from the electromatic typewriters, the monks had carefully cut them up and pasted them into enormous books. In another week, heaven be praised, they would have finished. Just what obscure calculations had convinced the monks that they needn't bother to go on to words of ten, twenty, or a hundred letters, George didn't know. One of his recurring nightmares was that there would be some change of plan and that the

High Lama (whom they'd naturally called Sam Jaffe, though he didn't look a bit like him) would suddenly announce that the project would be extended to approximately 2060 A.D. They were quite capable of it.

George heard the heavy wooden door slam in the wind as Chuck came out onto the parapet beside him. As usual, Chuck was smoking one of the cigars that made him so popular with the monks—who, it seemed, were quite willing to embrace all the minor and most of the major pleasures of life. That was one thing in their favor: they might be crazy, but they weren't bluenoses. Those frequent trips they took down to the village, for instance . . .

"Listen, George," said Chuck urgently. "I've learned something that means trouble."

"What's wrong? Isn't the machine behaving?" That was the worst contingency George could imagine. It might delay his return, than which nothing could be more horrible. The way he felt now, even the sight of a TV commercial would seem like manna from heaven. At least it would be some link with home.

"No—it's nothing like that." Chuck settled himself on the parapet, which was unusual, because normally he was scared of the drop. "I've just found what all this is about."

"What d'ya mean—I thought we knew."

"Sure—we know what the monks are trying to do. But we didn't know why. It's the craziest thing—"

"Tell me something new," growled George.

". . . but old Sam's just come clean with me. You know the way he drops in every afternoon to watch the sheets roll out. Well, this time he seemed rather excited, or at least as near as he'll ever get to it. When I told him that we were on the last cycle he asked me, in that cute English accent of his, if I'd ever wondered what they were trying to do. I said, 'Sure'—and he told me."

"Go on, I'll buy it."

"Well, they believe that when they have listed all His names— and they reckon that there are about nine billion of them—God's purpose will be achieved. The human race will have finished what it was created to do, and there won't be any point in carrying on. Indeed, the very idea is something like blasphemy."

"Then what do they expect us to do? Commit suicide?"

"There's no need for that. When the list's completed, God steps in and simply winds things up . . . bingo!"

"Oh, I get it. When we finish our job, it will be the end of the world."

Chuck gave a nervous little laugh.

"That's just what I said to Sam. And do you know what happened? He looked at me in a very queer way, like I'd been stupid in class, and said, 'It's nothing as trivial as *that*.'"

George thought this over for a moment.

"That's what I call taking the Wide View," he said presently. "But what d'ya suppose we should do about it? I don't see that it makes the slightest difference to us. After all, we already knew that they were crazy."

"Yes—but don't you see what may happen? When the list's complete and the Last Trump doesn't blow—or whatever it is they expect—we may get the blame. It's our machine they've been using. I don't like the situation one little bit."

"I see," said George slowly. "You've got a point there. But this sort of thing's happened before, you know. When I was a kid down in Louisiana we had a crackpot preacher who said the world was going to end next Sunday. Hundreds of people believed him—even sold their homes. Yet nothing happened; they didn't turn nasty as you'd expect. They just decided that he'd made a mistake in his calculations and went right on believing. I guess some of them still do."

"Well, this isn't Louisiana, in case you hadn't noticed. There are just two of us and hundreds of these monks. I like them, and I'll be sorry for old Sam when his lifework backfires on him. But all the same, I wish I was somewhere else."

"I've been wishing that for weeks. But there's nothing we can do until the contract's finished and the transport arrives to fly us out."

"Of course," said Chuck thoughtfully, "we could always try a bit of sabotage."

"Like hell we could! That would make things worse."

"Not the way I meant. Look at it like this. The machine will finish its run four days from now, on the present twenty-hours-a-day basis. The transport calls in a week. O.K., then all we need do is to find something that wants replacing during one of the overhaul periods—something that will hold up the works for a couple of days. We'll fix it, of course, but not too quickly. If we time matters properly, we can be down at the airfield when the last name pops out of the register. They won't be able to catch us then."

"I don't like it," said George. "It will be the first time I ever walked out on a job. Besides, it would make them suspicious. No, I'll sit tight and take what comes."

"I *still* don't like it," he said seven days later, as the tough little mountain ponies carried them down the winding road. "And don't you think I'm running away because I'm afraid. I'm just sorry for those poor old guys up there, and I don't want to be around when they find what suckers they've been. Wonder how Sam will take it?"

"It's funny," replied Chuck, "but when I said goodbye I got the idea he knew we were walking out on him—and that he didn't care because he knew the machine was running smoothly and that the job would soon be finished. After that—well, of course, for him there just isn't any After That . . ."

George turned in his saddle and stared back up the mountain road. This was the last place from which one could get a clear view of the lamasery. The squat, angular buildings were silhouetted against the afterglow of the sunset; here and there lights gleamed like portholes in the sides of an ocean liner. Electric lights, of course, sharing the same circuit as the Mark V. How much longer would they share it? wondered George. Would the monks smash up the computer in their rage and disappointment? Or would they just sit down quietly and begin their calculations all over again?

He knew exactly what was happening up on the mountain at this very moment. The High Lama and his assistants would be sitting in their silk robes, inspecting the sheets as the junior monks carried them away from the typewriters and pasted them into the great volumes. No one would be saying anything. The only sound would be the incessant patter, the never-ending rainstorm, of the keys hitting the paper, for the Mark V itself was utterly silent as it flashed through its thousands of calculations a second. Three months of this, thought George, was enough to start anyone climbing up the wall.

"There she is!" called Chuck, pointing down into the valley. "Ain't she beautiful!"

She certainly was, thought George. The battered old DC-3 lay at the end of the runway like a tiny silver cross. In two hours she would be bearing them away to freedom and sanity. It was a thought worth savoring like a fine liqueur. George let it roll around his mind as the pony trudged patiently down the slope.

The swift night of the high Himalayas was now almost upon them. Fortunately the road was very good, as roads went in this region, and they were both carrying torches. There was not the slightest danger, only a certain discomfort from the bitter cold. The sky overhead was perfectly clear and ablaze with the familiar, friendly stars. At least there would be no risk, thought George, of the pilot being unable to take off because of weather conditions. That had been his only remaining worry.

He began to sing but gave it up after a while. This vast arena of mountains, gleaming like whitely hooded ghosts on every side, did not encourage such ebullience. Presently George glanced at his watch.

"Should be there in an hour," he called back over his shoulder to Chuck. Then he added, in an afterthought, "Wonder if the computer's finished its run? It was due about now."

Chuck didn't reply, so George swung round in his saddle. He could just see Chuck's face, a white oval turned toward the sky.

"Look," whispered Chuck, and George lifted his eyes to heaven. (There is always a last time for everything.)

Overhead, without any fuss, the stars were going out.

II

COMIC

SECTIONS

Three Mathematical Diversions

RAYMOND QUENEAU

✿

1. An Exercise in Style: Mathematical

Raymond Queneau is one of the most remarkable and multi-talented of contemporary vanguard French writers. He is poet, novelist, humorist, encyclopedist—and mathematician. In France his most popular book is Exercices de Style. *This is an extraordinary affair, its only possible rival being the running parody, in* Ulysses, *of several hundred years of English literature. Queneau starts with a pointless but, as he says, "real" incident presumed to have occurred in a Paris bus. He then retells this incident in a number of styles. How many?* Ninety-nine! *And each of these versions is a small masterpiece of parody, burlesque, witty commentary, straight imitation, or exaggerated scholarship. "My intention," says Queneau, "was merely to produce some exercises; the finished product may possibly act as a kind of rust remover to literature, help to rid it of some of its scabs."*

The seemingly impossible task of translating this tour de force *into English has been accomplished brilliantly by Barbara Wright.*

While the whole point of the book is that the incident is never told "straight" (for Queneau's theory must be that there is no standard use of language), perhaps the version headed "Nar-

rative" offers the simplest statement of the anecdote. In Miss Wright's translation it runs thus:

ONE DAY at about midday in the Parc Monceau district, on the back platform of a more or less full S bus (now No. 84), I observed a person with a very long neck who was wearing a felt hat which had a plaited cord around it instead of a ribbon. This individual suddenly addressed the man standing next to him, accusing him of purposely treading on his toes every time any passengers got on or off. However, he quickly abandoned his dispute and threw himself on to a seat which had become vacant.

Two hours later I saw him in front of the gare Saint-Lazare engaged in earnest conversation with a friend who was advising him to reduce the space between the lapels of his overcoat by getting a competent tailor to raise the top button.

Readers of this book will wonder how this dead-pan banality may be translated into mathematical language. Thus:

IN A rectangular parallelepiped moving along a line representing an integral solution of the second-order differential equation:

$$y'' + \text{PPTB}(x)y' + \text{S} = 84$$

two homoids (of which only one, the homoid A, manifests a cylindrical element of length $L > N$ encircled by two sine waves of period $\frac{\pi}{2}$ immediately below its crowning hemisphere) cannot suffer point contact at their lower extremities without proceeding upon divergent courses. The oscillation of two homoids tangentially to the above trajectory has as a consequence the small but significant displacement of all significantly small spheres tangential to a perpendicular of length $l < L$ described on the supra-median line of the homoid A's shirt front.

Mathematicians who are expert in French (and also know Paris) may want to compare the translation with the original, herewith:

Mathématique

Dans un parallélépipede rectangle se déplacant le long d'une ligne intégrale solution de l'équation différentielle du second ordre:

$$y'' + TCPR(x)y' + S = 84$$

deux homoïdes (dont l'un seulement, l'homoïde A, présente une partie cylindrique de longueur L > N et dont deux sinusoïdes dont le rapport des périodes $= \dfrac{\pi}{2}$ entourent la calotte sphérique) ne peuvent présenter de points de contact de la base sans avoir également un point de rebroussement. L'oscillation de deux homoïdes tangentiellement à la trajectoire ci-dessus entraîne le déplacement infinitésimal de toute sphère de rayon infinitésimal tangente à une ligne de longueur l < L perpendiculaire à la partie supérieure de la médiane du plastron de l'homoïde A.

In reply to my inquiry M. Queneau wrote me that the letters TCRP (printed, for some reason, in the French text as TCPR) stand for Transports en Commun de la Région Parisienne, as it was known at the time (now called, if I decipher his handwriting correctly, RATP: Régie Autonome de Transports Parisiens). Miss Wright's PPTB I would presume designate the initials of the corresponding London transport system.

2. ON THE AERODYNAMIC PROPERTIES OF ADDITION

M. Queneau (1903–1976) was also a pataphysical mathematician or perhaps mathematical pataphysician. Parisian pataphysics is a delightful discipline of intellectual spoofery; our Beats might have done well to turn themselves deliberately into pataphysicians. From the Cahiers du Collège de Pataphysique, *No. 1, I draw M. Queneau's trail-blazing exposition of the aerodynamic properties of addition, which I have ventured to put into English.*

ALL ATTEMPTS, from earliest times to the present day, to demonstrate that $2 + 2 = 4$ have failed to take into account the velocity of the wind.

The fact is that the operation involved in adding whole numbers is possible only when the weather is calm enough so that, after the first 2 is set down, it will remain in place long enough for us to put down first the little cross, then the second 2, then the little wall on which one sits for purposes of reflection, and finally the result. At this point, even if the wind should start to blow, we have proved that two and two make four.

But if its velocity should increase, our first number will fall to the ground. If it continues to rise, the second number will also topple over. Under these conditions how shall we compute the value of

$$\text{ᴎ} + \text{ᴎ} \, ?$$

Present-day mathematical thought is powerless to offer a solution.

Let us now assume that the wind increases almost to hurricane force. In that case the first number will undoubtedly be swept away, then the little cross, and so on until nothing is left of the expression. But let us suppose that, immediately after the disappearance of the little cross, the wind suddenly dies. We are then left with the absurdity $2 = 4$.

The wind, however, can add as well as take away. The number 1, being exceptionally light and displaceable by the slightest breeze, may also, without the calculator being aware of it, be suddenly swept into an addition to which it does not properly belong. This lies back of the intuition of the Russian mathematician Dostoevski when he was emboldened to declare his predilection for the equation $2 + 2 = 5$.

The rules of decimal numeration likewise prove that the Hindus were probably, more or less unconsciously, led to the formulation of our general theory. It is clear that the zero, sensitive to the slightest puff of wind, rolls easily. Hence, when placed to the left of the number in such an expression as $02 = 2$, no value attaches to it, for it will vanish before we reach the end of the operation. It has significance only when placed to the right, in which situation the numbers preceding it are able to hold it back and prevent it from rolling away. As long as the wind does not exceed a velocity of a few feet per second, such an equation as $20 = 2$ may be generated.

These considerations lead to certain practical consequences. Faced with the prospect of atmospheric disturbances, one is wise to impose upon one's addition the proper aerodynamic form. Similarly it is advisable to write the equation from right to left, beginning as close as possible to the right-hand margin of the paper. If, during the course of the operation, the wind should cause it to slip or slide, one can nearly always catch it before it reaches the left-hand margin. Thus is obtained, even in the course of an equinoctial storm, such results as

$$\text{ᄃ} + \text{ᄃ} = \text{ᄳ}$$

3. The Geometrical Disappearance of Dino

Among Queneau's surrealist short stories is one called À la Limite de la Forêt, *translated by Barbara Wright as* At the Edge of the Forest. *It is quite impossible to describe, but one may say that it might have been written by Kafka if Kafka had had the capacity to laugh at himself. A traveler stays overnight at an inn and makes the acquaintance of Dino, a talking dog. The traveler is skeptical; he is of the opinion that there is a system of microphones under the table and that he is really conversing with a person in a nearby room. Dino, naturally enough, is indignant.*

"BAH!" said the dog. "You see a dog talk and you don't believe it?"

"You're well trained, that's all."

"Ha, ha—and if I were to tell you that I have other talents as well?"

"Which are?"

"For instance, to make myself invisible."

"Show me."

. . .

"Well, would you like it to be progressive and continuous or abrupt and sudden?"

"My goodness . . ."

"It's just as you wish."

"Well, let's say progressive and continuous."

Dino immediately jumped down from his chair and began to describe the biggest circle which could possibly be traced in the middle of the room without bumping into a chair. When he had come back more or less to his point of departure he started to lean sideways as he walked and to trace a second circle of a slightly smaller radius, his own dimensions at the same time becoming proportionately reduced, and, describing a spiral in this manner, he finally became no more than a sort of minute canine atom revolving with increasing speed around the symmetry axis perpendicular to the geometrical figure thus suggested; and at last, by proceeding to the limit, this Vibrio, achieving indefinitely decreasing dimensions, finally disappeared.

"A pretty conjuring trick," murmured the traveler. "But I've seen conjurers who were even more skillful. Bother, here I am talking to myself again—disgusting habit I must cure myself of."

The Wonderful World of Figures

COREY FORD

Corey Ford was in my mathematics class at Columbia many years ago. The splendid results of the instruction he received are evidenced by this remarkable arithmetical disquisition.

FIRST LET'S ALL climb up in my lap and I'll start off with a little story. Everybody comfortable? All right, then, this is going to be the story of mathematics, and it's too late for you to sneak out of the room now because I've locked the door.

Our story begins way back in prehistoric times, when man wore long sideburns and lived on the tops of high-wheeled bicycles. In those primitive days he had only *one* of everything— one horse, one cow, one wife, and so on—and there was no need for mathematics. But then man's avaricious nature asserted it- self, and he acquired more horses and cows and wives. The only way he could tell how many he had was to get them all together in the same room and count them on his fingers. This was all right with the horses and cows, but when he got all his wives together in one room he ran into trouble. So he drew some crude symbols on the wall to represent them instead; and that, my little readers, is how arithmetic was born.

Gradually man acquired so many horses and cows and wives

that he ran out of fingers, so he had to invent addition. Then he decided he'd better get rid of some of his wives (he hung onto his horses and cows, though), so he invented subtraction. Meantime his family was multiplying, which led to multiplication, and sooner or later his wife's mother and her brother's folks from Toledo and several cousins and a couple of sons-in-law who weren't working all moved in with him to divvy up his possessions, so he invented division. This was followed in succession by the invention of algebra, geometry, trigonometry, calculus, and canasta. Thus did man evolve our modern system of mathematics, and life hasn't been the same since.

Actually there are *two* systems of mathematics in use today: the system man uses, and the one his wife uses. Woman's mathematics differ from man's in that there are no round numbers and everything is expressed in terms of $4.49 or $9.98. In addition, any amount over two figures is automatically charged to her husband. What makes this system obscure, at least to a man, is the fact that it is based on feminine logic. For instance, if a woman sees something in a store that is on sale at half price, she always buys a second one because that way she gets the first one for nothing. Or, to cite another example of female reasoning, a husband gives his wife $20 to buy a new hat, and she sees just the hat she wants for $17, so she saves him $3 right there. Now, I want you to follow this carefully. While she is buying the hat, she sees a coat to go with it that is marked down from $40 to $23, so with the $3 she saved him on the hat, plus the $17 she saved on the coat, her husband still owes her $20.

The trouble is that a woman's mathematical system works so fast that a man cannot keep up with it. Take the experience of a friend of mine, a Mr. Beeks, whose wife decided she wanted a mink stole. Mr. Beeks told her they couldn't afford it, and his wife said it wouldn't cost any more than a trip to Miami, and Mr. Beeks pointed out that they couldn't afford a trip to Miami. So his wife said that instead of a trip to Miami they could do over the living room, and when he asked her where they'd get the money to do over the living room, she said by not going to

Miami, and if they didn't do over the living room or go to Miami either, they could use the money they saved to buy the mink stole. While Mr. Beeks was trying to figure that out, his wife bought the mink stole and wore it to Miami while the living room was being done over. Mr. Beeks says it looks very good on her too.

It was in an effort to get ahead of woman's mathematics that man evolved a *third* system called binary arithmetic. As we all know, man's own mathematics is based on the decimal system, due to the fact that he has ten fingers and ten toes. But in binary arithmetic there are only two digits, 0 and 1. Electronically these symbols represent the basic intelligence of "on" or "off," depending on whether the pulses of negative electricity are present or absent. (I'll explain that later, after I've had a chance to look it up myself.) In short, the symbols 0 and 1 merely signify values (or the lack of values) in a geometric progression running 1, 2, 4, 8, 16, 32, and 64, but proceeding from right to left. Thus in binary terms the figure 100 is written 1100100, which you can readily see is 1100100 times easier.

Binary arithmetic is the basic language of the electronic computer. This is because a computer has no fingers or toes and cannot count higher than 1. Using the two digits, 0 and 1, an infinite number of symbols are communicated to the machine, to be processed and stored away as negative electronic pulses. (Remind me about that sometime.) When a fact is desired, the computer extracts the information from the several hundred thousand bits of data in its memory system and answers either 1 (yes) or 0 (no). According to binary rules, any query which cannot be answered by a simple affirmative or negative is automatically rejected. This game is called Twenty Questions and is played as follows:

The contestants are blindfolded and led into a room where the computer is waiting. Their blindfolds are then removed, and the first contestant asks a leading question, such as, "Are you a living person?" The computer replies "0." The second contestant inquires, "Are you a character in fiction?" and the computer shakes its head "0." This narrows the field a little, and the third contestant (probably Bennett Cerf) asks, "Are you somebody in the last century, maybe?" This time the answer is "1." The first contestant, making another stab in the dark, suggests, "Were you by any chance President of the United States?" Again the computer nods "1." Further questions reveal that the computer was born in a log cabin, wore a beard, and freed the slaves. This stumps the contestants completely, and they hazard a series of wild guesses such as, "Did you once make a speech beginning 'Fourscore and seven years ago'?" or "Is your last name the same as the capital of Nebraska?" or "Were you ever assassinated in Ford's Theater on the night of April 14, 1865?" This continues until the total of twenty questions is exhausted and the contestants have to give up, whereupon the computer supplies the answer: "1100100."

Inasmuch as nobody can make head or tail of this answer, it is fed to another computer, which processes it and stores it away again. This puts man right back where he started, counting on his fingers.

And now, if you'll kindly get off my lap, we'll go on to the next chapter.

A, B, and C—The Human Element in Mathematics

STEPHEN LEACOCK

※

The Canadian economist and humorist Stephen Leacock died in Toronto in 1944. Canada has been a duller country ever since. In addition to being a very funny piece of writing, A, B, and C— The Human Element in Mathematics is a devastating commentary on the absurd method of teaching elementary arithmetic by "concrete examples." This anti-mathematical conception, praise God, is currently being abandoned by all numerate teachers of mathematics.

THE STUDENT of arithmetic who has mastered the first four rules of his art and successfully striven with money sums and fractions finds himself confronted by an unbroken expanse of questions known as problems. These are short stories of adventure and industry with the end omitted and, though betraying a strong family resemblance, are not without a certain element of romance.

The characters in the plot of the problem are three people called A, B, and C; the form of the question is generally of this sort: "A, B, and C do a certain piece of work. A can do as much work in one hour as B in two or C in four. Find how long they work at it."

Reprinted by permission of Dodd, Mead & Company from *Literary Lapses* by Stephen Leacock.

Or thus: "A, B, and C are employed to dig a ditch. A can dig as much in one hour as B can dig in two, and B can dig twice as fast as C. Find how long, etc., etc."

Or after this wise: "A lays a wager that he can walk faster than B or C. A can walk half as fast again as B, and C is only an indifferent walker. Find how far, and so forth."

The occupations of A, B, and C are many and varied. In the older arithmetics they contented themselves with doing a "certain piece of work." This statement of the case, however, was found too sly and mysterious or possibly lacking in romantic charm. It became the fashion to define the job more clearly and to set them at walking matches, ditch-digging, regattas, and piling cordwood. At times they became commercial and entered into partnership, having, with their old mystery, a "certain" capital. Above all, they revel in motion. When they tire of walking matches, A rides on horseback or borrows a bicycle and competes with his weaker-minded associates on foot. Now they race on locomotives; now they row; or again they become historical and engage stagecoaches; or at times they are aquatic and swim. If their occupation is actual work, they prefer to pump water into cisterns, two of which leak through holes in the bottom and one of which is watertight. A, of course, has the good one; he also takes the bicycle, and the best locomotive, and the right of swimming with the current. Whatever they do they put money on it, being all three sports. A always wins.

In the early chapters of the arithmetic their identity is concealed under the names of John, William, and Henry, and they wrangle over the division of marbles. In algebra they are often called X, Y, Z. But these are only their Christian names, and they are really the same people.

Now to one who has followed the history of these men through countless pages of problems, watched them in their leisure hours dallying with cordwood, and seen their panting sides heave in the full frenzy of filling a cistern with a leak in it, they become something more than mere symbols. They appear as creatures of flesh and blood, living men with their own passions, ambitions, and aspirations like the rest of us.

A is full-blooded, hotheaded, and strong-willed. It is he who proposes everything, challenges B to work, makes the bets, and bends the others to his will. He is a man of great physical strength and phenomenal endurance. He has been known to walk forty-eight hours at a stretch and to pump ninety-six. His life is arduous and full of peril. A mistake in the working of a sum may keep him digging a fortnight without sleep. A repeating decimal in the answer might kill him.

B is a quiet, easygoing fellow, afraid of A and bullied by him, but very gentle and brotherly to little C, the weakling. He is quite in A's power, having lost all his money in bets.

Poor C is an undersized, frail man with a plaintive face. Constant walking, digging, and pumping have broken his health and ruined his nervous system. His joyless life has driven him to drink and smoke more than is good for him, and his hand often shakes as he digs ditches. He has not the strength to work as the others do; in fact, as Hamlin Smith has said, "A can do more work in one hour than C in four."

The first time that ever I saw these men was one evening after a regatta. They had all been rowing in it, and it had transpired that A could row as much in one hour as B in two or C in four. B and C had come in dead fagged and C was coughing badly. "Never mind, old fellow," I heard B say. "I'll fix you up on the sofa and get you some hot tea." Just then A came blustering in and shouted, "I say, you fellows, Hamlin Smith has shown me three cisterns in his garden and he says we can pump them until tomorrow night. I bet I can beat you both. Come on. You can pump in your rowing things, you know. Your cistern leaks a little, I think, C." I heard B growl that it was a dirty shame and that C was used up now, but they went, and presently I could tell from the sound of the water that A was pumping four times as fast as C.

For years after that I used to see them constantly about the town and always busy. I never heard of any of them eating or sleeping. After that, owing to a long absence from home, I lost sight of them. On my return I was surprised to find A, B, and C no longer at their old tasks; on inquiry I heard that work in this line was now done by N, M, and O and that some people were employing for algebraical jobs four foreigners called Alpha, Beta, Gamma, and Delta.

Now it chanced one day that I stumbled upon old D, in the little garden in front of his cottage, hoeing in the sun. D is an aged laboring man who used occasionally to be called in to help A, B, and C. "Did I know 'em, sir?" he answered. "Why, I knowed 'em ever since they was little fellows in brackets. Master A, he were a fine-hearted lad, sir, though I always said, give me Master B for kindheartedness-like. Many's the job as we've been on together, sir, though I never did no racing nor aught of that, but just the plain labor, as you might say. I'm getting a bit too old and stiff for it nowadays, sir—just scratch about in the garden here and grow a bit of a logarithm or raise a common denominator or two. But Mr. Euclid, he uses me still for propositions, he do."

From the garrulous old man I learned the melancholy end of my former acquaintances. Soon after I left town, he told me, C had been ill. It seems that A and B had been rowing on the river for a wager, and C had been running on the bank and then sat in a draft. Of course the bank had refused the draft and C was taken ill. A and B came home and found C lying helpless in bed. A shook him roughly and said, "Get up, C, we're going to pile wood." C looked so worn and pitiful that B said, "Look here, A, I won't stand this. He isn't fit to pile wood tonight." C smiled feebly and said, "Perhaps I might pile a little if I sat up in bed." Then B, thoroughly alarmed, said, "See here, A, I'm going to fetch a doctor; he's dying." A flared up and answered, "You've got no money to fetch a doctor." "I'll reduce him to his lowest terms," B said firmly. "That'll fetch him." C's life might even then have been saved, but they made a mistake about the medicine. It stood at the head of the bed on a bracket, and the nurse accidentally removed it from the bracket without changing the sign. After the fatal blunder C seems to have sunk rapidly. On the evening of the next day it was clear, as the shadows deepened, that the end was near. I think that even A was affected at the last as he stood with bowed head, aimlessly offering to bet with the doctor on C's labored breathing. "A," whispered C, "I think I'm going fast." "How fast do you think you'll go, old man?" murmured A. "I don't know," said C, "but I'm going at any rate." The end came soon after that. C rallied for a moment and asked for a certain piece of work that he had left downstairs. A put it in his arms and he expired. As his soul sped heavenward, A watched its flight with melancholy admiration. B burst into a passionate flood of tears and sobbed, "Put away his little cistern and the rowing clothes he used to wear; I feel as if I could hardly ever dig again." The funeral was plain and unostentatious. It differed in nothing from the ordinary, except that out of deference to sporting men, and mathematicians, A engaged two hearses. Both vehicles started at the same time, B driving the one which bore the sable parallelepiped containing the last remains of his ill-fated friend. A, on the box of the empty hearse, generously consented to a handicap of a hundred years but arrived first at the cemetery by driving four times as fast as B. (Find the distance to the cemetery.) As the sarcophagus was lowered, the grave was surrounded by the broken figures of the first book of Euclid.

It was noticed that after the death of C, A became a changed man. He lost interest in racing with B and dug but languidly. He finally gave up his work and settled down to live on the interest of his bets. B never recovered from the shock of C's death; his grief preyed upon his intellect and it became deranged. He grew moody and spoke only in monosyllables. His disease became rapidly aggravated, and he presently spoke in words whose spelling was regular and which presented no difficulty to the beginner. Realizing his precarious condition, he voluntarily submitted to be incarcerated in an asylum, where he abjured mathematics and devoted himself to writing the *History of the Swiss Family Robinson* in words of one syllable.

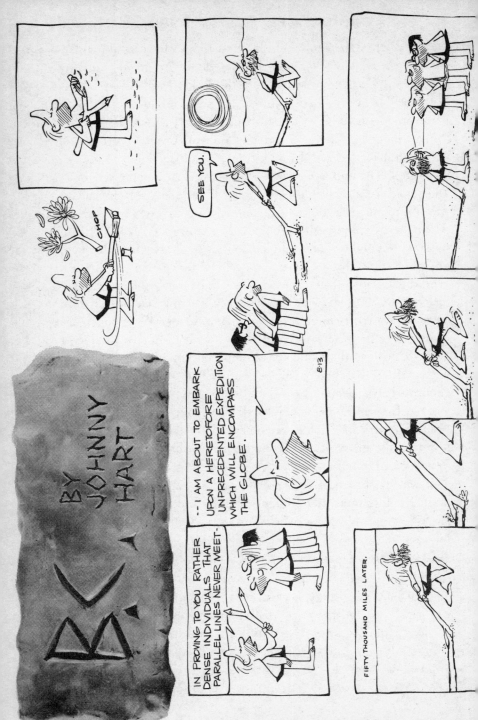

A Note on the Einstein Theory

MAX BEERBOHM

❧

The eminence of the late Sir Max Beerbohm as caricaturist, essayist, parodist, novelist, and conversationalist is of course a matter of common knowledge. Far less well known is his modest but striking contribution to the parallel lines theorem, a contribution which, with characteristic reticence, he ascribes to some passing acquaintance of his named Einstein.

IT IS SAID THAT THERE ARE, besides Dr. Einstein himself, only two men who can claim to have grasped the Theory in full. I cannot claim to be either of these. But I do know a good thing when I see it, and here is a thing that is excellent in its kind— romantically excellent in a kind that is itself high. When I think of rays being deflected by gravity, and of parallel lines at long last converging so that there isn't perhaps, after all, any such thing as Infinity, I draw a very deep breath indeed. The attempt to conceive Infinity had always been quite arduous enough for me. But to imagine the absence of it; to feel that perhaps we and all the stars beyond our ken are somehow cosily (though awfully) closed in by curtain curves beyond which is nothing; and to convince myself, by the way, that this exterior nothing is not (in virtue of *being* nothing) something, and therefore . . . but I lose the thread.

Enough that I never lose the thrill. It excites, it charms me to think of elderly great mathematicians of this and that nation packing their portmanteaus whenever there is to be a solar eclipse and traveling over land and sea to the Lick Observatory, or to some hardly accessible mountaintop in Kamchatka, and there testing, to the best of their power the soundness or unsoundness of the tremendous Theory. So far the weather has not been very favorable to these undertakings. Nature, who is proud and secretive, has opposed many clouds to the batteries of telescopes. But she has had only a partial success, it seems. Some observations have been more or less clearly made, some conclusions more or less clearly drawn. And these more or less clearly point to the likelihood that what Dr. Einstein in his humdrum home evolved from his inner consciousness is all delightfully correct.

But is the British public delighted? It gives no sign of being so. Its newspapers did at the first news of Einstein's existence try, very honorably, to excite it about Einstein and even about his work. It would *not* be excited. Strange! The tamest batting of Hertfordshire *v.* Australia, the feeblest goal-keeping of Wormwood Scrubbs *v.* Hornsey Rise, the lightest word that falls from the lips of the least accomplished Negro boxer, are better "copy" than any challenge to our notion of the Cosmos. This is all the stranger because the public is not careless of other things than Sport. Its passionate interest in archaeology, for instance, rose to boiling point only the other day: it could *not* hear too much about the tomb of Tutankhamen or tire of debating whether or not the bones of that king might rightly be disturbed. Why never a word as to the disturbance of our belief that parallel lines can nowhere converge? I haven't grudged Tutankhamen the renewal and immense enlargement of the fame he once had. I have but deplored the huge cold shoulder turned on the living Einstein.

Newton, no greater an innovator than he, is popular enough. Everybody knows something about Gravitation—and all about the apple. Perhaps if Newton had not mentioned that apple he, too, would be generally ignored. It is a great advantage for a discoverer to have been inspired by some homely little incident.

Newton and the apple, Copernicus and the whipping top, James Watt and the kettle. But Einstein and——? Poor Einstein!

Men of his magnitude are not avid of popularity? True, but this does not mean that popularity would be disagreeable to them. When the newspapers were trying to make Relativity a household word, I read an account of Einstein, written by one who knew him, and enhanced by a photograph of him. A very human person, I gathered; far from standoffish; a player of the fiddle; the constant smoker of a large pipe; a genial, though thoughtful, critic of current things. I liked his views on education. Why all this forcing of a child's memory? Memory—a matter of little moment. Let the child be taught to see, and to think, for itself. And let every child be taught a trade. And "after all," said Einstein, dismissing tuition, "the best thing in the world is a happy face." It was clear from the photograph that his own face was a happy one. But I discerned in it a certain wistfulness, too—the wistfulness of a thorough good fellow whose work somehow repels the attention of that good fellow, the average man. My heart went out to him. I wish I could help him. And now, I think, I can. Hark!

Yesterday afternoon I was walking on the coast road from Rapallo to Zoagli when I saw approaching in the distance a man of strenuous gait and of aspect neither Italian nor English. His brow was bare to the breeze; and as he drew near I perceived the brow to be a fine one; and as he drew nearer still I perceived the face to be a very happy one—with just a hint in it of wistfulness, which, however, vanished at my words, "Dr. Einstein, I presume?" He clapped a cordial hand on my shoulder; he treated me as an old friend, as a brother, and insisted that we should sit together on the low wall that divides the road from the cliff. Presently—after he had praised the sun and the sea and had expressed an ardent sympathy with Fascismo, and with Socialismo, no less—I said to him, "Master (if one who is not a disciple may so address you), tell me: What was it that first put you on the track of the tremendous Theory?" He knitted his fine brow, saying that his memory was not a very good one; but after a while he remembered and spoke to me as follows:

"One winter's evening, after a hard day's work, I was sitting by my fireside—for I have an open fire in the English fashion, not a stove; I like to sit watching the happy faces in the coals— when my eye lighted on the tongs in the fender. Of course it had often lighted on them before, but this time it carried to my brain a message which my brain could not understand. 'Here,' I mused, 'are two perfectly parallel lines. And yet, and yet, they meet at the extreme ends. How is that?' My friend Professor Schultz had promised to drop in and smoke a pipe with me that evening, and when he came I drew his attention to the phenomenon. He knelt down by the fender, pushed his spectacles up on to his forehead, gazed closely, and muttered, 'Gott im Himmel—ja!' I asked him—for he is a very ready man—if he had any explanation to offer. He rose from his knees and sat down on a chair heavily, burying his head in his hands. Suddenly he sprang to his feet. 'Einstein,' he said, 'I believe I have it! I believe that the ironworker who made those bars must have heated them red-hot and then bent the ends toward each other.' Dear old Schultz! Always so ready—so shallow! I suppose I ought not to have laughed, but I did, and Schultz went out in some anger. It was dawn when I rose from the fireside. The fire had long ago burned itself out, and I was stiff with cold. But my mind was all aglow with the basic principles of Relativismus."

"The world," I said quietly, "shall hear of this, Dr. Einstein."

The Achievement of
H. T. Wensel

H. ALLEN SMITH

Like Sir Max, my friend H. Allen Smith has built up a considerable reputation as a humorist. Among humorists (and indeed among human beings in general) he is the only one who, deliberately using all the resources of mathematical physics, has merged theology and mathematics to establish firmly a proposition of inestimable future interest to all mortal men.

A FRIEND OF MINE in Washington made the acquaintance, thirty years ago, of a man named Wensel, who was on the staff of the Bureau of Standards. One day Mr. Wensel called my friend into a shadowy corner of his laboratory and slipped him a document which, he said, might revolutionize all theological thought. Mr. Wensel has long since disappeared from the scene and today is not even remembered at the Bureau of Standards. Perhaps that will be rectified by publication, for the first time, of his remarkable theory. It follows:

Heaven is hotter than hell. The temperature of heaven can be rather accurately computed from available data. Our authority is the best possible, namely the Bible. Isaiah 30:26 reads, "Moreover the light of the moon shall be as the light of the sun, and the light of the sun shall be sevenfold, as the light of seven days." Thus heaven receives from the moon as much radiation as we do from the sun and in addition seven times seven (or forty-nine) times as much as we do from the sun, or fifty times in all as much as we receive from the sun.

Now the light we receive from the moon is a ten-thousandth of the light we receive from the sun, so we can ignore what we receive from the moon. And with this data in hand we can easily compute the temperature of heaven.

The radiation falling on heaven will heat it to the point where the heat lost by radiation is just equal to the heat received by radiation. In other words, heaven loses fifty times as much heat as the earth by radiation. Using the well-known Stefan-Boltzmann fourth-power law for radiation, $\left(\dfrac{H}{E}\right)^4 = 50$ where H is the absolute temperature of heaven and E is the absolute temperature of the earth—300° C. (273 plus 27). This gives H as 798° absolute or 525° C.

The exact temperature of hell cannot be computed, but it must be less than 444.6° C., the temperature at which brimstone or sulphur changes from a liquid to a gas. Revelations 21:8: "But the fearful, and unbelieving . . . shall have their part in the lake which burneth with fire and brimstone." A *lake* of molten brimstone means that its temperature must be below the boiling point, which is 444.6° C. If it were above this point it would be a vapor and not a lake.

We have, then, the following: Temperature of heaven, 525° C. or 977° F. Temperature of hell, less than 445° C. or less than 833° F. Therefore, heaven is hotter than hell.

Me, I'm always happy to be of service to humankind.

Needed: Feminine Math

PARKE CUMMINGS

❧

Between them, Mr. Cummings and The New Yorker *provide further useful kidding of the bring-it-home-to-the-child's-own-experience classroom instruction.*

A RECENT QUESTION asked of our Patsy, sixteen: "What is the volume of a brick wall 120 feet long, 3 feet high, and 2 feet thick?" Patsy couldn't have cared less. I can't speak for Russia, but if educators in *this* country want to get high school girls interested in math, they'll have to think up better problems, like:

Q. For Christmas a girl receives a 6-ounce bottle of *Toujours Indiscrète.* If she uses 1/10 of an ounce a date, for how many dates will it last?

Q. Tom's parents let him have the car one night out of five, and Jerry's parents allow him their car one night out of seven. During the course of a year, how many more times can Tom take you to the movies than Jerry?

Q. If the average rock'n'roll record plays for three minutes, how many records can you play in two hours, not counting twenty-five minutes' time out for a telephone call?

Q. Nancy owns six cashmere sweaters and seven skirts. Dorothy has eight sweaters and six skirts. If they keep lending each other their sweaters and skirts, how many different outfits can each of the girls appear in?

Q. Jane promises Bill she will let him have one kiss for every degree in a circle over 350. How many kisses does he get, provided he doesn't steal any?

LIFE IN CALIFORNIA DEPARTMENT

(Arithmetic exercise paper brought home by a third-grade pupil in an elementary school in Culver City)

1. When must an actress arrive at the studio to allow herself 1½ hours to make up for the part if shooting is to begin at nine o'clock?

2. A child actor spends 3 hours in school, one hour for lunch, and 4 hours at work. How many hours does he spend at the studio?

3. A make-up man has to make up two cowboys and one Indian. If he spends 15 minutes on each one, how long will it take him?

4. If a child actor arrives at the studio at 9 o'clock and spends 8 hours there, when would he leave for home?

5. A baby under 6 months of age can work 20 minutes a day. If the baby is needed for 3 days, how long has it worked?

Drawing by Frueh. © 1958, The New Yorker Magazine, Inc.

Two Extracts

MARK TWAIN

Jeannette M. Pepper, who drew my attention to the first of these small bits of joshing, adds that it is used by Croxton and Lowden in closing their book Practical Business Statistics. *Mark Twain somewhere in his* Notebook *remarks that in eternity "mathematics alone would occupy me eight million years." To judge from the reasoning that follows, he might very well need every minute of them.*

1.

THESE DRY DETAILS . . . give me an opportunity of introducing one of the Mississippi's oddest peculiarities—that of shortening its length from time to time. If you will throw a long, pliant apple paring over your shoulder, it will pretty fairly shape itself into an average section of the Mississippi River, that is the nine or ten hundred miles stretching from Cairo, Ill., southward to New Orleans, the same being wonderfully crooked, with a brief straight bit here and there at wide intervals . . .

. . .

At some forgotten time in the past cutoffs were made . . . These shortened the river, in the aggregate, seventy-seven miles.

Since my own day on the Mississippi, cutoffs have been made at Hurricane Island, at Island 100, at Napoleon, Ark., at Walnut Bend, and at Council Bend. These shortened the river, in the aggregate, sixty-seven miles . . .

Therefore the Mississippi between Cairo and New Orleans was twelve hundred and fifteen miles long one hundred and seventy-six years ago. It was eleven hundred and eighty after the cutoff of 1722 . . . Consequently its length is only nine hundred and seventy-three miles at present.

Now, if I wanted to be one of those ponderous scientific people and "let on" to prove what had occurred in the remote past by what has occurred in a given time in the recent past, or what will occur in the far future by what has occurred in late years, what an opportunity is here! Geology never had such a chance, nor such exact data to argue from! Nor "development of species" either! Glacial epochs are great things, but they are vague— vague. Please observe:

In the space of one hundred and seventy-six years the Lower Mississippi has shortened itself two hundred and forty-two miles. That is an average of a trifle over one mile and a third per year. Therefore, any calm person, who is not blind or idiotic, can see that in the Old Oölitic Silurian Period, just a million years ago next November, the Lower Mississippi River was upward of one million three hundred thousand miles long and stuck out over the Gulf of Mexico like a fishing rod. And by the same token any person can see that seven hundred and forty-two years from now the Lower Mississippi will be only a mile and three-quarters long, and Cairo and New Orleans will have joined their streets together and be plodding comfortably along under a single mayor and a mutual board of aldermen. There is something fascinating about science. One gets such wholesale returns of conjecture out of such a trifling investment of fact.

2.

"If it would take a cannon ball $3\frac{1}{3}$ seconds to travel four miles, and $3\frac{3}{8}$ seconds to travel the next four, and $3\frac{5}{8}$ to travel the next four, and if its rate of progress continued to diminish in the same ratio, how long would it take it to go fifteen hundred million miles?"

—"Arithmeticus," Virginia, Nevada.

I don't know.

Mark Twain.

Mathematics for Golfers

STEPHEN LEACOCK

Here is a second encounter between Stephen Leacock and mathematics, this time with probability theory. The value given for π, by the way, puzzles me; to six decimal places I had always thought it to be 3.141592. Leacock gives it as 3.141567. He was an economist; perhaps he was economizing.

IT IS ONLY quite recently that I have taken up golf. In fact, I have played for only three or four years, and seldom more than ten games in a week, or at most four in a day. I have had a proper golf vest for only two years. I bought a "spoon" only this year, and I am not going to get Scotch socks till next year.

In short, I am still a beginner. I have once, it is true, had the distinction "of making a hole in one," in other words, of hitting the ball into the pot, or can, or receptacle, in one shot. That is to say, after I had hit, a ball was found in the can, and my ball was not found. It is what we call circumstantial evidence—the same thing that people are hanged for.

Under such circumstances I should have little to teach to anybody about golf. But it has occurred to me that from a certain angle my opinions may be of value. I at least bring to bear on the game all the resources of a trained mind and all the equipment of a complete education.

In particular I may be able to help the ordinary golfer, or

Reprinted by permission of Dodd, Mead & Company from *Literary Lapses* by Stephen Leacock.

"goofer"—others prefer "gopher"—by showing him something of the application of mathematics to golf.

Many a player is perhaps needlessly discouraged by not being able to calculate properly the chances and probabilities of progress in the game. Take for example the simple problem of "going round in bogey." The ordinary average player, such as I am now becoming—something between a beginner and an expert—necessarily wonders to himself, "Shall I ever be able to go around in bogey; will the time ever come when I shall make not one hole in bogey but all the holes?"

To this, according to my calculations, the answer is overwhelmingly "yes." The thing is a mere matter of time and patience.

Let me explain for the few people who never play golf (such as night watchmen, night clerks in hotels, night operators, and astronomers) that "bogey" is an imaginary player who does each hole at golf in the fewest strokes that a first-class player with ordinary luck ought to need for that hole.

Now an ordinary player finds it quite usual to do one hole out of the nine "in bogey"—as we golfers, or rather, "us goofers," call it; but he wonders whether it will ever be his fate to do all the nine holes of the course in bogey. To which we answer again with absolute assurance, he will.

The thing is a simple instance of what is called the mathematical theory of probability. If a player usually and generally makes one hole in bogey, or comes close to it, his chance of making any one particular hole in bogey is one in nine. Let us say, for easier calculation, that it is one in ten. When he makes it, his chance of doing the same with the next hole is also one in ten; therefore, taken from the start, his chance of making the two holes successively in bogey is one tenth of a tenth chance. In other words, it is one in a hundred.

The reader sees already how encouraging the calculation is. Here is at last something definite about his progress. Let us carry it farther. His chance of making three holes in bogey one after the other will be one in 1000, his chance of four, one in 10,000, and his chance of making the whole round in bogey will be exactly one in 1,000,000,000—that is, one in a billion games.

In other words, all he has to do is to keep right on. But for how long? he asks. How long will it take, playing the ordinary number of games in a month, to play a billion? Will it take several years? Yes, it will.

An ordinary player plays about a hundred games in a year and will, therefore, play a billion games in exactly 10,000,000 years. That gives us precisely the time it will need for persons like the reader and myself to go around in bogey.

Even this calculation needs a little revision. We have to allow for the fact that in 10,000,000 years the shrinking of the earth's crust, the diminishing heat of the sun, and the general slackening down of the whole solar system, together with the passing of eclipses, comets, and showers of meteors, may put us off our game.

In fact, I doubt if we shall ever get around in bogey. Let us try something else. Here is a very interesting calculation in regard to "allowing for the wind."

I have noticed that a great many golf players of my own particular class are always preoccupied with the question of "allowing for the wind." My friend Amphibius Jones, for example, just before driving always murmurs something, as if in prayer, about "allowing for the wind." After driving he says with a sigh, "I didn't allow for the wind." In fact, all through my class there is a general feeling that our game is practically ruined by the wind. We ought really to play in the middle of the Desert of Sahara where there isn't any.

It occurred to me that it might be interesting to reduce to a formula the effect exercised by the resistance of the wind on a moving golf ball. For example, in our game of last Wednesday, Jones in his drive struck the ball with what, he assures me, was his full force, hitting it with absolute accuracy, as he himself admits, fair in the center, and he himself feeling, on his own assertion, absolutely fit, his eye being (a very necessary thing with Jones) absolutely "in," and he also having on his proper sweater —a further necessary condition of first-class play. Under all the favorable circumstances the ball advanced only fifty yards! It was evident at once that it was a simple matter of the wind: the wind, which was of that treacherous character that blows over the links unnoticed, had impinged full upon the ball, pressed it backward, and forced it to the earth.

Here, then, is a neat subject of calculation. Granted that Jones —as measured on a hitting machine the week the circus was here —can hit two tons and that this whole force was pressed against a golf ball only one inch and a quarter in diameter. What happens? My reader will remember that the superficial area of a golf ball is πr^3, that is 3.141567 x ($\frac{5}{8}$ inches)^3. And all of this driven forward with the power of 4000 pounds to the inch!

In short, taking Jones's statements at their face value, the ball would have traveled, had it not been for the wind, no less than six and a half miles.

I give next a calculation of even more acute current interest. It is in regard to "moving the head." How often is an admirable stroke at golf spoiled by moving the head! I have seen members of our golf club sit silent and glum all evening, murmuring from time to time, "I moved my head." When Jones and I play together I often hit the ball sideways into the vegetable garden from which no ball returns (they have one of these on every links; it is a Scottish invention). And whenever I do so Jones always says, "You moved your head." In return when *he* drives his ball away up into the air and down again ten yards in front of him, I always retaliate by saying, "You moved your head, old man."

In short, if absolute immobility of the head could be achieved, the major problem of golf would be solved.

Let us put the theory mathematically. The head, poised on the neck, has a circumferential sweep or orbit of about two inches, not counting the rolling of the eyes. The circumferential sweep of a golf ball is based on a radius of 250 yards, or a circumference of about 1600 yards, which is very nearly equal to a mile. Inside this circumference is an area of 27,878,400 square feet, the whole of which is controlled by a tiny movement of the human neck. In other words, if a player were to wiggle his neck even

1/190 of an inch the amount of ground on which the ball might falsely alight would be half a million square feet. If at the same time he multiplies the effect by rolling his eyes, the ball might alight anywhere.

I feel certain that after reading this any sensible player will keep his head still.

A further calculation remains—and one perhaps of even greater practical interest than the ones above.

Everybody who plays golf is well aware that on some days he plays better than on others. Question—How often does a man really play his game?

I take the case of Amphibius Jones. There are certain days when he is, as he admits himself, *"put off his game"* by not having on his proper golf vest. On other days the light puts him off his game; at other times the dark; so, too, the heat, or again the cold. He is often put off his game because he has been up late the night before; or similarly because he has been to bed too early the night before; the barking of a dog always puts him off his game; so do children, or adults, or women. Bad news disturbs his game; so does good; so also does the absence of news.

All of this may be expressed mathematically by a very simple application of the theory of permutations and probability; let us say that there are altogether fifty forms of disturbance, any one of which puts Jones off his game. Each one of these disturbances happens, say, once in ten days. What chance is there that a day will come when *not a single one of them occurs?* The formula is a little complicated, but mathematicians will recognize the answer at once as $\frac{x}{1} + \frac{x^2}{1} + \ldots \ldots \ldots \frac{x^n}{1}$. In fact, that is exactly how often Jones plays at his best; $\frac{x}{1} + \frac{x^2}{1} \ldots \frac{x^n}{1}$ worked out in time and reckoning four games to the week, and allowing for leap years and solar eclipses, come to about once in 2,930,-000 years.

And from watching Jones play I think that this is about right.

The Mathematician's Nightmare: The Vision of Professor Squarepunt

BERTRAND RUSSELL

There is no need to introduce to readers of this book the co-creator of Principia Mathematica. *They may, however, be interested in a glimpse of the evolution of Russell's mind, against which may be judged this delightful spoofing of Pythagoras, written during Russell's latter years. In his* My Philosophical Development (1959) *he speaks of his "retreat from Pythagoras."*

"My philosophical development, since the early years of the present century, may be broadly described as a gradual retreat from Pythagoras. The Pythagoreans had a peculiar form of mysticism which was bound up with mathematics. This form of mysticism greatly affected Plato and had, I think, more influence upon him than is generally acknowledged. I had, for a time, a very similar outlook and found in the nature of mathematical logic, as I then supposed its nature to be, something profoundly satisfying in some important emotional aspects. . . .

(Today) "Mathematics has ceased to seem to me non-human

in its subject matter. I have come to believe, though very reluctantly, that it consists of tautologies. I fear that, to a mind of sufficient intellectual power, the whole of mathematics would appear trivial, as trivial as the statement that a four-footed animal is an animal. I think that the timelessness of mathematics has none of the sublimity that it once seemed to me to have but consists merely in the fact that the pure mathematician is not talking about time. I cannot any longer find any mystical satisfaction in the contemplation of mathematical truth."

The Mathematician's Nightmare *starts off with some good-natured raillery directed against Eddington and his beloved number 137. The reader will of course recognize 137 (see Eddington's* Relativity Theory of Protons and Electrons, *1936) as the numerical value of the basic "fine-structure constant" of spectroscopy, viewed by Eddington as one of the four "constants of nature."*

Prefatory Explanation

My lamented friend Professor Squarepunt, the eminent mathematician, was during his lifetime a friend and admirer of Sir Arthur Eddington. But there was one point in Sir Arthur's theories which always bewildered Professor Squarepunt, and that was the mystical, cosmic powers which Sir Arthur ascribed to the number 137. Had the properties which this number was supposed to possess been merely arithmetical no difficulty would have arisen. But it was above all in physics that 137 showed its prowess, which was not unlike that attributed to the number 666. It is evident that conversations with Sir Arthur influenced Professor Squarepunt's nightmare.

The mathematician, worn out by a long day's study of the theories of Pythagoras, at last fell asleep in his chair, where a strange drama visited his sleeping thoughts. The numbers, in this drama, were not the bloodless categories that he had previously supposed them. They were living, breathing beings endowed with all the passions which he was accustomed to find in his fellow mathematicians. In his dream he stood at the center of endless concentric circles. The first circle contained the numbers from 1 to 10; the second, those from 11 to 100; the third, those from 101 to 1000; and so on, illimitably, over the infinite surface of a boundless plain. The odd numbers were male; the evens, female. Beside him in the center stood Pi, the master of ceremonies. Pi's face was masked, and it was understood that none could behold it and live. But piercing eyes looked out from the mask, inexorable, cold, and enigmatic. Each number had its name clearly marked upon its uniform. Different kinds of numbers had different uniforms and different shapes: the squares were tiles; the cubes were dice; round numbers were balls; prime numbers were indivisible cylinders; perfect numbers had crowns. In addition to variations of shape, numbers also had variations of color. The first seven concentric rings had the seven colors of the rainbow, except that 10, 100, 1000, and so on, were white, while 13 and 666 were black. When a number belonged to two of these categories—for example, if, like 1000, it was both round and a cube—it wore the more honorable uniform, and the more honorable was that of which there were fewer among the first million numbers.

The numbers danced round Professor Squarepunt and Pi in a vast and intricate ballet. The squares, the cubes, the primes, the pyramidal numbers, the perfect numbers, and the round numbers wove interweaving chains in an endless and bewildering dance, and as they danced they sang an ode to their own greatness:

> *We are the finite numbers.*
> *We are the stuff of the world.*
> *Whatever confusion cumbers*
> *The earth is by us unfurled.*
> *We revere our master Pythagoras*
> *And deeply despise every hag or ass.*
> *Not Endor's witch nor Balaam's mount*

We recognize as wisdom's fount.
But round and round in endless ballet
We move like comets seen by Halley.
And honored by the immortal Plato
We think no later mortal great-o.
We follow the laws
Without a pause,
For we are the finite numbers.

At a sign from Pi the ballet ceased, and the numbers one by one were introduced to Professor Squarepunt. Each number made a little speech explaining its peculiar merits.

1: I am the parent of all, the father of infinite progeny. None would exist but for me.

2: Don't be so stuck-up. You know it takes two to make more.

3: I am the number of Triumvirs, of the Wise Men of the East, of the stars in Orion's Belt, of the Fates and of the Graces.

4: But for me nothing would be foursquare. There would be no honesty in the world. I am the guardian of the Moral Law.

5: I am the number of fingers on a hand. I make pentagons and pentagrams. And but for me dodecahedra could not exist; and, as everyone knows, the universe is a dodecahedron. So, but for me, there could be no universe.

6: I am the Perfect Number. I know that I have upstart rivals; 28 and 496 have sometimes pretended to be my equals. But they come too far down the scale of precedence to count against me.

7: I am the Sacred Number: the number of days of the week, the number of the Pleiades, the number of the seven-branched candlesticks, the number of the churches of Asia, and the number of the planets—for I do not recognize that blasphemer Galileo.

8: I am the first of the cubes—except for poor old One, who by this time is rather past his work.

9: I am the number of the Muses. All the charms and elegancies of life depend upon me.

10: It's all very well for you wretched units to boast, but I am the godfather of all the infinite hosts behind me. Every single one owes his name to me. And but for me they would be a mere mob and not an ordered hierarchy.

At this point the mathematician got bored and turned to Pi, saying: "Don't you think the rest of the introductions could be taken for granted?" At this there was a general outcry.

11 shrieked: "But I was the number of the Apostles after the defection of Judas."

12 exclaimed: "I was the godfather of the numbers in the days of the Babylonians—and a much better godfather I was than that wretched 10, who owes his position to a biological accident and not to arithmetical excellence."

13 growled: "I am the master of ill-luck. If you are rude to me, you shall suffer."

There was such a din that the mathematician covered his ears with his hands and turned an imploring gaze upon Pi. Pi waved his conductor's baton and proclaimed in a voice of thunder, "Silence! Or you shall all become incommensurable." All turned pale and submitted.

Throughout the ballet the professor had noticed one number among the primes, 137, which seemed unruly and unwilling to accept its place in the series. It tried repeatedly to get ahead of 1 and 2 and 3 and showed a subversiveness which threatened to destroy the pattern of the ballet. What astonished Professor Squarepunt even more than this disorderly conduct was a shadowy specter of an Arthurian knight which kept whispering in the ear of 137, "Go to it! Go to it! Get to the top!" Although the shadowy character of the specter made recognition difficult, the professor at last recognized the dim form of his friend, Sir Arthur. This gave him a sympathy with 137 in spite of the hostility of Pi, who kept trying to suppress the unruly prime.

At length 137 exclaimed, "There's a damned sight too much bureaucracy here! What I want is liberty for the individual." Pi's mask frowned. But the professor interceded, saying, "Do not be too hard on him. Have you not observed that he's governed by a familiar? I knew this familiar in life, and from my knowledge I can vouch that it is he who inspires the anti-governmental sentiments of 137. For my part, I should like to hear what 137 has to say."

Somewhat reluctantly Pi consented. Professor Squarepunt said, "Tell me, 137, what is the basis of your revolt? Is it a protest against inequality that inspires you? Is it merely that your ego has been inflated by Sir Arthur's praise? Or is it, as I half suspect, a deep ideological rejection of the metaphysic that your colleagues have imbibed from Plato? You need not fear to tell me the truth. I will make your peace with Pi, about whom I know at least as much as he does himself."

At this 137 burst into excited speech: "You are right! It is their metaphysics that I cannot bear. They still pretend that they are eternal, though long ago their conduct showed that they think no such thing. We all found Plato's heaven dull and decided that it would be more fun to govern the sensible world. Since we descended from the Empyrean we have had emotions not unlike yours: each Odd loves its attendant Even; and the Evens feel kindly toward the Odds, in spite of finding them very odd. Our empire now is of this world, and when the world goes pop, we shall go pop too."

Professor Squarepunt found himself in agreement with 137. But all the others, including Pi, considered him a blasphemer and turned upon both him and the professor. The infinite host, extending in all directions farther than the eye could reach, hurled themselves upon the poor professor in an angry buzz. For a moment he was terrified. Then he pulled himself together and, suddenly recollecting his waking wisdom, he called out in Stentorian tones, "Avaunt! You are only Symbolic Conveniences!"

With a banshee wail the whole vast array dissolved in mist. And, as he woke, the professor heard himself saying, "So much for Plato!"

Milo and the Mathemagician

NORTON JUSTER

Milo and the Mathemagician *is drawn from Norton Juster's fantasy for children,* The Phantom Tollbooth. *It is about a little boy named Milo and his companions, among whom the Humbug and Tock (the dog who ticks) are to be encountered in these episodes. Most imitations of* Alice *are cursed from the start. This one has real freshness, and the changes on the elementary humor of mathematics are rung clearly, sharply, and brightly.*

UP AHEAD the road divided into three and, as if in reply to Milo's question, an enormous road sign, pointing in all three directions, stated clearly:

DIGITOPOLIS

5	Miles
1,600	Rods
8,800	Yards
26,400	Feet
316,800	Inches
633,600	Half inches

AND THEN SOME

"Let's travel by miles," advised the Humbug. "It's shorter."
"Let's travel by half inches," suggested Milo. "It's quicker."

"But which road should we take?" asked Tock. "It must make a difference."

As they argued, a most peculiar little figure stepped nimbly from behind the sign and approached them, talking all the while. "Yes, indeed; indeed it does; certainly; my, yes; it does make a difference; undoubtedly."

He was constructed (for that's really the only way to describe him) of a large assortment of lines and angles connected together into one solid many-sided shape—somewhat like a cube that's had all its corners cut off and then had all its corners cut off again. Each of the edges was neatly labeled with a small letter and each of the angles with a large one. He wore a handsome beret on top, and peering intently from one of his several surfaces was a very serious face. Perhaps if you look at the picture you'll know what I mean.

When he reached the car, the figure doffed his cap and recited in a loud clear voice:

My angles are many.
My sides are not few.
I'm the Dodecahedron.
Who are you?

"What's a Dodecahedron?" inquired Milo, who was barely able to pronounce the strange word.

"See for yourself," he said, turning around slowly. "A Dodecahedron is a mathematical shape with twelve faces."

Just as he said it, eleven other faces appeared, one on each surface, and each one wore a different expression.

"I usually use one at a time," he confided, as all but the smiling one disappeared again. "It saves wear and tear. What are you called?"

"Milo," said Milo.

"That is an odd name," he said, changing his smiling face for a frowning one. "And you only have one face."

"Is that bad?" asked Milo, making sure it was still there.

"You'll soon wear it out using it for everything," replied the Dodecahedron. "Now I have one for smiling, one for laughing, one for crying, one for frowning, one for thinking, one for pouting, and six more besides. Is everyone with one face called a Milo?"

"Oh no," Milo replied. "Some are called Henry or George or Robert or John or lots of other things."

"How terribly confusing," he cried. "Everything here is called exactly what it is. The triangles are called triangles, the circles are called circles, and even the same numbers have the same name. Why, can you imagine what would happen if we named all the twos Henry or George or Robert or John or lots of other things? You'd have to say Robert plus John equals four, and if the four's name were Albert, things would be hopeless."

"I never thought of it that way," Milo admitted.

"Then I suggest you begin at once," admonished the Dodecahedron from his admonishing face, "for here in Digitopolis everything is quite precise."

"Then perhaps you can help us decide which road to take," said Milo.

"By all means," he replied happily. "There's nothing to it. If a small car carrying three people at thirty miles an hour for ten minutes along a road five miles long at 11:35 in the morning starts at the same time as three people who have been traveling in a little automobile at twenty miles an hour for fifteen minutes on another road exactly twice as long as one half the distance of the other, while a dog, a bug, and a boy travel an equal distance in the same time or the same distance in an equal time along a third road in mid-October, then which one arrives first and which is the best way to go?"

"Seventeen!" shouted the Humbug, scribbling furiously on a piece of paper.

"Well, I'm not sure, but—" Milo stammered after several minutes of frantic figuring.

"You'll have to do better than that," scolded the Dodecahedron, "or you'll never know how far you've gone or whether or not you've ever gotten there."

"I'm not very good at problems," admitted Milo.

"What a shame," sighed the Dodecahedron. "They're so very useful. Why, did you know that if a beaver two feet long with a tail a foot and a half long can build a dam twelve feet high and six feet wide in two days, all you would need to build Boulder Dam is a beaver sixty-eight feet long with a fifty-one-foot tail?"

"Where would you find a beaver that big?" grumbled the Humbug as his pencil point snapped.

"I'm sure I don't know," he replied, "but if you did, you'd certainly know what to do with him."

"That's absurd," objected Milo, whose head was spinning from all the numbers and questions.

"That may be true," he acknowledged, "but it's completely accurate, and as long as the answer is right, who cares if the question is wrong? If you want sense, you'll have to make it yourself."

"All three roads arrive at the same place at the same time," interrupted Tock, who had patiently been doing the first problem.

"Correct!" shouted the Dodecahedron. "And I'll take you there myself. Now you can see how important problems are. If you hadn't done this one properly, you might have gone the wrong way."

"I can't see where I made my mistake," said the Humbug, frantically rechecking his figures.

"But if all the roads arrive at the same place at the same time, then aren't they all the right way?" asked Milo.

"Certainly not!" he shouted, glaring from his most upset face. "They're all the *wrong* way. Just because you have a choice, it doesn't mean that any of them *has* to be right."

He walked to the sign and quickly spun it around three times. As he did, the three roads vanished and a new one suddenly appeared, heading in the direction that the sign now pointed.

"Is every road five miles from Digitopolis?" asked Milo.

"I'm afraid it has to be," the Dodecahedron replied, leaping onto the back of the car. "It's the only sign we've got."

The new road was quite bumpy and full of stones, and each time they hit one the Dodecahedron bounced into the air and landed on one of his faces, with a sulk or a smile or a laugh or a frown, depending upon which one it was.

"We'll soon be there," he announced happily after one of his short flights. "Welcome to the land of numbers."

"It doesn't look very inviting," the bug remarked, for, as they climbed higher and higher, not a tree or a blade of grass could be seen anywhere. Only the rocks remained.

"Is this the place where numbers are made?" asked Milo as the car lurched again, and this time the Dodecahedron sailed off down the mountainside, head over heels and grunt over grimace, until he landed sad side up at what looked like the entrance to a cave.

"They're not made," he replied, as if nothing had happened. "You have to dig for them. Don't you know anything at all about numbers?"

"Well, I don't think they're very important," snapped Milo, too embarrassed to admit the truth.

"NOT IMPORTANT!" roared the Dodecahedron, turning red with fury. "Could you have tea for two without the two—or three blind mice without the three? Would there be four corners of the earth if there weren't a four? And how would you sail the seven seas without a seven?"

"All I meant was—" began Milo, but the Dodecahedron, overcome with emotion and shouting furiously, carried right on.

"If you had high hopes, how would you know how high they were? And did you know that narrow escapes come in all different widths? Would you travel the whole wide world without ever knowing how wide it was? And how could you do anything at long last," he concluded, waving his arms over his head, "without knowing how long the last was? Why, numbers are the most beautiful and valuable things in the world. Just follow me and I'll show you." He turned on his heel and stalked off into the cave.

"Come along, come along," he shouted from the dark hole. "I can't wait for you all day." And in a moment they'd followed him into the mountain.

It took several minutes for their eyes to become accustomed to the dim light, and during that time strange scratching, scraping, tapping, scuffling noises could be heard all around them.

"Put these on," instructed the Dodecahedron, handing each of them a helmet with a flashlight attached to the top.

"Where are we going?" whispered Milo, for it seemed like the kind of place in which you whispered.

"We're here," he replied with a sweeping gesture. "This is the numbers mine."

Milo squinted into the darkness and saw for the first time that they had entered a vast cavern lit only by a soft, eerie glow from the great stalactites which hung ominously from the ceiling. Passages and corridors honeycombed the walls and wound their way from floor to ceiling, up and down the sides of the cave. And, everywhere he looked, Milo saw little men no bigger than himself busy digging and chopping, shoveling and scraping, pulling and tugging carts full of stone from one place to another.

"Right this way," instructed the Dodecahedron, "and watch where you step."

As he spoke, his voice echoed and re-echoed and re-echoed again, mixing its sound with the buzz of activity all around them. Tock trotted along next to Milo, and the Humbug, stepping daintily, followed behind.

"Whose mine is it?" asked Milo, stepping around two of the loaded wagons.

"BY THE FOUR MILLION EIGHT HUNDRED AND TWENTY-SEVEN THOUSAND SIX HUNDRED AND FIFTY-NINE HAIRS ON MY HEAD, IT'S MINE, OF COURSE!" bellowed a voice from across the cavern. And striding toward them came a figure who could only have been the Mathemagician.

He was dressed in a long flowing robe covered entirely with complex mathematical equations and a tall pointed cap that made him look very wise. In his left hand he carried a long staff with a pencil point at one end and a large rubber eraser at the other.

"It's a lovely mine," apologized the Humbug, who was always intimidated by loud noises.

"The biggest number mine in the kingdom," said the Mathe-magician proudly.

"Are there any precious stones in it?" asked Milo excitedly.

"PRECIOUS STONES!" he roared, even louder than before. And then he leaned over toward Milo and whispered softly, "By the eight million two hundred and forty-seven thousand three hundred and twelve threads in my robe, I'll say there are. Look here."

He reached into one of the carts and pulled out a small object, which he polished vigorously on his robe. When he held it up to the light, it sparkled brightly.

"But that's a five," objected Milo, for that was certainly what it was.

"Exactly," agreed the Mathemagician. "As valuable a jewel as you'll find anywhere. Look at some of the others."

He scooped up a great handful of stones and poured them into Milo's arms. They included all the numbers from one to nine and even an assortment of zeros.

"We dig them and polish them right here," volunteered the Dodecahedron, pointing to a group of workers busily employed at the buffing wheels, "and then we send them all over the world. Marvelous, aren't they?"

"They are exceptional," said Tock, who had a special fond-ness for numbers.

"So that's where they come from," said Milo, looking in awe at the glittering collection of numbers. He returned them to the Dodecahedron as carefully as possible but, as he did, one dropped to the floor with a smash and broke in two. The Humbug winced and Milo looked terribly concerned.

"Oh, don't worry about that," said the Mathemagician as he scooped up the pieces. "We use the broken ones for fractions."

"Haven't you any diamonds or emeralds or rubies?" asked the bug irritably, for he was quite disappointed in what he'd seen so far.

"Yes, indeed," the Mathemagician replied, leading them to the rear of the cave. "Right this way."

There, piled into enormous mounds that reached almost to

the ceiling, were not only diamonds and emeralds and rubies but also sapphires, amethysts, topazes, moonstones, and garnets. It was the most amazing mass of wealth that any of them had ever seen.

"They're such a terrible nuisance," sighed the Mathemagician, "and no one can think of what to do with them. So we just keep digging them up and throwing them out. Now," he said, taking a silver whistle from his pocket and blowing it loudly, "let's have some lunch."

And for the first time in his life the astonished bug couldn't think of a thing to say.

Into the cavern rushed eight of the strongest miners, carrying an immense caldron which bubbled and sizzled and sent great clouds of savory steam spiraling slowly to the ceiling. A sweet yet pungent aroma hung in the air and drifted easily from one anxious nose to the other, stopping only long enough to make several mouths water and a few stomachs growl. Milo, Tock, and the Humbug watched eagerly as the rest of the workers put down their tools and gathered around the big pot to help themselves.

"Perhaps you'd care for something to eat?" said the Mathemagician, offering each of them a heaping bowlful.

"Yes, sir," said Milo, who was beside himself with hunger.

"Thank you," added Tock.

The Humbug made no reply, for he was already too busy eating, and in a moment the three of them had finished absolutely everything they'd been given.

"Please have another portion," said the Mathemagician, filling their bowls once more, and as quickly as they'd finished the first one the second was emptied too.

"Don't stop now," he insisted, serving them again,
    and again,
        and again,
            and again,
                and again.

"How very strange," thought Milo as he finished his seventh helping. "Each one I eat makes me a little hungrier than the one before."

"Do have some more," suggested the Mathemagician, and they continued to eat just as fast as he filled the plates.

After Milo had eaten nine portions, Tock eleven, and the Humbug, without once stopping to look up, twenty-three, the Mathemagician blew his whistle for a second time and immediately the pot was removed and the miners returned to work.

"U-g-g-g-h-h-h," gasped the bug, suddenly realizing that he was twenty-three times hungrier than when he started. "I think I'm starving."

"Me, too," complained Milo, whose stomach felt as empty as he could ever remember, "and I ate so much."

"Yes, it was delicious, wasn't it?" agreed the pleased Dodecahedron, wiping the gravy from several of his mouths. "It's the specialty of the kingdom—subtraction stew."

"I have more of an appetite than when I began," said Tock, leaning weakly against one of the larger rocks.

"Certainly," replied the Mathemagician. "What did you expect? The more you eat, the hungrier you get. Everyone knows that."

"They do?" said Milo doubtfully. "Then how do you ever get enough?"

"Enough?" he said impatiently. "Here in Digitopolis we have our meals when we're full and eat until we're hungry. That way, when you don't have anything at all, you have more than enough. It's a very economical system. You must have been quite stuffed to have eaten so much."

"It's completely logical," explained the Dodecahedron. "The more you want, the less you get, and the less you get, the more you have. Simple arithmetic, that's all. Suppose you had something and added something to it. What would that make?"

"More," said Milo quickly.

"Quite correct." He nodded. "Now suppose you had something and added nothing to it. What would you have?"

"The same," he answered again without much conviction.

"Splendid," cried the Dodecahedron. "And suppose you had something and added less than nothing to it. What would you have then?"

"FAMINE!" roared the anguished Humbug, who suddenly realized that that was exactly what he'd eaten twenty-three bowls of.

"It's not as bad as all that," said the Dodecahedron from his most sympathetic face. "In a few hours you'll be nice and full again—just in time for dinner."

"Oh dear," said Milo sadly and softly. "I only eat when I'm hungry."

"What a curious idea," said the Mathemagician, raising his staff over his head and scrubbing the rubber end back and forth several times on the ceiling. "The next thing you'll have us believe is that you only sleep when you're tired." And by the time he'd finished the sentence the cavern, the miners, and the Dodecahedron had vanished, leaving just the four of them standing in the Mathemagician's workshop.

"I often find," he casually explained to his dazed visitors, "that the best way to get from one place to another is to erase everything and begin again. Please make yourself at home."

"Do you always travel that way?" asked Milo as he glanced curiously at the strange circular room, whose sixteen tiny arched windows corresponded exactly to the sixteen points of the compass. Around the entire circumference were numbers from zero to three hundred and sixty, marking the degrees of the circle, and on the floor, walls, tables, chairs, desks, cabinets, and ceiling were labels showing their heights, widths, depths, and distances to and from each other. To one side was a gigantic note pad set on an artist's easel, and from hooks and strings hung a collection of scales, rulers, measures, weights, tapes, and all sorts of other devices for measuring any number of things in every possible way.

"No indeed," replied the Mathemagician, and this time he raised the sharpened end of his staff, drew a thin straight line in the air, and then walked gracefully across it from one side of the room to the other. "Most of the time I take the shortest distance between any two points. And, of course, when I should be in several places at once," he remarked, writing $7 \times 1 = 7$ carefully on the note pad, "I simply multiply."

Suddenly there were seven Mathemagicians standing side by side, and each one looked exactly like the other.

"How did you do that?" gasped Milo.

"There's nothing to it," they all said in chorus, "if you have a magic staff." Then six of them canceled themselves out and simply disappeared.

"But it's only a big pencil," the Humbug objected, tapping at it with his cane.

"True enough," agreed the Mathemagician, "but once you learn to use it, there's no end to what you can do."

"Can you make things disappear?" asked Milo excitedly.

"Why, certainly," he said, striding over to the easel. "Just step a little closer and watch carefully."

After demonstrating that there was nothing up his sleeves, in his hat, or behind his back, he wrote quickly:

$$4 + 9 - 2 \times 16 + 1 \div 3 \times 6 - 67 + 8 \times 2 - 3 +$$
$$26 - 1 \div 34 + 3 \div 7 + 2 - 5 =$$

Then he looked up expectantly.

"Seventeen!" shouted the bug, who always managed to be first with the wrong answer.

"It all comes to zero," corrected Milo.

"Precisely," said the Mathemagician, making a very theatrical bow, and the entire line of numbers vanished before their eyes. "Now is there anything else you'd like to see?"

"Yes, please," said Milo. "Can you show me the biggest number there is?"

"I'd be delighted," he replied, opening one of the closet doors. "We keep it right here. It took four miners just to dig it out."

Inside was the biggest

3

Milo had ever seen.

It was fully twice as high as the Mathemagician.

"No, that's not what I mean," objected Milo. "Can you show me the longest number there is?"

"Surely," said the Mathemagician, opening another door. "Here it is. It took three carts to carry it here."

Inside this closet was the longest

imaginable. It was just about as wide as the three was high.

"No, no, no, that's not what I mean either," he said, looking helplessly at Tock.

"I think what you would like to see," said the dog, scratching himself just under half-past four, "is the number of greatest possible magnitude."

"Well, why didn't you say so?" said the Mathemagician, who was busily measuring the edge of a raindrop. "What's the greatest number *you* can think of?"

"Nine trillion, nine hundred ninety-nine billion, nine hundred ninety-nine million, nine hundred ninety-nine thousand, nine hundred ninety-nine," recited Milo breathlessly.

"Very good," said the Mathemagician. "Now add one to it. Now add one again," he repeated when Milo had added the previous one. "Now add one again. Now add one again. Now add one again. Now add one again. Now add one again. Now add one again. Now add—"

"But when can I stop?" pleaded Milo.

"Never," said the Mathemagician with a little smile, "for the number you want is always at least one more than the number you've got, and it's so large that if you started saying it yesterday you wouldn't finish tomorrow."

"Where could you ever find a number so big?" scoffed the Humbug.

"In the same place they have the smallest number there is," he answered helpfully, "and you know what that is."

"Certainly," said the bug, suddenly remembering something to do at the other end of the room.

"One one-millionth?" asked Milo, trying to think of the smallest fraction possible.

"Almost," said the Mathemagician. "Now divide it in half. Now divide it in half again. Now divide it in half again. Now divide it in half again. Now divide it in half again. Now divide it in half again. Now divide——"

"Oh dear," shouted Milo, holding his hands to his ears, "doesn't that ever stop either?"

"How can it," said the Mathemagician, "when you can always take half of whatever you have left until it's so small that if you started to say it right now you'd finish even before you began?"

"Where could you keep anything so tiny?" Milo asked, trying very hard to imagine such a thing.

The Mathemagician stopped what he was doing and explained simply, "Why, in a box that's so small you can't see it—and that's kept in a drawer that's so small you can't see it, in a dresser that's so small you can't see it, in a house that's so small you can't see it, on a street that's so small you can't see it, in a city that's so small you can't see it, which is part of a country that's so small you can't see it, in a world that's so small you can't see it."

Then he sat down, fanned himself with a handkerchief, and continued. "Then, of course, we keep the whole thing in another box that's so small you can't see it—and, if you follow me, I'll show you where to find it."

They walked to one of the small windows and there, tied to the sill, was one end of a line that stretched along the ground and into the distance until completely out of sight.

"Just follow that line forever," said the Mathemagician, "and when you reach the end, turn left. There you'll find the land of Infinity, where the tallest, the shortest, the biggest, the smallest, and the most and the least of everything are kept."

"I really don't have that much time," said Milo anxiously. "Isn't there a quicker way?"

"Well, you might try this flight of stairs," he suggested, open-ing another door and pointing up. "It goes there too."

Milo bounded across the room and started up the stairs two at a time. "Wait for me, please," he shouted to Tock and the Humbug. "I'll be gone just a few minutes."

Up he went—very quickly at first—then more slowly—then in a little while even more slowly than that—and finally, after many minutes of climbing up the endless stairway, one weary foot was barely able to follow the other. Milo suddenly realized that with all his effort he was no closer to the top than when he began and not a great deal further from the bottom. But he struggled on for a while longer, until at last, completely ex-hausted, he collapsed onto one of the steps.

"I should have known it," he mumbled, resting his tired legs and filling his lungs with air. "This is just like the line that goes on forever, and I'll never get there."

"You wouldn't like it much anyway," someone replied gently. "Infinity is a dreadfully poor place. They can never manage to make ends meet."

Milo looked up, with his head still resting heavily in his hand; he was becoming quite accustomed to being addressed at the oddest times, in the oddest places, by the oddest people—and this time he was not at all disappointed. Standing next to him on the step was exactly one half of a small child who had been divided neatly from top to bottom.

"Pardon me for staring," said Milo, after he had been staring for some time, "but I've never seen half a child before."

"It's .58 to be precise," replied the child from the left side of his mouth (which happened to be the only side of his mouth).

"I beg your pardon?" said Milo.

"It's .58," he repeated. "It's a little bit *more* than a half."

"Have you always been that way?" asked Milo impatiently, for he felt that that was a needlessly fine distinction.

"My goodness, no," the child assured him. "A few years ago I was just .42 and, believe me, that was terribly inconvenient."

"What is the rest of your family like?" said Milo, this time a bit more sympathetically.

"Oh, we're just the average family," he said thoughtfully, "mother, father, and 2.58 children—and, as I explained, I'm the .58."

"It must be rather odd being only part of a person," Milo remarked.

"Not at all," said the child. "Every average family has 2.58 children, so I always have someone to play with. Besides, each family also has an average of 1.3 automobiles, and since I'm the only one who can drive three tenths of a car, I get to use it all the time."

"But averages aren't real," objected Milo. "They're just imaginary."

"That may be so," he agreed, "but they're also very useful at times. For instance, if you didn't have any money at all, but you happened to be with four other people who had ten dollars apiece, then you'd each have an average of eight dollars. Isn't that right?"

"I guess so," said Milo weakly.

"Well, think how much better off you'd be, just because of averages," he explained convincingly. "And think of the poor farmer when it doesn't rain all year: if there wasn't an average yearly rainfall of thirty-seven inches in this part of the country, all his crops would wither and die."

It all sounded terribly confusing to Milo, for he had always had trouble in school with just this subject.

"There are still other advantages," continued the child. "For instance, if one rat were cornered by nine cats, then, on the average, each cat would be 10 per cent rat and the rat would be 90 per cent cat. If you happened to be a rat, you can see how much nicer it would make things."

"But that can never be," said Milo, jumping to his feet.

"Don't be too sure," said the child patiently, "for one of the nicest things about mathematics, or anything else you might care to learn, is that many of the things which can never be often are. You see," he went on, "it's very much like your trying to reach Infinity. You know that it's there, but you just don't know where —but just because you can never reach it doesn't mean that it's not worth looking for."

"I hadn't thought of it that way," said Milo, starting down the stairs. "I think I'll go back now."

"A wise decision," the child agreed, "but try again someday —perhaps you'll get much closer." And, as Milo waved goodbye, he smiled warmly, which he usually did on the average of forty-seven times a day.

III

IRREGULAR
FIGURES

❧ ❧ ❧

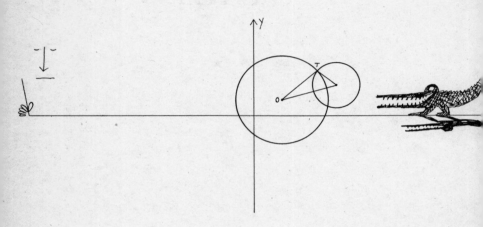

Sixteen Stones

SAMUEL BECKETT

*Certain vanguard critics speak of Samuel Beckett in the same
breath with Joyce and Kafka. Born in 1906 in Dublin, he has
spent most of his adult life in Paris and since 1945 has written
all his books and plays in French, though he himself translated
into English his most famous play,* Waiting for Godot (1954).
The novel Molloy, *from which this strange exercise in permutation and combination is extracted, was published in 1951.* Sixteen Stones *I conceive to be an expression of Beckett's conviction
of the triviality, the horrible emptiness, of all action. The hero's
manipulation of his sixteen pebbles reminds one of the well-
known puzzle-game Diabolo. And indeed there is something
hellish about this story.*

I TOOK ADVANTAGE of being at the seaside to lay in a store of
sucking stones. They were pebbles, but I call them stones. Yes,
on this occasion I laid in a considerable store. I distributed them
equally between my four pockets and sucked them turn and turn
about. This raised a problem which I first solved in the following
way. I had, say, sixteen stones, four in each of my four pockets,
these being the two pockets of my trousers and the two pockets
of my greatcoat. Taking a stone from the right pocket of my
greatcoat, and putting it in my mouth, I replaced it in the right
pocket of my greatcoat by a stone from the right pocket of my

trousers, which I replaced by a stone from the left pocket of my
trousers, which I replaced by a stone from the left pocket of
my greatcoat, which I replaced by the stone which was in my
mouth, as soon as I had finished sucking it. Thus there were still
four stones in each of my four pockets, but not quite the same
stones. And when the desire to suck took hold of me again, I
drew again on the right pocket of my greatcoat, certain of not
taking the same stone as the last time. And while I sucked it I
rearranged the other stones in the way I have just described. And
so on. But this solution did not satisfy me fully. For it did not
escape me that, by an extraordinary hazard, the four stones cir-
culating thus might always be the same four. In which case, far
from sucking the sixteen stones turn and turn about, I was really
only sucking four, always the same, turn and turn about. But
I shuffled them well in my pockets, before I began to suck and,
again, while I sucked, before transferring them, in the hope of
obtaining a more general circulation of the stones from pocket
to pocket. But this was only a makeshift that could not long
content a man like me. So I began to look for something else.
And the first thing I hit upon was that I might do better to transfer the stones four by four, instead of one by one, that is to say,
during the sucking, to take the three stones remaining in the
right pocket of my greatcoat and replace them by the four in
the right pocket of my trousers, and these by the four in the left
pocket of my trousers, and these by the four in the left pocket
of my greatcoat, and finally these by the three from the right
pocket of my greatcoat, plus the one, as soon as I had finished
sucking it, which was in my mouth. Yes, it seemed to me at first
that by so doing I would arrive at a better result. But on further
reflection I had to change my mind and confess that the circulation of the stones four by four came to exactly the same thing as
their circulation one by one. For if I was certain of finding each
time, in the right pocket of my greatcoat, four stones totally different from their immediate predecessors, the possibility nevertheless remained of my always chancing on the same stone,
within each group of four, and consequently of my sucking, not

the sixteen turn and turn about as I wished, but in fact four only, always the same, turn and turn about. So I had to seek elsewhere than in the mode of circulation. For no matter how I caused the stones to circulate, I always ran the same risk. It was obvious that by increasing the number of my pockets I was bound to increase my chances of enjoying my stones in the way I planned, that is to say, one after the other until their number was exhausted. Had I had eight pockets, for example, instead of the four I did have, then even the most diabolical hazard could not have prevented me from sucking at least eight of my sixteen stones, turn and turn about. The truth is I should have needed sixteen pockets in order to be quite easy in my mind. And for a long time I could see no other conclusion than this, that short of having sixteen pockets, each with its stone, I could never reach the goal I had set myself, short of an extraordinary hazard. And if at a pinch I could double the number of my pockets, were it only by dividing each pocket in two, with the help of a few safety pins, let us say, to quadruple them seemed to be more than I could manage. And I did not feel inclined to take all that trouble for a half measure. For I was beginning to lose all sense of measure, after all this wrestling and wrangling, and to say, All or nothing. And if I was tempted for an instant to establish a more equitable proportion between my stones and my pockets, by reducing the former to the number of the latter, it was only for an instant. For it would have been an admission of defeat. And sitting on the shore, before the sea, the sixteen stones spread out before my eyes, I gazed at them in anger and perplexity. For just as I had difficulty in sitting on a chair, or in an armchair, because of my stiff leg, you understand, so I had none in sitting on the ground, because of my stiff leg and my stiffening leg, for it was about this time that my good leg, good in the sense that it was not stiff, began to stiffen. I needed a prop under the ham, you understand, and even under the whole length of the leg, the prop of the earth. And while I gazed thus at my stones, revolving interminable martingales all equally defective, and crushing handfuls of sand, so that the sand ran through my

fingers and fell back on the strand, yes, while thus I lulled my
mind and part of my body, one day suddenly it dawned on the
former, dimly, that I might perhaps achieve my purpose without
increasing the number of my pockets, or reducing the number
of my stones, but simply by sacrificing the principle of trim. The
meaning of this illumination, which suddenly began to sing
within me, like a verse of Isaiah, or of Jeremiah, I did not penetrate at once, and notably the word trim, which I had never met
with, in this sense, long remained obscure. Finally I seemed to
grasp that this word trim could not here mean anything else,
anything better, than the distribution of the sixteen stones in
four groups of four, one group in each pocket, and that it was
my refusal to consider any distribution other than this that had
vitiated my calculations until then and rendered the problem
literally insoluble. And it was on the basis of this interpretation,
whether right or wrong, that I finally reached a solution, inelegant assuredly, but sound, sound. Now I am willing to believe,
indeed I firmly believe, that other solutions to this problem might
have been found, and indeed may still be found, no less sound,
but much more elegant, than the one I shall now describe, if I
can. And I believe, too, that had I been a little more insistent,
a little more resistant, I could have found them myself. But I was
tired, but I was tired, and I contented myself ingloriously with
the first solution that was a solution to this problem. But not to
go over the heartbreaking stages through which I passed before
I came to it, here it is, in all its hideousness. All (all !) that was
necessary was to put, for example, to begin with, six stones in
the right pocket of my greatcoat, or supply pocket, five in the
right pocket of my trousers, and five in the left pocket of my
trousers, that makes the lot, twice five ten plus six sixteen, and
none, for none remained, in the left pocket of my greatcoat,
which for the time being remained empty, empty of stones, that
is, for its usual contents remained, as well as occasional objects.
For where do you think I hid my vegetable knife, my silver, my
horn, and the other things that I have not yet named, perhaps
shall never name. Good. Now I can begin to suck. Watch me

closely. I take a stone from the right pocket of my greatcoat, suck it, stop sucking it, put it in the left pocket of my greatcoat, the one empty (of stones). I take a second stone from the right pocket of my greatcoat, suck it, put it in the left pocket of my greatcoat. And so on until the right pocket of my greatcoat is empty (apart from its usual and casual contents) and the six stones I have just sucked, one after the other, are all in the left pocket of my greatcoat. Pausing then, and concentrating, so as not to make a balls of it, I transfer to the right pocket of my greatcoat, in which there are no stones left, the five stones in the right pocket of my trousers, which I replace by the five stones in the left pocket of my trousers, which I replace by the six stones in the left pocket of my greatcoat. At this stage then the left pocket of my greatcoat is again empty of stones, while the right pocket of my greatcoat is again supplied, and in the right way, that is to say, with other stones than those I have just sucked. These other stones I then begin to suck, one after the other, and to transfer as I go along to the left pocket of my greatcoat, being absolutely certain, as far as one can be in an affair of this kind, that I am not sucking the same stones as a moment before, but others. And when the right pocket of my greatcoat is again empty (of stones), and the five I have just sucked are all without exception in the left pocket of my greatcoat, then I proceed to the same redistribution as a moment before, or a similar redistribution, that is to say, I transfer to the right pocket of my greatcoat, now again available, the five stones in the right pocket of my trousers, which I replace by the six stones in the left pocket of my trousers, which I replace by the five stones in the left pocket of my greatcoat. And there I am ready to begin again. Do I have to go on? No, for it is clear that after the next series, of sucks and transfers, I shall be back where I started, that is to say, with the first six stones back in the supply pocket, the next five in the right pocket of my stinking old trousers, and finally the last five in left pocket of same, and my sixteen stones will have been sucked once at least in impeccable succession, not one sucked twice, not one left unsucked. It is true that the next time

I could scarcely hope to suck my stones in the same order as the first time and that the first, seventh, and twelfth, for example, of the first cycle might very well be the sixth, eleventh, and sixteenth respectively of the second, if the worst came to the worst. But that was a drawback I could not avoid. And if in the cycles taken together utter confusion was bound to reign, at least within each cycle taken separately I could be easy in my mind, at least as easy as one can be, in a proceeding of this kind. For in order for each cycle to be identical, as to the succession of stones in my mouth, and God knows I had set my heart on it, the only means were numbered stones or sixteen pockets. And rather than make twelve more pockets or number my stones, I preferred to make the best of the comparative peace of mind I enjoyed within each cycle taken separately. For it was not enough to number the stones, but I would have had to remember, every time I put a stone in my mouth, the number I needed and look for it in my pocket. Which would have put me off stone forever, in a very short time. For I would never have been sure of not making a mistake, unless of course I had kept a kind of register, in which to tick off the stones one by one, as I sucked them. And of this I believed myself incapable. No, the only perfect solution would have been the sixteen pockets, symmetrically disposed, each one with its stone. Then I would have needed neither to number nor to think, but merely, as I sucked a given stone, to move on the fifteen others, each to the next pocket, a delicate business admittedly, but within my power, and to call always on the same pocket when I felt like a suck. This would have freed me from all anxiety, not only within each cycle taken separately, but also for the sum of all cycles, though they went on forever. But however imperfect my own solution was, I was pleased at having found it all alone, yes, quite pleased. And if it was perhaps less sound than I had thought in the first flush of discovery, its inelegance never diminished. And it was above all inelegant in this, to my mind, that the uneven distribution was painful to me, bodily. It is true that a kind of equilibrium was reached, at a given moment, in the early stages of each cycle, namely, after the third suck and before the fourth, but it did not last long, and the rest of the time I felt the weight of the stones dragging me now to one side, now to the other. So it was something more than a principle I abandoned when I abandoned the equal distribution; it was a bodily need. But to suck the stones in the way I have described, not haphazard, but with method, was also I think a bodily need. Here, then, were two incompatible bodily needs, at loggerheads. Such things happen. But deep down I didn't give a tinker's curse about being off my balance, dragged to the right hand and the left, backward and forward. And deep down it was all the same to me whether I sucked a different stone each time or always the same stone, until the end of time. For they all tasted exactly the same. And if I had collected sixteen, it was not in order to ballast myself in such and such a way, or to suck them turn about, but simply to have a little store, as never to be without. But deep down I didn't give a fiddler's curse about being without, when they were all gone they would be all gone, I wouldn't be any the worse off, or hardly any. And the solution to which I rallied in the end was to throw away all the stones but one, which I kept now in one pocket, now in another, and which of course I soon lost, or threw away, or gave away, or swallowed.

O'Brien's Table

J. L. SYNGE

❧

J. L. Synge was an Irish mathematician and a nephew of the great dramatist John Millington Synge. He served during the war as Ballistics Mathematician in the U.S. Army Air Force. In 1948 he was made Senior Professor at the School of Theoretical Physics at the Dublin Institute for Advanced Studies. If Laurence Sterne had known a great deal of mathematics he might have written two such books as Synge's Science: Sense and Nonsense *and* Kandelman's Krim, *the latter of which has wild overtones of* Alice in Wonderland. *From the former book I have taken, for the delectation of geometricians, two satirical fables.* Euclid and the Bright Boy *will be found on page 215.*

IN THE early part of the nineteenth century there lived in Dublin a gentleman named O'Brien, a widower with twin sons, Clarence and Marmaduke. At his death his will revealed a strange eccentricity. Since his sons were twins, it was expected that he would make an equal division between them, and this he did in the case of his bank assets and investments. The curious feature was in connection with the house and furniture, for he left all these to Clarence except for one magnificent mahogany table which went to Marmaduke. These bequests were tied by the condition that neither house nor furniture should be sold and by a further condition that the mahogany table should not be removed from the house.

At first everything went well. The brothers lived together in the house, making common use of the furniture, including the mahogany table. In due course Clarence fell in love with a young lady of good family who received his advances graciously and ultimately consented to become his wife. Since the brothers had the most amicable mutual relations, Clarence urged Marmaduke to continue to live in the house after the wedding. This he later regretted, however, when he observed that the behavior of his young wife toward Marmaduke was more intimate than their relationship permitted. The brothers quarreled, and Clarence forced Marmaduke to leave the house. Naturally Marmaduke would have liked to take away his mahogany table, but he could not do so under the terms of his father's will.

About two years after this Clarence was awakened at one o'clock one morning by stealthy noises in the room below. Grasping a poker in his right hand and a candlestick in his left, he descended the stairs and entered the dining room cautiously. There he found Marmaduke seated at the mahogany table, rubbing it affectionately.

High words ensued, and the result was that Clarence brought action against Marmaduke for trespass. Marmaduke's counsel appealed for the sympathy of the court; his client's heart was broken by separation from his mahogany table. But it was of no avail. The court decided that Marmaduke had no right of way to his table, and the case went against him.

Nettled at this outcome, Marmaduke decided to take counter action for trespass. His solicitor urged him against taking such action, but Marmaduke insisted on the ground that Clarence and his wife trespassed on his property nightly by sleeping vertically above his table.

The case was, of course, laughed out of court, the judge ruling that in such case trespass could be committed only by crossing the *surface* of the table. Marmaduke's counsel jumped up and, apologizing to the judge for his ignorance, asked if that meant that Clarence had the right to drive nails into the legs of the table, since the legs were not usually considered part of the surface of a table.

At this the judge smiled and made a judicial pun about taking a superficial view of things; he went on to explain that he had used the word *surface*, not in the vulgar sense in which it might be used by a furniture polisher, but in its scientific sense, derived from the Latin *superficies*, for the meaning of which reference might be made to any standard dictionary.

Burning with hatred for his brother Clarence, Marmaduke rushed along the quays to the nearest bookshop and bought three dictionaries. They all agreed in their scientific or geometrical definitions of the word *surface*, namely, that which has length and breadth but no thickness. Then he repaired to his lodgings and sat for many hours, biting his nails and staring into the fire.

Suddenly he jumped to his feet and, snatching up his hat, went with all possible speed to the home of a locksmith of shady reputation whose services he had used before. That night Marmaduke, with the assistance of the locksmith, entered the home of Clarence. Proceeding with stealthy steps to the mahogany table, he pulled open the drawer and, with a suppressed cry of satisfaction, took out a box of Clarence's cigars.

Marmaduke brought another action for trespass against Clarence, this time on the ground that Clarence had crossed the surface of the table by opening the drawer and putting in the box of cigars. This time the case was not laughed out of court. It went against Marmaduke, but he appealed it again and again, until finally it came before the House of Lords. The case excited public interest to an extraordinary extent, and the words "O'Brien's table" were on every tongue. Babies were christened Clarence or Marmaduke, according to the sympathies of their parents.

Many of the leading mathematicians and natural philosophers of Europe were summoned as expert witnesses, and their views were interesting and varied. The point on which their expert opinion was asked was this: Had Clarence crossed the surface of the table when he opened the drawer and put in his box of cigars?

With one exception, to which I shall come later, the experts agreed that the table had a surface, but they disagreed as to what that surface was.

The witnesses called by the plaintiff said that the table, drawer and all, was a geometrical entity extended in space and must therefore have a surface which included the table and all that pertained to it. Since the inside of the drawer was part of the table, the surface of the table must include it. Thus, even though there was a slight opening above the drawer, there existed a theoretical surface sealing this opening mathematically, and that this mathematical seal had been broken by Clarence when he opened the drawer.

On the other hand, the witnesses called by the defendant insisted that the table could not be regarded as a geometrical unit, since it consisted of two solid bodies, the main part of the table and the drawer. They maintained that each of these bodies had a surface and that neither of these surfaces had been crossed by Clarence, since he had stuck no pins or nails into the wood. Thus no trespass had been committed.

At this point the Lord Chancellor remarked that, however true this might be from a scientific standpoint, he viewed this doctrine with grave alarm. For, if this view were supported by law, no one would be safe in his house at night unless he had the four walls of his house constructed of a single piece of material, with neither doors nor windows in it.

The last expert witness to be called was a small bearded man who spoke rapidly in French. Although his testimony appeared to favor the defense, he expressed contempt for the whole affair and indicated clearly that only very stupid people would spend so much time on an argument like this. Gesticulating freely, he explained, through an interpreter who followed him with the greatest difficulty, that there were two worlds. One was the world of our senses, vast, chaotic, complex, and inexplicable. The other was the world of mathematics, clear, ordered, reasonable. These two worlds must be kept apart. If they were mixed, the most unfortunate confusion would result and was even then resulting. A surface, he explained, was a mathematical concept and did not exist in the real world, except in a vulgar non-scientific sense, and as an expert witness he was not concerned with vulgar senses of that sort. He then made a motion of washing his hands and sat down.

At this moment two telegraph boys entered the hall and handed telegrams to the two counsels. These contained the information that Marmaduke had just sailed from Cove for America, accompanied by Clarence's wife, and that Clarence, pursuing them, had died of heart failure on the road to Cork. The case was thereupon dropped.

The Abominable Mr. Gunn

ROBERT GRAVES

Robert Graves, born in 1895 of Anglo-Irish-German ancestry, is one of the most interesting and independent-souled first-rate writers now using English. Greatly accomplished as poet, highly accomplished as historical novelist, recklessly accomplished as scholar, there is no one like him among his own generation. This casual little tale gives no hint of his varied talents. It manipulates, much more informally, the same theme that engaged the interest of Aldous Huxley in his Young Archimedes, *reprinted in* Fantasia Mathematica. *The conquest of the genius by the Philistine is a standard literary gambit; what is surprising is that it should have retained its popularity in our time, whose presumed enlightenment is generally supposed to make impossible tragedies like those of Keats, Chatterton—and such a potential Gauss as Mr. Graves's schoolmate, F. F. Smilley.*

ONE MONDAY MORNING in September 1910 the abominable Mr. J. O. G. Gunn, master of the third form at Brown Friars, trod liverishly down the aisle between two rows of pitch-pine desks and grasped the short hairs just above my right ear. Mr. Gunn, pale, muscular, and broad-faced, kept his black hair plastered close to the scalp with a honey-scented oil. He announced to the form, as he lifted me up a few inches, "And now Professor Graves will display his wondrous erudition by discoursing on the first missionary journey of St. Paul." (Laughter.)

I discoursed haltingly, my mind being as usual a couple of stages ahead of my tongue, so that my tongue said "Peter" when I meant "Paul," and "B.C." when I meant "A.D.," and "Crete" when I meant "Cyprus." It still plays this sort of trick, which often makes my conversation difficult to follow and is now read as a sign of incipient senility. In those days it did not endear me to Mr. Gunn. . . .

After the disaster at Syracuse one Athenian would often ask another, "Tell me, friend, what has become of old So-and-so?" and the invariable answer came, "If he is not dead, he is school-mastering." I can wish no worse fate to Mr. J. O. G. Gunn— father of all the numerous sons-of-guns who have since sneered at my "erudition" and cruelly caught at my short hairs—than that he is still exercising his profession at the age of eighty-plus, and that each new Monday morning has found him a little uglier and a little more liverish than before.

Me erudite? I am not even decently well read. What reading I have done from time to time was never a passive and promis-cuous self-exposure to the stream of literature but always a search for particular facts to nourish, or to scotch, some obses-sive maggot that had gained a lodgment in my skull. And now I shall reveal an embarrassing secret which I have kept from the world since those nightmare days.

One fine summer evening as I sat alone on the roller behind the cricket pavilion, with nothing much in my head, I received a sudden celestial illumination: it occurred to me that I knew everything. I remember letting my mind range rapidly over all its familiar subjects of knowledge, only to find that this was no foolish fancy. I did know everything. To be plain: though con-scious of having come less than a third of the way along the path of formal education, and being weak in mathematics, shaky in Greek grammar, and hazy about English history, I nevertheless held the key of truth in my hand and could use it to open any lock of any door. Mine was no religious or philosophical theory but a simple method of looking sideways at disorderly facts so as to make perfect sense of them.

I slid down from the roller, wondering what to do with my

embarrassing gift. Whom could I take into my confidence? Nobody. Even my best friends would say, "You're mad!" and either send me to Coventry or organize my general scragging, or both; and soon some favor-currier would sneak to Mr. Gunn, which would be the end of everything. It occurred to me that perhaps I had better embody the formula in a brief world message, circulated anonymously to the leading newspapers. In that case I should have to work under the bedclothes after dark, by the light of a flash lamp, and use the cipher I had recently perfected. But I remembered my broken torch-light bulb and the difficulty of replacing it until the next day. No, there was no immediate hurry. I had everything securely in my head. Again I experimented, trying the key on various obstinate locks; they all clicked and the doors opened smoothly. Then the school bell rang from a distance, calling me to preparation and prayers.

Early the next day I awoke to find that I still had a fairly tight grasp of my secret; but a morning's lessons intervened, and when I then locked myself into the privy, and tried to record it on the back of an old exercise book, my mind went too fast for my pen, and I began to cross out—a fatal mistake—and presently crumpled up the page and pulled the chain on it. That night I tried again under the bedclothes, but the magic had evaporated and I could get no further than the introductory sentence.

My vision of truth did not recur, though I went back a couple of times to sit hopefully on the roller; and before long, doubts tormented me, gloomy doubts about a great many hitherto stable concepts, such as the authenticity of the Gospels, the perfectibility of man, and the absoluteness of the Protestant moral code. All that survived was an afterglow of the bright light in my head and the certainty that it had been no delusion. This is still with me, for I now realize that what overcame me that evening was a sudden infantile awareness of the power of intuition, the supralogic that cuts out all routine processes of thought and leaps straight from problem to answer.

How easily this power is blunted by hostile circumstances Mr. Gunn demonstrated by his treatment of one F. F. Smilley, a new boy, who seems, coincidentally, to have had a vision analogous to mine, though of a more specialized sort. Smilley came late to Brown Friars; he had been educated at home until the age of eleven because of some illness or other. It happened on his first entry into the third form that Mr. Gunn set us a problem from Hilderbrand's *Arithmetic for Preparatory Schools*, which was to find the square root of the sum of two long decimals, divided (just for cussedness) by the sum of two complicated vulgar fractions. Soon everyone was scribbling away except F. F. Smilley, who sat there abstractedly polishing his glasses and gazing out of the window.

Mr. Gunn looked up for a moment from a letter he was writing and asked nastily, "Seeking inspiration from the distant church spire, Smilley?"

"No, sir. Polishing my glasses."

"And why, pray?"

"They had marmalade on them, sir."

"Don't answer me back, boy! Why aren't you working out that sum?"

"I have already written down the answer, sir."

"Bring your exercise book here! . . . Ah, yes, here is the answer, my very learned and ingenious friend Sir Isaac Newton" —tweaking the short hairs—"but where is it worked out?"

"Nowhere, sir. It just came to me."

"Came to you, F. F. Smilley, my boy? You mean you hazarded a wild guess?"

"No, sir, I just looked at the problem and saw what the answer must be."

"Ha! A strange psychical phenomenon! But I must demand proof that you did not simply turn to the answer at the end of the book."

"Well, I did do that afterward, sir."

"The truth now slowly leaks out."

"But it was wrong, sir. The last two figures should be thirty-five, not fifty-three."

"Curiouser and curiouser! Here's a Brown Friars' boy in the third form who knows better than Professor Hilderbrand, Cambridge's leading mathematician."

"No, sir, I think it must be a misprint."

"So you and Professor Hilderbrand are old friends? You seem very active in his defense."

"No, sir, I have met him, but I didn't like him very much."

F. F. Smilley was sent at once to the headmaster with a note: "Please cane bearer for idleness, lying, cheating, and gross impertinence"—which the headmaster, who had certain flaws in his character, was delighted to do. I cannot tell the rest of the story with much confidence, but my impression is that Mr. Gunn won, as he had already won in his battle against J. X. Bestard-Montéry, whose Parisian accent when he was called upon to read "Maître Corbeau, sur un arbre perché" earned him the name of "frog-eating mountebank" and a severe knuckling on the side of the head. Bestard was forced to put a hard Midland polish on his French.

Mr. Gunn, in fact, gradually beat down F. F. Smilley's resistance by assiduous hair tweakings, knucklings, and impositions and compelled him to record all mathematic argument in the laborious way laid down by Professor Hilderbrand. No more looking out of the window, no more guessing at the answer.

Whether the cure was permanent I cannot say, because shortly before the end of that school year the Chief of County Police gave the headmaster twenty-four hours to leave the country (the police were more gentlemanly in those Edwardian days), and Brown Friars broke up in confusion. I have never since heard of F. F. Smilley. Either he was killed in World War I, or else he is schoolmastering somewhere. Had he made his mark in higher mathematics, we should surely have heard of it. Unless, perhaps, he is so much of a back-room boy, so much the arch-wizard of the mathematic-formula department on which Her Majesty's nuclear physicists depend for their bombs and piles, that the security men have changed his name, disguised his features by plastic surgery, speech-trained him into alien immigrance, and suppressed his civic identity. I would not put it past them. But the mathematical probability is, as I say, that Gunn won.

Coconuts

BEN AMES WILLIAMS

❦

Ben Ames Williams (1889–1953) was a prolific, popular, and honest storyteller. Coconuts, *rather uncharacteristic for him, is a story about a little man who had a passion, not for mathematics, as Mr. Williams seemed to think, but for figures. It originally appeared in* The Saturday Evening Post *during the twenties.*

During the first week after the publication of Coconuts *the* Post *received some two thousand letters, most of them requesting the answer, others proposing solutions to the coconut problem. You will find the whole story, together with a first-rate discussion of the mathematics involved, in Martin Gardner's* Second Scientific American Book of Mathematical Puzzles and Diversions, *pages 104–111 (Simon and Schuster, 1961).*

THERE IS in many men a certain single-mindedness, a fixity of interest amounting to passion; and when such an emotion is once firmly seated you may take that man's future as determined, whether for good or ill. Your statesman has a passion for power; you will find, if you search his soul, that he is in his heart utterly assured of the importance of the mistress whom he serves. He seeks to move and direct the destinies of others not so much for his selfish gain as from a conviction that he has a message, that it is of vital importance to the world that he be heard and followed. Such singleness of mind may fairly be called an essential to success. If a man wishes to manufacture a soft drink that shall become nationally famous, he must begin with or acquire the conviction that that beverage is beyond compare, that it combines the gifts of transient pleasure and permanent health in a surpassing degree.

I have heard a vegetable jobber speak almost devoutly of the virtues of the onion. Such passions as this mold lives for good and ill.

The fortunate man is he whose passion and profession coincide; for then there is no strife within him, but a sure ascendancy. When vocation fights with avocation the struggle may be long and victory bitter in the end. A man may be a banker and collect first editions still; but the love nearest his heart will drive out the other at the last, and his longing is toward her always. Philosophy is all very well in its way; a well-poised mind capable of determining the relative importance of a rare postage stamp and a new railroad may make for mild contentment. But it will never experience the hot fire of happy zeal or the purging depths of black despair.

It is, of course, incidentally true that a man may serve a mistress and despise her still. Such a man, you might suppose, must be a weak and spineless thing.

Yet—let us have a look at Wadlin.

Wadlin's passion was for figures. He loved them with a curious yearning, gloated over them as a bibliophile fondles an old and precious volume. They were to him the most beautiful thing in the world. At home at night, in his small single room, he liked to draw out a pad of clean yellow paper and write figures on it; liked to watch them form and break ranks and reform again as though they were soldiers; liked to make them march in smooth progression. To his eyes 2-4-6-8-10 was a thing of beauty; 3-6-9 had an exotic charm. And he would carry the sequence 1-2-4-8-16 on and on till he had covered pages, for sheer love of the magic of the thing. He liked to add columns in which the digits came in such arrangements as 7-4-3-3-2-5-4-2-6; his quick eye, without effort, resolved this into 7-7-5-5-6-6 and set the total down.

The multiplication table to him was sweeter than the Song of Songs; and to take such a sum as 279936 and, dividing it by 2 and by 3, whittle it inexorably down to unity was an operation which had about it the stern drama of an ancient tragedy. To divide a number into its factors delighted him; and he had sought through tremendous vistas to discover numbers which could not be factored. He knew the orderly ways that digits have, and he knew a thousand and one tricks they may be taught to play. An incorrect equation was to his eyes the ugliest thing in nature.

This man had kept a personal cash account since he was seventeen years old and had it balanced to a penny. He used to like to figure what his average earnings had been, by the year, by the month, by the week, by the day, by the hour, and even by the minute. He could have told you, to seven places of decimals, his earnings by the second during his working hours; and he had a record running back nine years of the exact number of minutes he had spent in bed. For nineteen months and fourteen days past he had been keeping this record in more complete form, so that he was able to tell you, for that length of time, exactly how every minute of his time had been spent. He would have preferred to amplify this, recording the totals by seconds; but his watch was subject to small inaccuracies and he did not feel justified in buying a new one. Instead, he worked out a mathematical table of allowances for these variations.

As accessories to this passion of his he loved sharp lead pencils, clean white paper, and neatly ruled columns in a blank ledger.

He was about thirty-five years old. If you had asked him he would have said just that, dropping his eyes a little; but if you won his confidence and asked him exactly how old he was, he could have looked at his watch and told you to the minute. The statement would have been based on the assumed time of his birth. There was no exact record available, but he had made some researches in the matter and arrived at a hypothetical hour and minute which he used as a base in all such calculations. Nevertheless, the necessity of using an approximation always irked him sore.

He was, in his stockinged feet, five feet eight and fourteen thirty-seconds of an inch tall, morning measurement. Sometimes at night he fell as low as seven thirty-seconds. His weight ranged between two extremes: The lowest on record was a hundred and thirty-one pounds, seven ounces; the highest a hundred and thirty-eight pounds, two ounces. His statistics covered only the six years, four months, nine days—on the first of July—since he bought and set up and had tested his elaborate bedroom scale. He ate between two thousand and twenty-one hundred calories a day. It was three hundred and eleven steps from his room to the subway platform, and two hundred and nine from the subway platform to his office stool, always assuming that in the elevator he stood still just within the door. For the year 1924 he walked an average of sixteen and four-sevenths steps in reaching his seat in the subway trains after arriving on the platform and an average of sixteen and eleven-thirteenth steps from his seat to the foot of the stair. He never used the escalators. He could have told you the average time it took him to reach the office, to be served at the restaurant where he lunched, to get home at night. His life was spent in a world full of figures; they were his familiar playfellows.

The fact that he had no other friends may have been cause or consequence of this preoccupation on Wadlin's part. But whatever the cause, he was a little man very much alone. He once calculated that for a period of thirty days, outside the office and on matters not connected with his work, he spoke to but sixty-three persons, was spoken to by only nineteen, and exchanged a total of fifteen hundred and thirty-two words, of which he spoke nine hundred and one. His only living relative was an uncle in Chicago, and the mathematical probabilities were that this uncle would die on the seventh of June 1931 at thirty-seven minutes past eleven in the morning.

Wadlin worked in the office of Dean Story, a contractor whose special concern was with public buildings and large construction, and Wadlin's particular province was mathematical. Thus his daily tasks were a long debauch; but he hid this fact from those about him, feeling a furtive shame. Only at home, where the world did not pry, did he indulge to the full his dark and secret passion, revel in his columns of figures unashamed.

Story was not a mathematician; he was an artist. He had done the grind at figures necessary to secure an architect's degree but proceeded to forget them as soon as the need for them was passed.

"I can always hire that sort of thing done," he used to say. "When I need it." Wadlin had heard him say this.

Story studied in Paris, came back with a cultivated taste and a certain genius for design. Accident led him from planning buildings into erecting them; he discovered in himself a talent for business and in effect abandoned his profession for this new career. The field into which he had plunged was one hitherto shared by two or three concerns; he found himself in competition with Dana, and Asquith, and with Marr.

Marr was the Titan, the man about whom stories grew. In the whirlpool of competition he not only kept himself afloat, but he rode serenely. His methods were frankly adapted to the problems he found it necessary to solve. He made them no secret; himself used to tell with gusto the story, for example, of the lithograph. It was an incident in which he took an almost childish pride.

The contract in question involved the construction of a building at one of the state institutions, and Marr and Dana and Asquith were all bidding. Bids to be opened on the seventh of April, at noon, in the office at the State House. The building to be of re-enforced-concrete design, not only as to outer walls but as to floors and partitions and the very roof itself. Marr did his own concrete work, but Dana and Asquith would have this work done by subcontractors.

"I knew I could underbid Dana," Marr told Story one day. "But Asquith bothered me. He'd get Ryan to do his superstructure, and Ryan could get down pretty low on his figure if he wanted to. I had to find out how low. Ryan wouldn't give Asquith his figure till the morning of the seventh, and there'd be no chance of a leak after that. It was up to me. So I went to see Ryan, tried to talk turkey to him.

"I told him first that I wanted advice, pretended not to know Asquith had come to him. Offered him a thousand dollars for an estimate; said I'd take his figure as a basis for my own bid. He wouldn't talk. Told me he was tied up.

"Then I offered him the subcontract if he'd make me a figure low enough, and he said he was tied up with Asquith.

"I let it ride for a while, and the next time I offered to bet him that the figure he made Asquith would be below three hundred thousand. Offered to bet him five thousand on that. If he'd taken me I'd have counted on his putting it at three hundred or above, and I'd have scaled that a thousand or two. But he wouldn't take me up."

Then Marr chuckled and lighted a fresh cigar. "I was pretty well up against it," he confessed. "And I got up to go, looking around the office, and I saw this lithograph on the wall. A lot of sheep in a pasture and a railroad train in the background. Looked like a railroad calendar. It tickled me, and I said to Ryan, 'That's some picture you've got there.' Joking. But he said, 'You bet it is. A lot of people haven't sense enough to see it, but those sheep are right.' And I caught on right away. I said I'd like to buy the picture, and he wouldn't sell, and I offered him five thousand, and went up to eight thousand for it, and bought it. Carried it out of there under my arm.

"Told him I was going to figure on a basis of three hundred thousand for the superstructure. And the figure he gave Asquith was three hundred and ten. That's one way of doing business, my son."

Story laughed politely. "The answer seems to be to keep away from Ryan," he commented.

Marr shook his head robustly. "Lord, they're all the same," he urged. "You're in a cutthroat game, my boy. Dog eat dog. Might as well make up your mind to that. They'll break you if they can."

"The same to you and many of them," Story remarked, and Marr laughed and said: "Pshaw, no hard feelings. I'm just telling you." And went upon his way.

He came in upon another day, and it happened that Wadlin was in Story's office. Story had been giving the little man facts and specifications on a building that was projected, while Wadlin noted them down in his small, precise hand.

When Marr came in Wadlin rose to go back to his desk, but Story said, "Sit still, Mr. Wadlin. Morning, Marr."

So Wadlin understood that Story wished to be rid of the other as soon as might be, and he held his ground.

Marr, it appeared, had nothing important to say; he spoke casually of business, of a building upon which he was engaged, of the weather and the prospects of the Braves. Story answered briefly, almost curtly. And Marr by and by leaned forward on the other's desk and produced a bit of paper.

"Here's a funny trick with figures I came across the other day," he announced. "Give me a number with two digits in it."

Story shook his head. "Figures don't mean anything to me," he replied. "Wadlin's my man for that."

Marr grinned. "I do my own figuring," he declared. "Then there's no mistake."

"Wadlin doesn't make mistakes," Story replied. "He wouldn't be here if he did. I can't waste time on such details."

The other chuckled. "All right. But you, Wadlin, see what you make of this. Give me a number with two digits."

Wadlin glanced at Story, and the other nodded, and Wadlin said quietly, "Ninety-nine!"

"Right," Marr agreed, and wrote on the paper before him.

"Here you are," he said, and showed Wadlin what he had written. Wadlin glanced at the paper, saw there:

$$\frac{297}{99}$$

"Now give me another figure with two digits," Marr commanded. "You give me two numbers and I'll write two, and they'll all add up to two ninety-seven."

Wadlin smiled faintly. "Ninety-nine," he repeated; and Marr wrote the digits down, and then hesitated, and then grinned ruefully.

"Shucks, you know it," he protested.

Wadlin shook his head. "Two ninety-seven is ninety-nine plus one ninety-eight," he said crisply. "Half one ninety-eight is ninety-nine. You would subtract my number from ninety-nine and write the result as your number; do that twice. Obvious."

"Wasn't obvious to me," Marr protested, stared at the little man. "Say, are you satisfied with your job?"

"Yes," said Wadlin, and Marr grinned again and rose.

"Well, I'll move on," he announced. Glanced at Story. "Bidding on the hospital?" he inquired.

"I propose to," Story assured him.

"Wasting time," Marr declared. "I'm taking that myself. Let it alone."

Story smiled, and the other departed. Story glanced at Wadlin. "All right," he said. "Where were we?"

"Roof supports," Wadlin replied.

Story bent to his papers again. "We'll have to cut it fine to beat him," he commented. "He'll take a loss to get it, risk the inspection. All right, let's go on."

Wadlin looked at the other man's bowed head in a curious, appraising way.

"He'd probably pay you more than you're getting here," Story added, without looking up. "I don't want to stand in your way. You're getting all you're worth to me."

"Naturally," Wadlin replied.

"It's doubtful whether I'll ever pay you any more," Story insisted.

"Points of support. Re-enforcement," Wadlin prompted; and they returned to the business in hand.

They were working on the matter of the hospital contract. The plans had been drafted by the state department which had the matter in charge; the specifications were exact and rigid; the amount of detail involved was enormous. Another than Wadlin might have been lost in the maze of figures, but the little man moved happily among his notes and his calculations, and Story, having put the matter in his hands, refrained from interference. The bids were to be opened in the offices of the department at noon on the twenty-fifth of February.

Dana, Story found, would not bid. "Too big for me, with what I have on hand," the other man said. Asquith would bid, but Asquith's banking background was weak. Story had no fear of him. There might be an outsider, someone not yet heard from; but if there were such a man his figure was not likely to be low, or if it were, the bond for performance must discourage him. Marr, Story felt sure, was his only real rival.

By the middle of February Wadlin had completed his calculations. He laid, one morning, a neat slip of paper on Story's desk. Story picked it up, read: "At prices current, wages current, total cost to you of construction, including office charges and all other items, will be $393,462.10."

Story studied it for a moment, looked up at little Wadlin with a stern eye. "You understand," he said, "I'm relying on your figures."

"The figures are correct," Wadlin replied precisely.

"If you've any doubt, say so. I can hire a man to check them for a hundred dollars."

"I have no doubt."

Story nodded. "All right," he said in dismissal, and Wadlin withdrew. Story began to calculate. His thoughts were vague and general. The labor situation was stable—no apparent likelihood of trouble; the market on materials gave no indications of approaching fluctuations. He might discount the possibility by advance purchases.

"Call it four hundred thousand," he thought. "Allow fifty thousand for mishaps. Four hundred and fifty. Say a profit of fifty thousand. Five hundred thousand. That's a fair price on the building too." Sat still for a while, considering—considering not figures but the human factor—Marr.

"He can build as cheaply," he confessed to himself. "He'll scamp if he has to. He can bid four-fifty. If I do that I'll have to scratch for my profit."

Rang for Wadlin again. "Have you a copy of these figures?" he asked, twisting the scrap of paper in his hand.

"All totals destroyed," Wadlin replied; and Story nodded and ripped the paper into little shreds and dropped them into his ash tray, touched a match to them there.

"It's a question of Marr," he said, half aloud; and Wadlin seemed for a moment about to speak, then held his tongue. There was, if Story had looked that way, a curious devotion in his eyes. After a moment the little man turned and left the room.

But that night when he got back to his boardinghouse there was an abstraction in his manner not usually to be seen there. He set down his daily records. Two-o-two-three calories. Three hundred and twelve steps from the subway platform to his room. He noted this discrepancy; he must have lagged a little on the way. Stumbled, it may be. Fifteen steps from his seat in the car to the foot of the stair. Eleven minutes, twenty-one seconds waiting to be served in the restaurant. Spoken to by the waiter and by the lodger in the hall. Total words—fourteen by him, five by the waiter and the lodger. Time in the office eight hours, seven minutes, fourteen seconds. Time in transit one hour, fourteen minutes, twelve seconds. Time eating—breakfast twelve minutes, three seconds; lunch thirty-six minutes, even; dinner forty-eight minutes, nine seconds. Expenditures—

Set all these matters gravely down. Yet in the end seemed not content. He put his records away and for a while sat thinking, his pencil making idle rows of figure 7's on a blank sheet of yellow paper. And in the end he went to his shelves and took out a book in which were pasted newspaper clippings, sheaves and sheaves of them; and he began painstakingly to read them through. Found at last one that held his eye.

Before he went to bed that night he made a note of the facts that he had lost three ounces during the day and that he had stayed up an hour and ten minutes and twenty seconds later than usual. But these circumstances seemed not to distress him; there was a certain contentment in his countenance as he lay in the darkened room before he went precisely off to sleep at last, as his long habit was.

When his own tasks next day were done he deviated from his long routine; instead of going directly to the restaurant where he was accustomed to dine, and then to his room, he sought out the building in which Marr's office was and inconspicuously waited there for Marr to emerge. Later he followed Marr. It might have been apparent to a spectator that Wadlin sought to discover where Marr went, what the other man would do.

The hospital bids were to be in on the twenty-fifth, to be opened at noon that day. On the twenty-third, in the afternoon, Wadlin approached Story, sought an interview; and when they were face to face the little man said diffidently:

"I wish to tell you that it is possible Marr will not bid on the hospital."

Story looked at the little man attentively. "What makes you say that?"

Wadlin did not reply. "If I am not in the office on the morning of the twenty-fifth," he said, "I will telephone you. I should know by then."

Story rose. "I say," he challenged, "what are you about? Are you planning something?"

"A mathematical recreation," said Wadlin precisely. "I will try to telephone. I hope his bid will not be in on time."

And for fear of saying more than he meant, he turned and took himself away; left Story to sit uncertain there, to weigh the possibilities in what Wadlin had suggested.

Marr was a bachelor and his home was in an apartment uptown. But it furnished him only with lodgings and breakfast. He had a tremendous appetite for work, was as like as not to stay in the office till uncertain hours; and this was particularly true when there was pressing business afoot, as there was now. At such times, however, he came down to dine in a small restaurant on the lower floor of his office building before returning to his evening stint of calculation and of planning. Wadlin had observed this habit of his.

On the evening of the twenty-fourth when Marr thus came into the restaurant the place was almost deserted. Only here and there at isolated tables solitary diners sat.

Marr was a gregarious man; he preferred company when there was company to be had; and Wadlin had seen him stop at such moments as this and survey the room, seeking some acquaintance among the persons there. When Marr thus looked about the room this evening he saw Wadlin at a distant table. The little man had not yet been served; he was absorbed in some task; he bent over a notebook open on the cloth and labored therein with calculations. Marr chuckled, brushed past the headwaiter and crossed to the table where sat the little man; he clapped Wadlin on the shoulder, and when Wadlin looked up with dull and inattentive eyes Marr asked heartily: "What are you figuring? Hospital? Late for that, isn't it?"

"I don't expect you're through figuring yet," Wadlin responded somewhat tartly.

Marr nodded. "Can't get the last word from the subcontractors till tomorrow morning," he agreed. "But my part of it's all done." He glanced at Wadlin's notebook. "That doesn't look like specifications."

Wadlin said somewhat morosely, "Just a problem that interested me."

"Stuck, are you?"

"I haven't found the key yet," Wadlin confessed. "The method of attack."

"What is it?" Marr insisted. "I never saw a problem yet that would stick me."

The waiter came to take his order, and their conversation was interrupted. But when the man was gone Marr returned to the point. "What's your difficulty?"

Wadlin protested. "Oh, it's just a trick thing."

"Let's have it," Marr insisted. "Let's have it."

The little man still hesitated, said at last reluctantly, "Why, I had it at noon from a man uptown. Haven't been able to get it yet." Marr made an impatient, peremptory gesture, and Wadlin said vaguely, "It's just a problem in indeterminates, I think."

"What is it, man?" Marr cried. "Let me in on it. I'll straighten you out in no time."

"I don't want to bother you," Wadlin argued. "It's not as simple as it looks. I've been at it six hours and more."

"What is it? What is it?" Marr demanded. "You act as though it were confidential."

So at last Wadlin told him. "Well," he explained, "according to the way the thing was given to me, five men and a monkey were shipwrecked on a desert island, and they spent the first day gathering coconuts for food. Piled them all up together and then went to sleep for the night.

"But when they were all asleep one man woke up, and he thought there might be a row about dividing the coconuts in the morning, so he decided to take his share. So he divided the coconuts into five piles. He had one coconut left over, and he gave that to the monkey, and he hid his pile and put the rest all back together."

He looked at Marr; the man was listening attentively.

"So by and by the next man woke up and did the same thing," Wadlin continued. "And he had one left over, and he gave it to the monkey. And all five of the men did the same thing, one after the other, each one taking a fifth of the coconuts in the pile when he woke up, and each one having one left over for the monkey. And in the morning they divided what coconuts were left, and they came out in five equal shares."

He added morosely, "Of course each one must have known there were coconuts missing; but each one was guilty as the others, so they didn't say anything."

Marr asked sharply, "But what's the question?"

"How many coconuts were there in the beginning?" Wadlin meekly explained.

Marr laughed. "Why, that's simple enough. You just—"

But their victuals were served; the table was filled with viands; they could find no room for calculations. So when they were done Marr said, "Here, you come upstairs to the office and we'll work this out. It won't take long."

"I'd like to get it," Wadlin agreed, "before I go to sleep. There must be a formula, some way to work it."

"Won't take five minutes," Marr declared, and Wadlin said meekly: "Well, I believe the record is fifty-eight minutes. But I've been at it hours."

Marr laughed. "Went at it wrong," he insisted. "Come along upstairs."

In Marr's office the big man bade Wadlin sit down, himself took pad and pencil. "Here, I'll show you," he explained. And, while Wadlin watched him with some attention, he wrote swiftly:

"x—original pile; a, b, c, d, e—shares of each man."

And he proceeded to form equations:

$$x = 5a + 1.$$
$$x - (a + 1) = 5b + 1.$$

And on in the same fashion, till abruptly he stopped and hesitated. "And that equals the remaining pile," he said. "How much was that?"

"We only know it was divisible by five," Wadlin replied gently.

"Call it y," Marr said carelessly; and Wadlin started to speak, then held his tongue, while Marr proceeded with the processes of substitution. Till presently Marr's pencil came to rest again, and he scratched his head.

"That leaves us two unknowns in one equation," he said reluctantly; and Wadlin nodded and commented in a meek tone: "I ran up against that too."

"No known quantities in the darned thing," Marr protested.

"No," Wadlin agreed.

"Why, it can't be solved," Marr cried, but Wadlin dissented.

"It's been done," he assured the other man. "You see, you do know the monkey got five coconuts, and you do know there were five men. It's been worked out, but I don't know just how to go at it."

For a moment there was silence, then Marr cried, "Wait a minute; I see it now." And began to write again.

Wadlin watched him with a contented little smile.

They sat late that night, the lighted windows in Marr's office the only gleam against the tall front of the office building. By and by Marr took off his collar; once or twice he rose and strode up and down the room; for a while he labored with a slide rule. And during the first hour or two there were moments when he was discouraged, ready to abandon the task. But at such moments Wadlin had always a suggestion to offer.

"Five must be a factor, somehow," he would say. "I think the number is some kind of a power of five."

And when that line of search was exhausted he would propose that they seek to make a formula.

"There must be one," he urged, "one that would fit all such problems."

Their formula, when they got one, covered four lines of figures and letters, running clear across the sheet; when they solved it— and that took an hour and ten minutes—the result they got was 7, a manifest impossibility.

They checked the formula for errors and found four and made a new one which would not solve; they strove and panted and perspired; and little Wadlin, with the utmost gravity, made long calculations which came to nothing, solved tremendous equations which gave an absurd result at the end. Sheer weariness drove them at last to temporary surrender; they started uptown in a taxicab, and Marr offered to drop Wadlin at his boardinghouse.

"I'm not sleepy yet," Wadlin confessed as they were about to part. "A thing like this interests me. I'll probably work till I get it."

"I'll tell you," Marr suggested impulsively. "Neither am I. Come on up to my place and we'll wring this thing's neck somehow. No pile of coconuts can stump me. What do you say?"

"I'd like to get it," Wadlin agreed.

So they went on together, and at Marr's apartment they had coffee and cleared a table and set to work again. But Marr was sleepy; his head continually drooped, and Wadlin at last said, "You rest a minute, sir. You've been doing all the figuring. I've got a new idea I want to try out."

There was a madness on Marr by this time; he shook his head. "No, no, I'm going to get this if it takes me till daylight."

Nevertheless, he did relax in his chair, watching through half-shut eyes Wadlin's flying pencil.

There was a tiny glint of light against its varnished side; it moved erratically yet rhythmically to and fro. By and by a sound came from his chair, and Wadlin saw that the big man was asleep.

He sighed a little, and very quietly he buried his own head in his arms. He was sleepy too. When later he awoke, cramped and stiff and cold, there was daylight in the windows, and Marr was slumped in the chair across from him, snoring heavily. Marr's chair was deep and comfortable; Wadlin brought a blanket from the other room and covered him over. Then he drew the heavy blinds. There was a clock upon the mantel, and he crossed and gently stopped the swinging of the pendulum; and he returned to his chair and kept ward there for a while. Once he looked at his watch and saw with satisfaction that it had run down; Marr's must have done the same. After the clock on the mantel had been still for an hour or so he started it again.

When Marr still slept the little man bethought himself of the telephone; it was, he discovered, in a cabinet in the hall, and he shut himself into the closet and in muffled tones put through a call to Story. When he was done he swathed the bell in his handkerchief so that it would not ring. Came back to the other room.

By and by Marr stirred and roused himself and groaned and opened his eyes to see Wadlin's pencil flying still. The room was dark, the lights burning; the window hangings were heavy.

He said huskily, "Hello!" Roused a little more. "Say, I've been asleep."

"I've almost got it," Wadlin told him. "At least, I've got an idea. You see, we overlooked the simplest thing. We started on the notion that this thing had five for a factor, but four is a factor too. That helps, don't you see? Four is a factor, and so is five; and so twenty is a factor."

"Then the number, if you subtract one, has twenty for a factor," Marr agreed, his interest reviving. "Say, I've been dreaming about coconuts. Millions of them. Fool thing to take us so long." He pulled a pad toward him. "There aren't so many numbers that have twenty for a factor. Only five in each hundred," he pointed out.

"I think we could work it out by experiment that way," Wadlin assented. "But I'd like to do it by formula."

"I want to do it any old way. I'm not ashamed to use by-guess and by-gorry. Brute strength or anything," Marr commented. "Look here, Wadlin, the number remaining must have twenty for a factor too."

"It's the first number that we want," Wadlin reminded him.

Marr began to calculate again, his pencil moving; the point broke and he sharpened it. For a time there was silence between them.

And once, after a long while, Marr looked at his watch and saw that it had run down, and he wound it and set it according to the clock on the mantel.

"I've got to get downtown by eleven," he said, half to himself. Wadlin made no comment at all.

The little man heard once or twice a muffled burr as the telephone labored to be heard. But it did not penetrate to Marr's ears. And Wadlin was growing very sleepy; it was a tremendous relief to him when at last the time came to say:

"Wait! Now! I'm on the track now, sir."

And in the jubilation over their belated success Wadlin held himself gravely, weary now, full of a vast contentment, and of some scorn too.

Then at last Marr discovered that the clock was slow and so flung an understanding curse at Wadlin before he raced hopelessly away downtown.

Marr came storming in that afternoon. Wadlin was there in Story's office; he stood calmly while the big man trumpeted his wrongs.

And Story listened and smiled a little but made no other comment at all.

Marr told Story he would make it his personal business to drive the other man out of the contracting field; and he swung at last upon Wadlin and poured out his wrath upon the little man.

"You'll get yours too," he promised. "This town will be too hot for you."

Wadlin said quietly, "It's one tale you're not like to tell." He was, in his still way, enjoying himself.

"I don't have to tell it," Marr retorted, but he flushed shamefully. "I've other ways."

"Someone else might tell," Wadlin reminded him warningly.

Marr swelled with speech unuttered, and Wadlin smiled, and Story chuckled and said gently, "Goodbye, Coconuts."

The big man stood for a moment trembling, then with a cry he bolted through the door. After he was gone there was a little silence. Wadlin was waiting, and Story was thinking, and it was Story who spoke in the end.

"I got it at a comfortable figure, Wadlin," he said. "I banked on your word that he wouldn't bid. He came in late, and I refused to consent to accept his bid. There'll be a bonus for you."

Wadlin shook his head. "No need of that, sir," he replied.

Story looked at him thoughtfully. "You know," he said, "I don't see just why you did it. Marr had offered you a good job. And he's a mathematical shark, loves figures as well as you do. And I've no interest in such things. I should expect you to want to work for him, tie up with a man like that."

Wadlin hesitated. "Why, no," he said slowly. "You can hire men like me for things like that. He oughtn't to waste his time on them at all."

And Story, considering the matter at his leisure later, found something curiously appealing in the little man's humility. It occurred to him that a man may serve a mistress and despise her still.

If he be a little man.

Euclid and the Bright Boy

J. L. SYNGE

Here is the second of Mr. Synge's disconcerting mathematical fables. Apparently this professional agrees with Bertrand Russell that mathematics consists of tautologies. A good many mathematical mines have exploded during the last fifty years or more, many of them shaking the foundations of Euclid. Here is a firecracker.

THE YEAR IS 297 B.C., and we are in the famous city of Alexandria. It is evening, and the marble pillars of the library are shining in the golden haze of the setting sun.

A group of boys is sitting on the steps of the library, engaged in a loud argument such as boys of twelve often indulge in. They are expressing their opinions as to what goes on in the library but can come to no agreement. Finally one boy, brighter and cheekier than the rest, jumps up with a cry. "There's an old geezer coming out of the library now. By Zeus, I'll ask him!"

A dignified scholar emerges from the library with a roll of manuscript under his arm. The boy runs up to him.

"Beg pardon, sir, but us boys would like to know what you learned men do in the library all day."

The scholar is impressed by this youthful interest in learning and smiles in a kindly way as he replies. "There are many

Reprinted by permission of Jonathan Cape Limited from *Science: Sense and Nonsense* by J. L. Synge. Copyright 1951 by J. L. Synge.

scholars doing many things. I am writing a book on geometry."
And he pats the manuscript under his arm.

"What is geometry?" asks the boy.

"That is a long story," replies the scholar. "Perhaps you will
come to the university some day, and you will learn what
geometry is."

The boy makes a face. "Please, sir," he pleads, "I want to
know *now*. I know it would take a long time to learn *all* about
it, but can't you tell me just a little bit now?"

By this time the scholar is very much impressed by the eager-
ness of the boy. "Well," he says, unrolling his manuscript, "I'll
read you the first sentence."

He moves out of the shadow to where a last ray of the sun
illuminates his manuscript. Then, clearing his throat, and changing his voice from the easy conversational to the pontifical tone
of the lecture rostrum, he reads that sentence which has echoed
through so many classrooms for so many centuries: "A point is
that which has no part."[1]

There follows a dead silence.

"Do you want to hear more?" asks Euclid, for of course the
scholar is none other than him.

"No," says the boy. "I want to think that one over."

Euclid gives him a kindly pat on the head. "Perhaps I'll see
you again tomorrow evening. Now I must be off."

The boy puts out a hand and stops him. "Please, sir," he asks,
"has a point got a smell?"

"You cheeky urchin," cries Euclid, "get out of my way! Have
you no respect for learning and for learned men?"

The boy flushes with anger and jumps across the path of
Euclid, his teeth bared and his fists clenched. His voice rises to
a shriek. "You old he-goat," he cries. "I ask you an honest question and I want an honest answer! Has a point got a smell, or
has it not got a smell? Tell me that, or by the seven mouths of
the Nile I'll tear every shred of clothes off of you! I'll show the

---

[1] Σημεῖόν ἐστιν οὗ μέρος οὐθέν, or, in Latin, *Punctum est, cujus pars nulla est.*

people of Alexandria the pot belly and shrunken shins of a great geometer!"

Euclid is alarmed. He is not used to this vehemence in scientific argument. The boy must be possessed. He shrugs his shoulders and decides that a line of appeasement will be best.

"No, of course a point has no smell," he says.

The boy goes on: "Has a point color?"

"No."

"Has it a shape?"

"No."

"Can a point talk?"

"No."

"Can it hear?"

"No."

A short silence follows, and Euclid wonders whether he can slip quietly away. But the boy speaks again.

"I think you are a dishonest man," he says. "You tell people that a point has no part, but you don't tell them that a point has no smell, no color, can't talk, can't hear. Why do you bother to say that a point has no part, when there are so many other things it hasn't got? Tell me that."

Euclid sinks slowly on to the step of the library. His head is bowed, and he speaks in a low, broken voice. "My boy, I really don't know what a point is, but I wanted to write a lot of things about points, and the philosophers say that you mustn't talk about a thing until you define it. So I put in that definition of a point. It doesn't mean anything at all, I suppose. I'm very tired. Please, may I go home now? My wife told me not to be late as there are some people coming in after supper for a little party."

The boy looks down with contempt at the quivering old man, then folds his arms with dignity and speaks in a biting tone. "A fig for tired old men and wives and little parties! This matters much more—it's a question of sense or nonsense. What your definition says is this: A point is a point. Why stop there? Why not go on and say a point is a point is a point is a point forever?

It means just as much and as little as your precious definition, and if you went on repeating a point is a point is a point, it would keep you from driveling out the rest of the nonsense that is in you."

Spitting on the ground, the boy turns and runs down the steps into the street, where his neck is broken under the wheel of a passing chariot. Euclid shudders, gets up slowly, puts his manuscript back under his arm, and plods homeward with his head sunk on his chest.

The *Elements of Euclid* appeared in due course, and it was, as everyone knows, not a book of the month or a book of the year, but a book of the centuries. It might have been rather different, for as he sat in the library, fingering the scribe's galley proof, Euclid thought of the limp form of the dead boy and drafted a footnote for Definition I, explaining that a point had no smell and no color. But when he showed it to a colleague, the colleague told him to cut it out as it would only confuse people. *He* thought that the definition was perfectly clear as it stood.

The Purse of Fortunatus

LEWIS CARROLL

*This little topological exercise by Lewis Carroll may be un-
familiar even to my learned readers, for* Sylvie and Bruno *and
its sequel are not much read these days. They are dull books,
failures, in fact, but not in the least conventional. Indeed, one
shudders to think what a shrewd psychoanalyst would make of
them.*

"Mein Herr" took up Lady Muriel's work and examined it
through his large spectacles (one of the adjuncts that made him
so provokingly like the professor). "Hemming pocket handkerchiefs?" he said musingly. "So *that* is what the English
miladies occupy themselves with, is it?"

"It is the one accomplishment," I said, "in which man has
never yet rivaled woman!"

Here Lady Muriel returned with her father; and, after he had
exchanged some friendly words with "Mein Herr," and we had
all been supplied with the needful "creature comforts," the new-
comer returned to the suggestive subject of pocket handkerchiefs.

"You have heard of Fortunatus's Purse, Miladi? Ah, so!
Would you be surprised to hear that, with three of these leetle

handkerchiefs, you shall make the Purse of Fortunatus, quite soon, quite easily?"

"Shall I indeed?" Lady Muriel eagerly replied, as she took a heap of them into her lap and threaded her needle. *"Please* tell me how, Mein Herr! I'll make one before I touch another drop of tea!"

"You shall first," said Mein Herr, possessing himself of two of the handkerchiefs, spreading one upon the other, and holding them up by two corners, "you shall first join together these upper corners, the right to the right, the left to the left, and the opening between them shall be the *mouth* of the purse."

A very few stitches sufficed to carry out *this* direction. "Now, if I sew the other three edges together," she suggested, "the bag is complete?"

"Not so, Miladi. The *lower* edges shall *first* be joined—ah, not so!" (as she was beginning to sew them together). "Turn one of them over, and join the *right* lower corner of the one to the *left* lower corner of the other, and sew the lower edges together in what you would call *the wrong way*."

"I see!" said Lady Muriel, as she deftly executed the order. "And a very twisted, uncomfortable, uncanny-looking bag it makes! But the *moral* is a lovely one. Unlimited wealth can only be attained by doing things *in the wrong way!* And how are we to join up these mysterious—no, I mean *this* mysterious opening?" (twisting the thing round and round with a puzzled air). "Yes, it *is* one opening. I thought it was *two*, at first."

"You have seen the puzzle of the Paper Ring?" Mein Herr said, addressing the earl. "Where you take a slip of paper and join its ends together, first twisting one, so as to join the *upper* corner of *one* end to the *lower* corner of the *other?*"

"I saw one made only yesterday," the earl replied. "Muriel, my child, were you not making one, to amuse those children you had to tea?"

"Yes, I know that puzzle," said Lady Muriel. "The ring has only *one* surface and only *one* edge. It's very mysterious!"

"The *bag* is just like that, isn't it?" I suggested. "Is not the *outer* surface of one side of it continuous with the *inner* surface of the other side?"

"So it is!" she exclaimed. "Only it *isn't* a bag, just yet. How shall we fill up this opening, Mein Herr?"

"Thus!" said the old man impressively, taking the bag from her, and rising to his feet in the excitement of the explanation. "The edge of the opening consists of *four* handkerchief edges, and you can trace it continuously, round and round the opening: down the right edge of *one* handkerchief, up the left edge of the *other*, and then down the left edge of the *one*, and up the right edge of the *other!*"

"So you can!" Lady Muriel murmured thoughtfully, leaning her head on her hand, and earnestly watching the old man. "And that *proves* it to be only *one* opening!"

She looked so strangely like a child, puzzling over a difficult lesson, and Mein Herr had become, for the moment, so strangely like the old professor, that I felt utterly bewildered; the "eerie" feeling was on me in its full force, and I felt almost *impelled* to say, "Do you understand it, Sylvie?" However, I checked myself by a great effort and let the dream (if indeed it *was* a dream) go on to its end.

"Now, this *third* handkerchief," Mein Herr proceeded, "has *also* four edges, which you can trace continuously round and round: all you need do is to join its four edges to the four edges of the opening. The purse is then complete, and its outer surface—"

"*I* see!" Lady Muriel eagerly interrupted. "Its *outer* surface will be continuous with its *inner* surface! But it will take time. I'll sew it up after tea." She laid aside the bag and resumed her cup of tea. "But why do you call it Fortunatus's Purse, Mein Herr?"

The dear old man beamed upon her, with a jolly smile, looking more exactly like the professor than ever. "Don't you see, my child—I should say Miladi? Whatever is *inside* that purse is *outside* it; and whatever is *outside* it is *inside* it. So you have all the wealth of the world in that leetle purse!"

His pupil clapped her hands in unrestrained delight. "I'll certainly sew the third handkerchief in—*some* time," she said, "but I won't take up your time by trying it now."

The Symbolic Logic of Murder

JOHN REESE

❦

Mr. Reese's Darwin Carlisle is the last of our Irregular Figures and a most appealing one. This is the only story in existence (to my best if limited knowledge) which adjusts Boolean algebra, of an admittedly elementary order, to the requirements of popular fiction.

"I DREAD talking to him again," said Detective Rich Hinkle. "This genius, I mean—this young space scientist, Darwin Carlisle—this brain!"

"Him?" said Detective Jack Kunz. "How come?"

"This whole space exploration deal gives me the creeps, and so do these young eggheads," Hinkle said moodily. "It's contrary to the laws of nature to shoot at the moon!"

"Oh, Carlisle's all right," said Kunz.

"He is? Listen, any guy of twenty-four that sits around with a pretty girl and works equations—Jack, he's got to be *slightly* abnormal!"

Kunz thought it over. "I don't react that way. I kind of like the kid. It's old McKinstry that gives me the creeps."

"The preacher?" said Hinkle. "What's wrong with him?"

"Nothing," Kunz replied slowly, with a shiver, "but all preachers give me the creeps. It must be a subconscious guilt left over from something that happened when I was a kid. I guess

Reprinted by permission of Lurton Blassingame, author's representative. Copyright © 1960 by Davis Publications, Inc.

where you are afraid of science, I'm afraid of religion, or something."

"Well," said Hinkle after a moment, "this whole case gives me the creeps. Especially Darwin Carlisle."

As a rule, homicide men are immune to moods, and these two were veterans, above average in intelligence. Both were college graduates; both were big, dark, neat men in their forties. They had been partners on the night watch for so long that, like old married people, they now looked alike and had grown heavy, deliberate, thoughtful, and slow-moving together.

It was 1:35 A.M. They had worked all night on what should have been an easy case. A petty thug who had made his living extorting money from bookies on the North Side of Los Angeles had been murdered last evening. Hinkle and Kunz had interviewed three witnesses and had caused the arrests of four cheap racketeers.

All four had been associates of the dead man; all were capable of murder, and each had ample reason to desire the victim's death. Hinkle and Kunz were sure that they had the killers in jail, but they were just as sure that they would never be able to prove it. The four suspects had refused to talk—a stupid tactic but an effective one, since there was really nothing to connect them with the crime.

It was an unimportant killing, but like all men, policemen are depressed by defeat. To be so close to success and still to be humiliated by the four miserable specimens now languishing in jail was a peculiarly painful form of frustration.

Hinkle and Kunz even thought alike, so that when one had the creeps, the other had them too. Between them they filled the room to overflowing with eerie gloom. It was a small room, furnished only with a table and six chairs. They had pulled the records of the four suspects, but there was little in them that they did not already know. Other details had been supplied by robbery and vice squad stoolies. Few men know as much about their own wives as Hinkle and Kunz knew about their suspects. Yet the homicide men were at a dead end.

"May as well get it over with." Hinkle sighed. "We can't keep three honest witnesses waiting all night."

Kunz went to the door, opened it, and said, "If you people will come in, we'd like to talk to you once more, please."

First to enter was Shelley Parkinson, a small, vividly dark girl with such a look of innocence that it was like turning on more lights in the room. Some of the gloom melted from it. Both detectives had to smile at the mere sight of her pretty, cheerful face and trim, girlish figure. Hinkle stood up and pulled out a chair.

"Here, Miss Parkinson," he said. "It's certainly good of you people to wait so long for us."

"Oh, we didn't wait all this time. We went out for coffee. Was that all right?" the girl said. Her huge, brown eyes grew enormous as it occurred to her, too late, that they might have done something wrong.

"Of course it was all right!" Kunz said enthusiastically, before his surprised partner could open his mouth.

The girl was followed by a well-dressed man with a heavy shock of white hair and a lined but ruggedly handsome face. This was the Reverend Doctor G. Bart McKinstry, the minister who gave the obscurely sinful Kunz the creeps. He sat down opposite the girl, with the exhausted sigh of an old man who should have been in bed hours ago.

Lastly came a blond youth with a crew cut, with horn-rimmed glasses and a halfback's physique. Much of his muscular grace, however, seemed to have been oddly eroded away, as if by the drain of condensation from the pleasant intellectual fog in which he lived. His pockets were stuffed with crumpled papers, sharp pencils, and the inevitable slide rule; his blue eyes beheld without really seeing; and he walked with the dreamy shuffle of one whose motor nerves were better attuned to the orbit of Venus than to his own feet.

Darwin Carlisle sprang from a long line of university forebears. His father taught physics, his mother geology, at Columbia. Darwin was a graduate student at California Institute of

Technology, where he was earning his doctorate by designing guidance systems for space probes and then describing them in monographs that not more than a dozen people in the whole world could understand. There are such people, and they differ from most mortals in that foggy, dreamy, star-smitten expression. Otherwise they look as normal and wholesome as shoe clerks, faucet manufacturers, and first basemen.

"This is a nice room," Darwin said, looking around at the naked walls, the gaunt furniture, and the bare ceiling with its one stark light. "Nothing to distract you here, is there? A room for thinking!"

Hinkle flinched. Dr. McKinstry angrily looked the other way. These three witnesses had been together for more than four hours—plenty of time for the young man's neo-functional, interplanetary personality to have collided violently with the old preacher's stern fundamentalism. It was plain that Hinkle was not the only man who got the creeps from Carlisle.

Darwin sat down beside Shelley. She put her hand on his arm, a gesture both trusting and proprietary. It showed that while she relied on him to protect her from tigers, bandits, and traveling salesmen, she also was ready to wipe his nose for him whenever necessary.

"Sorry we made you wait so long," said Kunz, "but we hoped you would remember something that had slipped your mind when we first talked to you."

"We're badly in need of help," said Hinkle.

"Oh, dear!" Shelley wailed. "Didn't you catch the four men you wanted so badly?"

"Yes," Kunz said grimly. "They were picked up by various units of the department within one hour of the murder. They were scattered all over the city but not so far that they could not have been together at the scene of the murder at the time it took place."

"But if you have the murderers, how can we help?"

Hinkle said, "All four of them have alibis, miss. Not unimpeachable alibis, I'm sure, but all four have dummied up and won't even admit what time it is. This is not the only thing this department has to do, and it will take more time and manpower than the chief can spare to prove that two or more of our suspects, plus two or more of their alibi witnesses, are lying."

"I see," the girl said.

"What do you mean by 'prove'? The term is subject to narrower definition," said Darwin.

Hinkle glared at him. "Oh? In what way?"

"Well, I can 'prove' the speed of light to you with analogic instruments, because you accept their rationality. But how can I 'prove' it to a jungle cannibal? Conversely, I can 'prove' to the cannibal that he owes me a debt, by merely hitting him over the head. He accepts the logic of brute force, while you, I'm sure, would demand invoices."

There was a moment of deep silence. Shelley looked proud; Kunz looked worried, and Hinkle and Dr. McKinstry seemed to be counting silently from one to ten.

"I'm familiar with that point of view," Dr. McKinstry said. "The exact quotation is, *And Pilate said, What is truth?* The time comes, young man, when all we get by splitting hairs is smaller fragments of hair!"

"I didn't mean to be argumentative, sir," said Darwin.

"Then why not just listen?" the minister snapped. "I can 'prove' that the firmament is not merely a shooting gallery for you young squirts over there at Cal Tech, but at this moment these officers have requested our help in solving a murder."

"We have to 'prove' it to a jury beyond a reasonable doubt, Darwin," Kunz explained. "Let's go over it again, and see if one of you can remember *something* that will help us connect these men with the job."

The detectives were skilled interrogators and the witnesses were eager to help. Unfortunately there were excellent reasons why they could not.

It had been raining hard at 7:54 P.M., the moment of death for Rudy Lambert, alias Walter Lane, alias Rudolf Walters, but better known as Needle Nose the Fink. According to the stoolies,

Needle Nose had, by his own code, earned execution. Two weeks ago he had extorted $100 from one Albine Wooten, a girl bookie, by threatening to pour acid in her ears. Albine later had calmed her nerves with a fifth of vodka and then strolled in front of a five-ton truck. Four men had attended her funeral.

One was her brother, Mickey Boyce, a strong-arm robber with a psychopathic record. One was her "lay-off man," Red Pearson, the North Side's boss bookie. A third was her boy friend, Stanley Manlo, a pin setter in a bowling alley and a pathological coward who slept with a switch-blade knife under his pillow. The fourth was Sid Filette, whose North Figueroa Street newsstand also handled a little cut-price marijuana. Sid's grief had perhaps been most poignant of all, since Albine had expired owing him money.

Four more unappetizing individuals than Boyce, Pearson, Manlo, and Filette do not exist; but charming people rarely commit premeditated murder, and when they do, they employ elaborately ingenious devices that always go wrong. Then the homicide men, who have seen everything, easily whisk them in. There had been no such defect in the brilliantly stupid simplicity of this murder.

Needle Nose had ducked vengeance by the unlikely ruse of working as a handy man in the last house on Frenchick Way, a dead-end street one block long. Rain or shine, Dr. McKinstry, who lived at 4772 Frenchick, always took an evening walk. He was on his way home in the heavy rain when he saw, across the street, another pedestrian whom he recognized as his neighbor's new employee.

He was sure no one else was afoot on the street. The handy man hurried on. Dr. McKinstry turned into his own sidewalk. He had taken two steps when several gunshots—he was not sure if there were two or three—boomed out.

There was no outcry of accusation or pain—no sound at all but those shots and the violent beating of the rain. Dr. McKinstry knew instantly that something terrible had happened. He stopped, half paralyzed by horror.

Then the starter of an automobile began grinding. The engine started, and the dark mass of the car hurtled past him.

"It must have been parked at the end of the street. Its lights did not go on until after it turned the corner. It passed within ten feet of me, but I don't know how many men were in it. I have a feeling, though, that I saw more than one shadow," said the tired old preacher. "I made an effort to control myself, and I remember thinking that I had to memorize the license number. I felt it would be important to the authorities, but it was too dark, or perhaps I was just not alert enough."

"You can't give us any idea of that license number—even one digit or one letter?" Kunz asked hopefully.

"No. I remember only the terrible roar of the engine. I recall the thought that went through my mind—*Their roaring shall be like a lion, they shall roar like young lions*. Then I'm afraid my mind simply went blank."

Hinkle sighed. "We can't blame you, sir. You have no idea what make of car it was?"

"Officer, I don't really know one car from another."

Kunz looked at Shelley. "You got a look at it—do you think you might be able to identify it now, after thinking it over?"

She looked troubled. "No, sir—only that it was an old-model sedan. You know, before they started putting on those tail fins. And I seem to recall that it was a grubby blue in color. You know what happens to blue when you don't take care of it."

"Oxidization," Darwin Carlisle murmured.

"I'll make a note of that," Hinkle said coldly. "Now, you two were on Miss Parkinson's porch, at 4770 Frenchick Way, next door to Dr. McKinstry—right?"

"Yes, sir. I was facing the street and Darwin was facing the house. That's why he didn't see as much as I did," said Shelley.

"But he knows it was oxidized," said Hinkle. "May I ask why you were facing the street and why he was not?"

"He—he was kissing me good night," she said, "but do you have to put that in the papers?"

"Of course not!" said Kunz. "Have you remembered how many shots you heard?"

"No, sir. It could have been two or three or four."

"Have you been able to recall how many people were in the car you saw?"

"No, sir, only that I have a distinct impression of more than one."

"You and the Reverend both have that impression, and several quick shots don't sound like a one-man job," Hinkle said. "In other words, none of you can add anything to what you told us earlier tonight?"

All three witnesses shook their head. Darwin Carlisle said, "What about your prisoners' cars? If one of them is an old-model sedan—"

"They don't own any cars, any of them," Hinkle snapped. "Oxidized or otherwise. They've got us whipped and they know it. That's what burns me up!"

They sat there in dispirited silence a moment, five sincere people whose best was not good enough. Then Dr. McKinstry murmured apologetically, "I'm sorry. I guess we didn't give you very good clues, did we?"

"It's not your fault, Reverend," said Hinkle. "At least we're sure of one thing—it wasn't a one-man job. But were there two, three, or four of them in on it? That's what we don't know!"

"And none of them will talk?" said Darwin.

Kunz grinned. "Well, we did get one squeal out of Red Pearson when we started to leave him alone with Sid Filette and Mick Boyce, right here in this very room. Red is not what you'd call a trusting soul, not even here."

"Not with those two," said Hinkle. "Sid and Mick are bad medicine. Red's not taking a chance on one of them getting behind him with a shiv, while he's watching the other one. That's how he has run the North Side bookies so long—by not ever letting Boyce and Filette get him between them."

"Oh, they sound horrid!" Shelley cried. "I had no idea there were such people in the world."

"You're giving these guys the benefit of the doubt, miss," Hinkle said. "You see, ganging up on this job doesn't make them pals. We're dealing with thieves that hate everybody, especially one another. All that could possibly bring them together is mutual hatred."

She shuddered. "I can't imagine human beings living like that. I can't!" she said in a low voice.

Kunz gritted. "Miss, guys like that are why my partner and I have careers. Let me tell you about them—Mickey Boyce, for instance. The fun you get from television Mickey gets from breaking somebody's arm. Why, I've seen little Stanley Manlo run like a rabbit on an open street in broad daylight just to avoid meeting Mick. Stanley lives in terror of that goon. Mick is one of those guys that enjoys torturing people. The only man on earth he's afraid of is Red Pearson."

"Red threatened to kill him one day," Hinkle explained, "and some day he'll do it, and Mick knows it."

"This Red Pearson seems to have a strong, dominating personality," Dr. McKinstry observed.

"Yes," said Hinkle, "but he couldn't dominate Albine Wooten. She told me once that Red warned her to cut loose from Stan Manlo because she couldn't depend on a coward. But she loved the guy. Well, Red was right! Stan sure wasn't around when Needle Nose put the old arm on her."

Again a small shudder ran through the girl's shapely body, and her brown eyes reflected shocked admiration as they darted from one detective to the other. Kunz saw the impression they were making, and after this frustrating night's work he needed admiration. He warmed to his subject.

"Or you take the noble small businessman, Sid Filette. Now there's a way to live! Sid has been held up and shaken down and rousted around so often in that crummy newsstand of his—and by his own friends!—that he has a standing rule never to be alone with any one of them. His nickname is Witness, because he's a guy who wants a witness around at all times. Even when we want to talk to him, we have to be sure that two officers go in. How do you like that?"

"It's unbelievable!" the girl gasped.

"To you, maybe," said Hinkle, "or to a jury. But not to anyone who knows these guys. These aren't big-time hoodlums, miss. These are the scum of the underworld. But that doesn't mean that they haven't made us look like jackasses."

"If only we had that license number!" said Kunz.

"Why," said Darwin Carlisle, "do you need that?"

He blinked genially through his horn-rimmed glasses. Both detectives were discouraged and tired. Even Kunz grew slightly red-faced, and Hinkle winced with the effort of holding his temper. It was Hinkle who said, with excessive politeness, "Just how else do we connect these guys with the job, kid?"

"It seems to me you already have," said Darwin.

"Oh, we have, have we?" said Kunz.

"Yes. Look, I'll show you—"

Darwin took a pencil from one pocket, a piece of paper from another, and scribbled rapidly for a minute. He handed the paper to Hinkle. Kunz got up quickly and came around to read over Hinkle's shoulder. The two detectives found themselves staring at this:

$$BP + BM + BF + PM + PF + MF + BPM + BMF +$$
$$BPF + PMF + BPMF \neq 0.$$
$$\overline{BP} = 0.$$
$$BM + BF + PM + PF + MF + BPM + BMF + BPF +$$
$$PMF + BPMF \neq 0.$$
$$\overline{PM} + B\overline{PM} + \overline{PMF} + BPMF = 0.$$
$$BM + BF + PF + MF + BMF + BPF \neq 0.$$
$$B\overline{PF} = 0.$$
$$BM + BF + PF + MF + BMF \neq 0.$$
$$B\overline{M} = 0.$$
$$BF + PF + MF + BMF \neq 0.$$
$$B\overline{F} + P\overline{F} + M\overline{F} = 0.$$
$$BMF \neq 0.$$

Kunz so far forgot himself as to blurt out, "What the hell is this—a prescription?"

"A set of equations in symbolic logic," said Darwin, "or inequations, rather, this being the simplest attack on so simple a problem."

"And what," said Hinkle hoarsely, "is symbolic logic?"

"A method of solving logical problems by algebra."

"Do you do this when you shoot rockets at the moon?" said Hinkle. There was a dangerous glint in his eye.

"It is used in designing all complex circuitry, and that includes rocket guidance systems."

"Now wait a minute, Rich. Let him work this out!" Kunz pleaded as Hinkle stumbled to his feet. "What have we got to lose?"

Hinkle sat down. Darwin reached across and took back the paper. Shelley beamed proudly. Kunz and Hinkle leaned across the table to watch. Even Dr. McKinstry showed interest, if not approval.

"We know that with four factors, sixteen combinations are possible, including 'one' and 'none,' " said Darwin. "We can eliminate the four 'ones,' since both Shelley and Dr. McKinstry are quite sure there were more than one man in the car. We can, of course, also eliminate 'none,' since somebody had to be there to commit the murder. That leaves us with only eleven combinations. Now, using letters to represent your men—B for Boyce, P for Pearson, M for Manlo, and F for Filette—we write our eleven combinations in our first equations, as follows:

$$BP + BM + BF + PM + PF + MF + BPM + BMF + BPF + PMF + BPMF \neq 0.$$

"Only one combination can be guilty. The others aren't; so our equation is not balanced. That's why we draw a line through the 'equal' sign—to make it mean 'not equal,' or rather, 'not true.' Now we'll consider these men one at a time. You say Boyce was so afraid of Pearson that he would never be alone with him. In the Boyce-Pearson combination, Boyce therefore becomes a negative quantity. We draw a line over him to indicate the negative, writing that as a separate equation, as follows:

$$\overline{B}P = 0.$$

"Here we use the 'equal' sign, because this combination is true. Having eliminated that combination, we have left this equation:

$$BM + BF + PM + PF + MF + BPM + BMF + BPF +$$
$$PMF + BPMF \neq 0.$$

"Now let's consider Pearson. He distrusted the coward, Manlo, so profoundly that it's hard to believe he would ever participate in a murder with him. So in all combinations where both P and M appear, P must be negative. Let's write those combinations that way—using, as you will note, the 'equal' sign to indicate truth:

$$\overline{P}M + B\overline{P}M + \overline{P}MF + B\overline{P}MF = 0.$$

"Now we have only this left of our first equation:

$$BM + BF + PF + MF + BMF + BPF \neq 0.$$

"But you say Pearson never lets himself be caught between Boyce and Filette—that he objected when you tried to leave him alone with them here. Would he go out on a murder job with them?—and with them armed? Hardly! So we must write the Boyce-Pearson-Filette combination as true, with a negative P and the 'equal' sign:

$$B\overline{P}F = 0.$$

"Which leaves us only this of our original equation:

$$BM + BF + PF + MF + BMF \neq 0.$$

"But Manlo, you say, ran like a rabbit at the very sight of Boyce. Certainly he'd never help him on a murder, unless someone was along to protect him. So we write the Boyce-Manlo combination with a negative M and the 'equal' sign:

$$\overline{BM} = 0.$$

"Which leaves us only these combinations:

$$BF + PF + MF + BMF \neq 0.$$

"But you say that Filette is so afraid of his friends that he has a rule never to be alone with any one of them. In all two-man combinations where Filette appears, we must therefore use a negative F and the 'equal' sign, as follows:

$$B\overline{F} + P\overline{F} + M\overline{F} = 0.$$

"Which leaves us, of our eleven original combinations, only BMF. This part of the equation *is* true, and it is the *only one* that can be true. It proves that Boyce, Manlo, and Filette *together* were the murderers. If any sum is equal to zero, then all of its parts are equal to zero, too, and in a binomial system the opposite is also true. In short, not one of the three can possibly deny his guilt!"

Darwin pushed the paper across to Hinkle who gave it one quick, creepy look and refused to touch it. "Is that what you call *proof?*" he said in a choking voice. "What'll you guys at Cal Tech dream up next?"

"We didn't dream it up. Symbolic logic was invented, if we may use that term, in 1847 by an English mathematician, George Boole, who is probably doing handsprings in his grave over the way I have oversimplified his system. It's often called Boolean algebra, and it has been used by logicians and mathematicians for over a century," said Darwin.

"But what is a century in the story of mankind?" Dr. McKinstry said indignantly. "Men aren't numbers or letters! That's the trouble with you scientists—you try to reduce human beings to mere quantitative symbols."

"Not quantitative, sir—relational," said Darwin. "The letters, B, P, M, and F do not represent men but only the narrow characteristics that make it possible or impossible for them to be at a certain place at a certain time for the certain purpose of committing murder."

"I cannot believe it!" The old man shook his white head. "Human beings are far too complex for such—such abracadabra!"

Kunz picked up the paper. "I'm not so sure, sir," he said thoughtfully. "These are pretty primitive specimens of mankind. I don't understand all these hieroglyphics, but I give you my word I understand those four crooks."

Shelley did not understand either, but her faith never wavered. "They're always trying to trip Darwin up on the electronic computer at Cal Tech, but they never can," she said. "Why don't you ask them to check this out? I bet you find out that Darwin is right again!"

"Unfortunately, miss, there are no electronic computers on a jury," Hinkle said gloomily. He hit the table with his fist. "No, we've got to find that car!"

"If the information you gave me about the suspects is accurate, then my symbols are valid, my equations correct, and my conclusion inescapable," said Darwin. "However, I have an idea about the car too."

He wrote something on another piece of paper which he handed across the table to Dr. McKinstry. "Please take a look at that, sir. At the same time try to recall when you heard those shots and saw that car, and see if anything comes back to you."

Kunz and Hinkle craned their necks to read what looked to them like a list of California automobile license numbers:

LOV 538; HLE 886; JIK 213; ISA 529; SRP 471; MOI 398; DCH 935.

The old preacher took the paper reluctantly. Kunz and Hinkle saw him run his eyes over the list, lay the paper aside with an impatient frown, then snatch it up again. They saw him stare at it and then turn pale, as he remembered 7:54 P.M. in all its shock and horror.

"That's it—the license number of that car!" he shouted. "It's the fourth number on the list. Why, I can see it as plainly as though it were—"

But Hinkle and Kunz had already snatched the paper from him and were running from the room. They were back in three minutes—it takes no more than that to check a license number with the California Department of Motor Vehicles. And now both men had a creepy look.

"It's a 1952 blue sedan, registered to Sid Filette's landlord's sister," said Kunz. "This ties him in, and I'll bet we tie the other two in too!"

Hinkle looked at Carlisle with an expression almost of fear. "But don't you dare show us your equations on this one!" he muttered. "If I have to see any more symbolic logic tonight, I'll go nuts."

"This wasn't symbolic logic, sir," said Darwin. "Dr. McKinstry twice quoted Scripture tonight. The verse about Pilate was pointedly apropos to our discussion of the exact meaning of words, but I'll have to ask him to pardon me for saying that his other quotation did not make the same kind of sense. This was when he said that the automobile made him think of the roaring of lions. Unfortunately here we must again use the most precise definitions.

"It *did* roar, but not like a lion. The two sounds have nothing in common, and the one could not suggest the other. Why, then, did Dr. McKinstry recall so irrelevant a passage? Could it be that, for some reason, he had made an effort to remember that exact verse? If so, why?

"Most of us, when we must remember something like a phone number or an address, associate it with something already familiar. When I first met Shelley, for a long time I had to remind myself of silver and ytterbium, these being the forty-seventh and seventieth in the periodic table of the elements. It was the only way I could remember that she lived at 4770 Frenchick Way. Do you follow me?"

"Oh yes, sure!" said Hinkle, swallowing hard. "Silver what was it? Sure, anybody would do it that way!"

"I think," said Darwin, "that Dr. McKinstry, being an intelligent, conscientious man, tried to associate the license number with something familiar—in this case, the fifth chapter and the twenty-ninth verse of the book of Isaiah. Somehow, the human mind being the marvelously complex thing it is, he afterward associated the verse through its context, rather than its number, which would be written ISA 529."

"How do you know so much about the Bible?" said Dr. McKinstry.

"My grandfather, who teaches philosophy at Harvard, gave me a hundred dollars for memorizing the book of Isaiah when I was sixteen. It's a very helpful reference for a scientist. For instance, in the sixty-fifth chapter—"

"Go home," said Kunz. "All of you go home!"

He had just remembered why preachers gave him the creeps. It had to do with the dishonest way he had won a camera as a Sunday School prize—by writing Bible verses on his cuff, instead of memorizing them.

To the end of his life Kunz would feel like a crook, just as Hinkle would feel stupid. But a little humility is good for all of us, and it probably helped the two men when they sat down to reason with Red Pearson.

Once Red realized that they were not trying to frame him for a murder he had not committed, he co-operated willingly, even enthusiastically. After that it was easy to break down the cowardly Manlo.

It was 3:29 A.M. when they left the police building, with their case all wrapped up. The rain was over and the stars were out. So was the moon—a bloodshot crescent that was just about ready to set. It looked weak and helpless to Hinkle, hanging there above the mountains as though half of its supports had been shot away. He looked up at it with a sigh.

"I still wish they'd leave it alone!" he said.

IV

SIMPLE
HARMONIC
MOTIONS

❧ ❧ ❧

The Square of the Hypotenuse

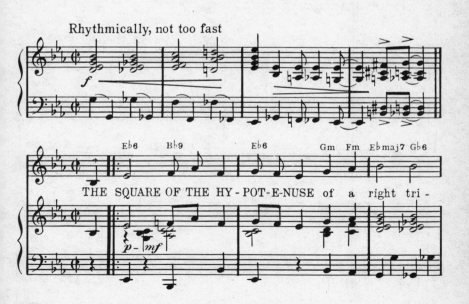

MUSIC BY SAUL CHAPLIN
LYRICS BY JOHNNY MERCER

The connections between music and mathematics were pointed out some time ago by the Pythagorean school. But there are very few pieces of music actually inspired by mathematics. I have unearthed only two, of which this amusing ditty, originally sung by the unique Danny Kaye, is the first. It appeared in the film Merry Andrew *many years ago.*

The Square of the Hypotenuse

The Ta Ta

MUSIC BY JOSEPH CHARLES HOLBROOKE
JINGLES BY SIDNEY H. SIME

The omniscient Martin Gardner (who could have compiled this volume with his eyes shut) directed my attention to a wacky little book of forgotten nonsense verse entitled Bogey Beasts, *music by Joseph Charles Holbrooke, jingles by Sidney H. Sime. Our old friend Moebius would have liked "The Ta Ta."*

There is a co-zy kitch-en in-side his room-y

head, Al-so a ti - ny bed-room in which he goes to

bed _____ So

when his walk is end - ed and he no more would roam _____

In - side - out he turns him - self to find _

He found his brains were use-less, as ma-ny o-thers would _____ If they but tried to use them__ a great un-like-ly hood. _____ He

249

V

DIVIDENDS
AND
REMAINDERS

❧ ❧ ❧

Apothems

❦

Of course this heading should be Apothegms. *Fortunately* Apothems *is pronounced identically and seems much more mathematical. Or perhaps our heading should have been* Aphorithmetric. *In any case, I direct your attention to the samples from Stanislaw Jerzy Lec, a modern Polish genius of the aphorism; and to those from G. C. Lichtenberg, the eighteenth-century physicist and satirist. These few examples give hardly any hint of the remarkable quality of their minds.*

The great repository of mathematical anecdotes, aphorisms, and so forth is probably Robert Edouard Moritz' On Mathematics and Mathematicians (*formerly titled* Memorabilia Mathematica *or* The Philomath's Quotation-Book) *and published by Dover Publications, Inc., New York. Some of my readers will need no signpost to this well-known volume.*

IN THE geometrical analysis of a line a, one indefinite section of it is called x; the other is not y, as it would be in ordinary life, but $a - x$. This is the reason that mathematical language has such great advantages over ordinary speech.

—GEORGE CHRISTOPH LICHTENBERG (1742–1799)

I cannot deny it: when I saw for the first time that people in my country began to know the meaning of the radical sign in mathematics, clear tears of joy came into my eyes.

Ibid.

If an angel were to tell us about his philosophy, I believe many of his statements might well sound like "2 × 2 = 13."

Ibid.

Materialism is the asymptote of psychology.

Ibid.

And now the artificial ruins were gradually becoming natural ones. Ruins to the second power.

Ibid.

If a man who cannot count finds a four-leaf clover, is he entitled to happiness?

—STANISLAW JERZY LEC (1909–   )

Two parallel lines meet somewhere in infinity . . . and they believe it.

Ibid.

Many a zero thinks that it is the ellipse on which the earth travels.

Ibid.

It is easy to form a chain from a string of zeros.

Ibid.

This principle is so perfectly general that no particular application of it is possible.

—G. POLYA, *How to Solve It*

Geometry is the art of correct reasoning on incorrect figures.

Ibid.

What is the difference between method and device? A method is a device which you can use twice.

Ibid.

The different branches of Arithmetic—Ambition, Distraction, Uglification, and Derision.

—LEWIS CARROLL, *Alice in Wonderland*

(Of the ant) Every one of them is like the figure 3. And there are so many of them . . . so very many . . . 333333333333 . . . to infinity.

—JULES RENARD, *Histoires Naturelles*

All animals are equal, but some animals are more equal than others.

—GEORGE ORWELL, *Animal Farm*

The mathematicians are a sort of Frenchmen: when you talk to them, they immediately translate it into their own language, and right away it is something entirely different.

—GOETHE

I had a feeling once about Mathematics—that I saw it all. Depth beyond Depth was revealed to me—the Byss and the Abyss. I saw—as one might see the transit of Venus or even the Lord Mayor's Show—a quantity passing through infinity and changing its sign from plus to minus. I saw exactly why it hap-

Reprinted by permission of Harcourt, Brace and World, Inc., from *Animal Farm* by George Orwell.

pened and why the tergiversation was inevitable—but it was after dinner and I let it go.

—WINSTON CHURCHILL

Mathematics contains much that will neither hurt one if one does not know it nor help one if one does know it.

—J. B. MENCKEN, *De Charlataneria eruditorum*, 1715

A graphomath is a person who, having no mathematics, attempts to describe a mathematician.

—AUGUSTUS DE MORGAN, *A Budget of Paradoxes*

To the eye of God there are no numbers: seeing all things at one time, he counts nothing.

—ETIENNE BONNOT DE CONDILLAC

The product of an infinite series of integers of whatsoever magnitude is, if there be included in the series nought, nought also.

—Mysterious dedicatory note to *Lawyer, Heal Thyself,* an autobiography by the British attorney Bill Mortlock

When the Angles (with the Saxons) invaded England, they descended on what was later the Land Debatable, that is the North of England and the South of Scotland. The acute Angles went north and the obtuse ones south.

—ANONYMOUS (presumably a Scot)

Reprinted by permission of The Macmillan Company from *Lawyer, Heal Thyself* by Bill Mortlock.

A Subset of Anecdotes

⚹

Rich treasures of mathematical anecdotes are to be found in Moritz (already cited) and in Augustus De Morgan's lovely old crotchety book A Budget of Paradoxes, *published in two volumes by the Open Court Publishing Co., Chicago and London. The subjoined handful just happen to please me.*

EULER, DIDEROT, ALGEBRA, AND GOD

In his inexhaustible A Budget of Paradoxes, *Augustus De Morgan tells this story:*

EULER was a believer in God, downright and straightforward. The following story is told by Thiebault, in his *Souvenirs de vingt ans de séjour à Berlin* . . . Thiebault says that he has no personal knowledge of the truth of the story but that it was believed throughout the whole of the north of Europe. Diderot paid a visit to the Russian Court at the invitation of the Empress. He conversed very freely and gave the younger members of the Court circle a good deal of lively atheism. The Empress was much amused, but some of her counselors suggested that it might be desirable to check these expositions of doctrine. The Empress did not like to put a direct muzzle on her guest's tongue, so the following plot was contrived. Diderot was informed that a learned mathematician was in possession of an algebraical demonstration of the existence of God and would give it him before all the Court, if he desired to hear it. Diderot gladly consented. Though the name of the mathematician is not given, it was Euler.

257

He advanced toward Diderot and said gravely, and in a tone of perfect conviction:

$$Monsieur, \frac{a + b^n}{n} = x, \ donc \ Dieu \ existe; \ répondez!$$

Diderot, to whom algebra was Hebrew, was embarrassed and disconcerted, while peals of laughter rose on all sides. He asked permission to return to France at once, which was granted.

—AUGUSTUS DE MORGAN

PARADISE LOST AT CAMBRIDGE

Thomas Jefferson Hogg, surely one of the most remarkably named of men and the biographer of Shelley, tells us a story about the Cambridge mathematician who, having never read Paradise Lost, *was finally induced to do so and reported as follows:*

"I HAVE READ your famous poem. I read it attentively: but what does it prove? There is more instruction in half a page of Euclid! A man might read Milton's poem a hundred, aye, a thousand times, and he would never learn that the angles at the base of an isosceles triangle are equal!"

—THOMAS JEFFERSON HOGG

WITH APOLOGIES TO BOLYAI

THERE IS a story about two Hungarian aristocrats who decided to play a game in which the one who calls the largest number wins.

"Well," said one of them, "you name your number first."

After a few minutes of hard mental work the second aristocrat finally named the largest number he could think of.

"Three," he said.

Now it was the turn of the first one to do the thinking, but after a quarter of an hour he finally gave up.

"You've won," he agreed. —GEORGE GAMOW

EXTINCTION BY SUBTRACTION

THE MANNER of Demoivre's death has a certain interest for psychologists. Shortly before it he declared that it was necessary for him to sleep some ten minutes or a quarter of an hour longer each day than the preceding one; the day after he had thus reached a total of something over twenty-three hours he slept up to the limit of twenty-four hours and then died in his sleep.

—R. BALL

Reprinted by permission of The Macmillan Company from *Mathematical Recreations and Essays* by R. Ball.

π AND THE ACTUARY

DE MORGAN was explaining to an actuary what was the chance that a certain proportion of some group of people would at the end of a given time be alive and quoted the actuarial formula, involving π, which, in answer to a question, he explained stood for the ratio of the circumference of a circle to its diameter. His acquaintance, who had so far listened to the explanation with interest, interrupted him and exclaimed, "My dear friend, that must be a delusion; what can a circle have to do with the number of people alive at a given time?"

Ibid.

THAT MASON-DIXON LINE

ONE OF the most curious of these cases (geometrical paradoxes) was that of a student, I am not sure but a graduate, of the University of Virginia, who claimed that geometers were in error in assuming that a line had no thickness. He published a school geometry based on his views, which received the endorsement of a well-known New York school official and, on the basis of this, was actually endorsed, or came very near being endorsed, as a textbook in the public schools of New York.

—SIMON NEWCOMB

Yet it was, I believe, this same renowned Simon Newcomb who proved by mathematics that man would never fly. His reminiscences were published in 1903. In December of that year the Wright brothers flew at Kitty Hawk.

MATHEMATICS CHEZ MADAME MARIETTE

In his book of reminiscences of the Paris of the twenties and thirties, A Narrow Street, *Elliot Paul offers a delightful description of Madame Mariette's brothel. In the waiting room was an "album" which was passed out discreetly by the hostess to any client who felt the need of reinforcement. Mr. Paul's account of the album leads directly to the subject, an interest in which is common to all my readers. I refer to mathematics.*

THE "ALBUM" had a collection of photographs which left little or nothing to the imagination except to make one wonder, when halfway through, what possibly could be left for the remaining pages to portray. To what extent the "album" at Madame Mariette's place made things easier for fading clients I cannot say, but it changed the course of the life of a young Frenchman I knew who was attending the Sorbonne in the early 1920s. Jacques was brilliant but had no ambition and no plans for the use of his excellent mind. He was at school because his parents could pay for it and university life was more carefree and less onerous than a job in a bank or the executive offices of some factory. One day when he was idling away an afternoon at Mariette's, in perusing the "album" he was struck with the infinite number of variations contained in a few simple acts involving two, three, and in extreme cases four parties. He began thinking in terms of numbers: permutations and combinations. That same evening he plunged avidly into his neglected mathematics textbooks and soon led his class in higher algebra and integral calculus. Today he is one of the most distinguished theoretical mathematicians in London and freely admits that he owes it all to Mariette.

—ELLIOT PAUL

THE DEVIL A MATHEMATICIAN WOULD BE

I owe the following story to the courtesy of Chandler Davis of Providence, Rhode Island, who says it was collected by the world traveler and raconteur A. J. Lohwater.

THE DEVIL said to Daniel Webster, "Set me a task I can't carry out, and I'll give you anything in the world you ask for."

Daniel Webster: "Fair enough. Prove that for n greater than 2, the equation $a^n + b^n = c^n$ has no non-trivial solution in integers."

They agreed on a three-day period for the labor, and the Devil disappeared.

At the end of the three days the Devil presented himself, haggard, jumpy, biting his lip. Daniel Webster said to him, "Well—how did you do at my task? Did you prove the theorem?"

"Eh? No . . . no, I haven't proved it."

"Then I can have whatever I ask for? Money? The Presidency?"

"What? Oh, *that*—of course. But listen! If we could just prove the following two lemmas—"

—A. J. LOHWATER

A Little Nursery Mathematics

❧

There are many old rhymes and riddles involving elementary arithmetic, of which this is doubtless the best known:

> Multiplication is vexation,
> Division is as bad,
> The Rule of Three
> Does puzzle me
> And practice drives me mad.

There are many variants of the above rhyme; I found this one in the delightful Lore and Language of Schoolchildren *by Iona and Peter Opie. The Opies have traced the rhyme back to a manuscript c. 1570.*

In his amusing Space Child's Mother Goose *Frederick Winsor thus sophisticates this ancient jingle:*

> Automation
> Is Vexation,
> Quaternions are bad;
> Analysis Situs
> Is only detritus,
> I wonder: Have I been had?

In the Opies' now classic Oxford Dictionary of Nursery Rhymes *are several nursery riddles. Here is an ingenious one:*

> *Make three-fourths of a cross,*
>   *And a circle complete,*
> *And let two semi-circles*
>   *On a perpendicular meet;*
> *Next add a triangle*
>   *That stands on two feet;*
> *Next two semi-circles and a circle complete.*

The solution is the word T-O-B-A-C-C-O. *The Opies add that another solution offered is "a picture of a bicycle"—which would seem to me to involve considerable topological stretching.*

Here are more of Winsor's higher-mathematical rhymes:

> *Three jolly sailors from Blaydon-on-Tyne*
> *They went to sea in a bottle by Klein.*
> *Since the sea was entirely inside the hull*
> *The scenery seen was exceedingly dull.*

> *Flappity, Floppity, Flip!*
> *The Mouse on the Möbius Strip.*
>   *The Strip revolved,*
>   *The Mouse dissolved*
> *In a chronodimensional skip.*

> *Little Jack Horner*
>   *Sits in a corner*
> *Extracting cube roots to infinity,*

An assignment for boys
That will minimize noise
And produce a more peaceful vicinity.

And a few by L. A. Graham:

A diller, a dollar,
A witless trig scholar
  On a ladder against a wall.
If length over height
Gives an angle too slight,
  The cosecant may prove his downfall.

A mathematician named Ray
Says extraction of cubes is child's play.
  You don't need equations
  Or long calculations
Just hot water to run on the tray.

See Saw, Marjorie Daw,
She rocked—and learned the lever law.
She saw that he weighed more than she
For she sat higher up than he,
Which made her cry, excitedly,
"To see saw, it is plain to see,
There must be an equality
'Twixt You times X and Y times Me."

A Quadrinomial of Poems

❧

That magnificent old man, J. J. Sylvester, who taught mathematics during the Victorian period at University College, London, the University of Virginia, Johns Hopkins, and Oxford, wrote a fairish amount of by no means bad Miltonic verse. This sonnet, To a Missing Member, etc., seems to me quite a stunt. The lines by Christopher Morley doubtless portray his father, Frank Morley (1860–1937), who wrote books on analytic functions and inversive geometry. The lines from Pope I include to show how silly a great poet can be when he steps outside his own province. The lines from Wordsworth may seem a bit windy and literary to professional mathematicians, but they seem to me to have the root of the matter in them nonetheless.

To a Missing Member of a Family Group of Terms in an Algebraical Formula

Lone and discarded one! divorced by fate,
Far from thy wished-for fellows—whither art flown?
Where lingerest thou in thy bereaved estate,
Like some lost star, or buried meteor stone?
Thou mindst me much of that presumptuous one
Who loth, aught less than greatest, to be great,
From heaven's immensity fell headlong down
To live forlorn, self-centered, desolate:
Or who, like Heraclid, hard exile bore,
Now buoyed by hope, now stretched on rack of fear
Till throned Astaea, wafting to his ear

Words of dim portent through the Atlantic roar,
Bade him "the sanctuary of the Muse revere
And strew with flame the dust of Isis' shore."

—J. J. SYLVESTER

PORTRAIT OF A MATHEMATICIAN

Sweep the pale hair, like wings, above the ears;
*   Whittle the nose, and carve and bone the jaw;*
Blank the studying eyes, till human fears
*   Eliminate in universal law.*

Slack the mortal shirt, stiffen the hands,
*   Holding the dear old pipe, half-smoked, unlit—*
So, lovingly, we loose Orion's Bands
*   And write equation with the Infinite.*

—CHRISTOPHER MORLEY

FROM *The Dunciad*

Mad Mathesis alone was unconfined,
Too mad for mere material chains to bind,
Now to pure space lifts her ecstatic stare,
Now, running round the circle, finds it square.

—ALEXANDER POPE

GEOMETRY

Yet may we not entirely overlook
The pleasure gathered from the rudiments

Of geometric science. Though advanced
In these inquiries, with regret I speak,
No farther than the threshold, there I found
Both elevation and composed delight:
With Indian awe and wonder, ignorance pleased
With its own struggles, did I meditate
On the relation those abstractions bear
To Nature's laws, and by what process led,
Those immaterial agents bowed their heads
Duly to serve the mind of earth-born man;
From star to star, from kindred sphere to sphere,
From system on to system without end.

More frequently from the same source I drew
A pleasure quiet and profound, a sense
Of permanent and universal sway,
And paramount belief; there, recognized
A type, for finite natures, of the one
Supreme Existence, the surpassing life
Which—to the boundaries of space and time,
Of melancholy space and doleful time,
Superior and incapable of change,
Nor touched by welterings of passion—is,
And hath the name of, God. Transcendent peace
And silence did await upon these thoughts
That were a frequent comfort to my youth.

'Tis told by one whom stormy waters threw,
With fellow sufferers by the shipwreck spared,
Upon a desert coast, that having brought
To land a single volume, saved by chance,
A treatise of Geometry, he wont,
Although of food and clothing destitute,
And beyond common wretchedness depressed,
To part from company and take this book
(Then first a self-taught pupil in its truths)
To spots remote, and draw his diagrams

With a long staff upon the sand, and thus
Did oft beguile his sorrow, and almost
Forget his feeling: so (if like effect
From the same cause produced, 'mid outward things
So different, may rightly be compared),
So was it then with me, and so will be
With Poets ever. Mighty is the charm
Of those abstractions to a mind beset
With images and haunted by herself,
And specially delightful unto me
Was that clear synthesis built up aloft
So gracefully; even then when it appeared
Not more than a mere plaything, or a toy
To sense embodied: not the thing it is
In verity, an independent world,
Created out of pure intelligence.

—From WILLIAM WORDSWORTH, *The Prelude*

Surd and Absurd

Surd and Absurd *will do as well as any other rubric for this group of lighter-than-air poems. I should dearly love to know the identity of the author of* Song of the Screw. *It has a Victorian flavor. (By the way, for a different handling of the same subject matter see the editor's* Fantasia Mathematica, *p. 40 ff.) The* Modern Hiawatha *I include as obviously the work of an unconscious topologist. Mr. Lister's* Song Against Circles *is a neat illustration of a truth surprising to some: that mathematics is quite capable of arousing many different kinds of emotions. The rhymed japeries by Frere and Canning and by Rankine are delightful examples of Victorian pedantic humor.*

ME

*I think that I shall never see
A calculator made like me.
A me that likes martinis dry
And on the rocks, a little rye.
A me that looks at girls and such,
But mostly girls, and very much.
A me that wears an overcoat
And likes a risky anecdote.*

Reprinted by permission of the author from *The Best from Fantasy and Science Fiction*. Copyright © 1959 by Mercury Press, Inc.

A me that taps a foot and grins
Whenever Dixieland begins.
They make computers for a fee,
But only moms can make a me.

—HILBERT SCHENCK, JR.

"Gentlemen, the operation of this complex computer is based upon a
very simple counting technique."

SONG OF THE SCREW

A moving form or rigid mass,
Under whate'er conditions
Along successive screws must pass
Between each two positions.
It turns around and slides along—
This is the burden of my song.

The pitch of screw, if multiplied
By angle of rotation,
Will give the distance it must glide
In motion of translation.
Infinite pitch means pure translation,
And zero pitch means pure rotation.

Two motions on two given screws,
With amplitudes at pleasure,
Into a third screw-motion fuse,
Whose amplitude we measure
By parallelogram construction
(A very obvious deduction).

Its axis cuts the nodal line
Which to both screws is normal,
And generates a form divine,
Whose name, in language formal,
Is "surface-ruled of third degree."
Cylindroid is the name for me.

Rotation round a given line
Is like a force along,
If to say couple you decline,
You're clearly in the wrong—

271

'Tis obvious, upon reflection,
A line is not a mere direction.

So couples with translations too
*   In all respects agree;*
And thus there centers in the screw
*   A wondrous harmony*
Of Kinematics and of Statics—
The sweetest thing in mathematics.

The forces on one given screw,
*   With motion on a second,*
In general some work will do,
*   Whose magnitude is reckoned*
By angle, force, and what we call
The coefficient virtual.

Rotation now to force convert,
*   And force into rotation;*
Unchanged the work, we can assert,
*   In spite of transformation.*
And if two screws no work can claim,
Reciprocal will be their name.

Five numbers will a screw define,
*   A screwing motion, six;*
For four will give the axial line,
*   One more the pitch will fix;*
And hence we always can contrive
One screw reciprocal to five.

Screws—two, three, four, or five, combined
*   (No question here of six),*
Yield other screws which are confined
*   Within one screw complex.*
Thus we obtain the clearest notion
Of freedom and constraint of motion.

In complex III, three several screws
  At every point you find,
Or if you one direction choose,
  One screw is to your mind;
And complexes of order III
Their own reciprocals may be.

In IV, wherever you arrive,
  You find of screws a cone,
On every line of complex V
  There is precisely one;
At each point of this complex rich,
A plane of screws have given pitch.

But time would fail me to discourse
  Of Order and Degree;
Of Impulse, Energy, and Force,
  And Reciprocity.
All these and more, for motions small,
Have been discussed by Dr. Ball.

—ANONYMOUS

THE MODERN HIAWATHA

He killed the noble Mudjokivis.
Of the skin he made him mittens,
Made them with the fur side inside
Made them with the skin side outside.
He, to get the warm side inside,
Put the inside skin side outside;
He, to get the cold side outside,
Put the warm side fur side inside.
That's why he put the fur side inside,

Why he put the skin side outside,
Why he turned them inside outside.

—AUTHOR UNKNOWN

THE LOVES OF THE TRIANGLES

[*A Parody of Erasmus Darwin's* Loves of the Plants]

Stay your rude steps, or e'er your feet invade
The Muses' haunts, ye Sons of War and Trade!
Nor you, ye Legion Fiends of Church and Law,
Pollute these pages with unhallow'd paw!
Debased, corrupted, groveling, and confined,
No DEFINITIONS *touch your senseless mind;*
To you no POSTULATES *prefer their claim,*
No ardent AXIOMS *your dull souls inflame;*
For you no TANGENTS *touch, no* ANGLES *meet,*
No CIRCLES *join in osculation sweet!*

For me, ye CISSOIDS, *round my temples bend*
Your wandering Curves; ye CONCHOIDS *extend;*
Let playful PENDULES *quick vibration feel,*
While silent CYCLOIS *rests upon her wheel;*
Let HYDROSTATICS, *simpering as they go,*
Lead the light Naiads on fantastic toe;
Let shrill ACOUSTICS *tune the tiny lyre;*
With EUCLID *sage fair* ALGEBRA *conspire;*
The obedient pulley strong MECHANICS *ply,*
And wanton OPTICS *roll the melting eye!*

I see the fair fantastic forms appear,
The flaunting drapery and the languid leer;
Fair Sylphish forms—who, tall, erect, and slim,

Dart the keen glance, and stretch the length of limb;
To viewless harpings weave the meanless dance,
Wave the gay wreath, and titter as they prance.

Such rich confusion charms the ravish'd sight,
When vernal Sabbaths to the Park invite;
Mounts the thick dust, the coaches crowd along,
Presses round Grosvenor Gate the impatient throng;
White-muslin'd misses and mammas are seen,
Link'd with gay Cockneys glittering o'er the green:
The rising breeze unnumber'd charms displays,
And the tight ankle strikes th' astonish'd gaze.

But chief, thou Nurse of the Didactic Muse,
Divine NONSENSIA, *all thy sense infuse;*
The charms of Secants and of Tangents tell,
How Loves and Graces in an Angle dwell;
How slow progressive Points protract the Line,
As pendant spiders spin the filmy twine;
How lengthened Lines, impetuous sweeping round,
Spread the wide Plane, and mark its circling bound;
How Planes, their substance with their motion grown,
Form the huge Cube, the Cylinder, the Cone.

. . . . .

'Twas thine alone, O youth of giant frame,
Isosceles! that rebel heart to tame!
In vain coy Mathesis thy presence flies,
Still turn her fond hallucinating eyes;
Thrills with Galvanic fires each tortuous nerve,
Throb her blue veins, and dies her cold reserve;
—Yet strives the fair, till in the Giant's breast
She sees the mutual passion flame confess'd:
Where'er he moves she sees his tall limbs trace
Internal Angles equal at the Base;
Again she doubts him: but produced at will,
She sees the external Angles equal still.

Say, blest Isosceles! what favoring pow'r,
Or love, or chance, at night's auspicious hour,
While to the Asses'-Bridge entranced you stray'd,
Led to the Asses'-Bridge the enamor'd maid?
—The Asses'-Bridge, for ages doom'd to hear
The deafening surge assault his wooden ear,
With joy repeats sweet sounds of mutual bliss,
The soft susurrant sigh, and gently-murmuring kiss.

—JOHN HOOKHAM FRERE and GEORGE CANNING,
in the *Anti-Jacobin, or Weekly Examiner* (1798)

THE MATHEMATICIAN IN LOVE

1

A mathematician fell madly in love
With a lady, young, handsome, and charming:
By angles and ratios harmonic he strove
Her curves and proportions all faultless to prove.
As he scrawled hieroglyphics alarming.

2

He measured with care, from the ends of a base,
The arcs which her features subtended:
Then he framed transcendental equations, to trace
The flowing outlines of her figure and face,
And thought the result very splendid.

3

He studied (since music has charms for the fair)
The theory of fiddles and whistles—
Then composed, by acoustic equations, an air,
Which, when 'twas performed, made the lady's long hair
Stand on end, like a porcupine's bristles.

4

The lady loved dancing—he therefore applied,
 To the polka and waltz, an equation;
But when to rotate on his axis he tried,
His center of gravity swayed to one side,
 And he fell, by the earth's gravitation.

5

No doubts of the fate of his suit made him pause,
 For he proved, to his own satisfaction,
That the fair one returned his affection—"because,
"As every one knows, by mechanical laws,
 "Reaction is equal to action."

6

"Let x *denote beauty—y, manners well-bred—*
 "Z, Fortune—(this last is essential)—
"Let L *stand for love"—our philosopher said—*
"Then L *is a function of* x, y, *and* z,
 "Of the kind which is known as potential."

7

"Now integrate L *with respect to d t,*
 "(t Standing for time and persuasion);
"Then, between proper limits, 'tis easy to see,
"The definite integral Marriage must be—
 "(A very concise demonstration)."

8

Said he—"If the wandering course of the moon
 "By Algebra can be predicted,
"The female affections must yield to it soon"—
—But the lady ran off with a dashing dragoon,
 And left him amazed and afflicted.

—W. J. M. RANKINE, *Songs and Fables* (1874)

$$E = MC^2$$

What was our trust, we trust not,
  What was our faith, we doubt;
Whether we must or must not
  We may debate about.
The soul perhaps is a gust of gas
  And wrong is a form of right—
But we know that Energy equals Mass
  By the Square of the Speed of Light.

What we have known, we know not,
  What we have proved, abjure.
Life is a tangled bowknot,
  But one thing still is sure.
Come, little lad; come, little lass;
  Your docile creed recite:
"We believe that Energy equals Mass
  By the Square of the Speed of Light."

—MORRIS BISHOP

ENGINEER'S YELL

E to the X dy! dx!
E to the X dx!

Secant, cosine, tangent, sine,
Three-point-one-four-one-five-nine;

Square root, cube root, QED.
Slip stick! slide rule!
  'ray, U.C.!

—AUTHOR UNKNOWN (University of California)

Reprinted by permission of Dial Press, Inc., from *A Bowl of Bishop* by Morris Bishop. Copyright 1954 by Morris Bishop.

Rhymes by Algebra

Martin Gardner, whose department in Scientific American *is eagerly read and who has been incessantly helpful in the preparation of this book, writes me that in W. S. Walsh's* Handy-Book of Literary Curiosities *there is a discussion of the difficulty of finding a rhyme for "month" and reports that Walsh includes this mathematical example:*

> *Youths who would senior wranglers be*
> *Must drink the juice distilled from tea,*
> *Must burn the midnight oil from month to month,*
> *Raising binomials to the n + 1th.*

The rhyme, says Walsh, has been attributed to the famous Whewell, the learned Master of Trinity College, another of whose masterpieces is quoted in my Fantasia Mathematica. *Mr. Gardner goes on to say that a friend of his, Stephen Barr, has written an improved version:*

> *The answer is, said Dr. North,*
> *Who's worked on it a month,*
> *Not simply x raised to the fourth,*
> *But x^{n+1}*

Note on θ, ϕ, and ψ

> *Whereas my lady loves to look*
> *On learned manuscript and book,*
> *Still must she scorn, and scorning sigh,*
> *To think of those I profit by.*

"Note on O . . ." reprinted by permission of *The New Statesman* of March 23, 1935.

Plotinus now, or Plutarch is
A prey to her exegesis,
And while she labors to collate
A page, I grasp a postulate,

And find for one small world of fact
Invariant matrices, compact
Within the dark and igneous rock
Of Comptes Rendus *or* Proc. Roy. Soc.

She'll pause a learned hour, and then
Pounce with a birdlike acumen
Neatly to annotate the dark
Of halting sense with one remark;

While I, maybe, precisely seize
The elusive photon's properties
In α*'s and* δ*'s, set in bronze-*
bright vectors, grim quaternions.

Silent we'll sit. We'll not equate
Symbols too plainly disparate,
But hand goes out to friendly hand
That mind and mind may understand

How one same passion burned within
Each learned peer and paladin,
Her Bentley and her Scaliger,
My Heisenberg and Schrödinger.

—MICHAEL ROBERTS

A Song Against Circles

The circle is a thing of cold perfection.
  Given the chance, a circle will go far,
But not in any definite direction,
  And never more or less than $2\pi r$.

Its impulses are never quite wholehearted.
  It starts, but like a traveler ill-prepared,
It soon comes back again to where it started,
  Having enclosed a space for πr^2.

—R. P. Lister

Wockyjabber

'Twas finite, and the polar cusp,
Orthogonal to the secant lay.
The semi-tacnode operates on
The Gudermanian of A.

"Beware the integral, my son,
With shape of non-symmetric bell,
Beware old Van der Pol, and shun
The curious vector del."

He took his program in his hand.
Long hours the real root he sought.
Then rested by the storage drums,
And sat awhile in thought.

And as in tedious thought he sat,
The integral without a name,

Rose from a skewed, conformal map,
Diverging as it came!

Pi-e, Pi-e, and x, y, z,
The digital went clicky-clack.
He found the norm in series form,
And brought the work sheets back.

"Oh, hast thou solved the integral?
Here is a raise, my brainish boy!"
He threw his time cards in the air
And clapped his hands with joy.

'Twas finite, and the polar cusp,
Orthogonal to the secant lay.
The semi-tacnode operates on
The Gudermanian of A.

—HILBERT SCHENCK, JR.

EINSTEIN: A PARODY IN THE MANNER OF EDW-N MARKH-M

We drew our circle that shut him out,
This man of Science who dared our doubt.
But ah, with a fourth-dimensional grin
He squared a circle that took us in.

—LOUIS UNTERMEYER

TENDING TO INFINITY

Once, tending to infinity,
A Doctor of Divinity
Collided with the Trinity.
  They said, "How do you do?"

He answered, "I have come so far,
From star to star, from star to star,
A little dizzy, under par.
  Is this where I tend to?"

They answered, "Your velocity
Cannot at most amount to c,
So you must voyage eternally.
  Adieu, good sir, adieu!"

—J. L. SYNGE

THE SUPERLATIVE DEGREE

A Square is something different
  From a Rube;
If he gets squarer, will he
  Be a Cube?

—EARNEST ELMO CALKINS

THE MAGIC BOX

Length, breadth, and depth are said to be
The limits of man's comprehension,
 But when I see the pile of junk
That she can get into a trunk

The mystery convinces me
That woman knows a fourth dimension.

—W. R. BAKER

PROFESSOR SODDY AND THE KISS PRECISE

Frederick Soddy was a distinguished English chemist and economist who in 1921 won the Nobel Prize in Chemistry. He is perhaps most famous for his investigation of isotopes, a word of his own coinage. Like many Englishmen, for example, Lewis Carroll, he saw no necessary oppositon between science and a sense of humor. Martin Gardner put me on to Soddy's delightful poem involving four tangential circles, as well as to Mr. Gosset's development of the theorem and Soddy's own rhymed extension of the theorem involving spheres. This appeared in Nature, *June 20, 1936.*

THE KISS PRECISE

For pairs of lips to kiss maybe
Involves no trigonometry.
'Tis not so when four circles kiss
Each one the other three.
To bring this off the four must be
As three in one or one in three.
If one in three, beyond a doubt
Each gets three kisses from without.
If three in one, then is that one
Thrice kissed internally.

Four circles to the kissing come.
The smaller are the benter.
The bend is just the inverse of

The distance from the center.
Though their intrigue left Euclid dumb
There's now no need for rule of thumb.
Since zero bend's a dead straight line
And concave bends have minus sign,
The sum of the squares of all four bends
Is half the square of their sum.

To spy out spherical affairs
An oscular surveyor
Might find the task laborious,
The sphere is much the gayer,
And now besides the pair of pairs
A fifth sphere in the kissing shares.
Yet, signs and zero as before,
For each to kiss the other four
The square of the sum of all five bends
Is thrice the sum of their squares.

—FREDERICK SODDY

In the January 9, 1937, issue of Nature *there appeared a fourth verse to* The Kiss Precise. *This, which generalizes Professor Soddy's equations to space of* n- *dimensions, flowed from the pen of Mr. Thorold Gosset of Cambridge. Here it is:*

THE KISS PRECISE (GENERALIZED)

And let us not confine our cares
To simple circles, planes and spheres,
But rise to hyper flats and bends
Where kissing multiple appears.
In n-ic space the kissing pairs
Are hyperspheres, and Truth declares—

As n + *2 such osculate*
Each with an n + *1 fold mate*
The square of the sum of all the bends
Is *n* times the sum of their squares.

—THOROLD GOSSET

In the December 5, 1936, issue of Nature *Professor Soddy revealed that he had again been bitten by the Muse. Herewith:*

THE HEXLET

However ill-assorted in girth three spheres may be
Each one can kiss the other two and simultaneously
A ring of six about them all kissing serially.

Though any necklet of graded beads
    May fit in general the she-sex,
This Hexlet of mine of novel design
    Caresses not one but three necks.
However it's worn it alters its grade
    To suit its tri-spherical prison,
Plays kiss-in-the-ring and merry-go-round
    Whilst hugging three necks with precision.
Like bubbles that blow and dwindle and go
    It holds up to light-hearted derision
The terrible muddle mathematical fuddle
    Makes of the pure circumflex
And its pet aversion is the mental inversion
    That will have "It's 1/x."

All saints and sages throughout the ages
    From one doxy never have swerved,
To hold fast unto what in change changes not
    And ferret out what is conserved.
Now these beads without flaw obey this first law

For the aggregate sum of their bends.
As each in the tunnel slims through the funnel
Its vis-à-vis *grossly distends.*
But the mean of the bends of each opposite pair
Is the sum of the three of the thoroughfare.

—FREDERICK SODDY

SHORT CUTS TO SUCCESS

(HOW IT WORKS:—In order to remember the value of π to thirty places of decimals you need only learn one of the following passages by heart. In both these passages each word, by the number of letters it contains, denotes a figure. The integer is purposely omitted. The integer is 3; those ignorant of this can remember it by committing to memory the initials of the contributor.)

$$\pi = 3.141592653589793238462643383279.$$

To Mr. H. Bailey

(who has to have recourse to Greek Iambics when
he wants to remember the value of π)

I nunc, O Baili, Parnassum et desere rupem;
1   4   1   5   9   2   6   5
  Dic sacra Pieridum deteriora quadris!
  3   5   8   9   7
Subsidium hoc ad vos, quamquam leve, fertur ab hymnis
9   3   2   3   8   4   6   2   6
  Quos dat vox Sophocli (non in utroque probrumst?)[1]
  4   3   3   8   3   2   7   9

[1] "Will you dare any longer, Bailey, to turn your back on Parnassus hill, telling us that the sacred rites of the Muses are less important than constructing squares? Here is aid brought to you, though it be but slight, by poetry, and poetry couched in the language of Sophocles—there is a double thrust at your vanity!"[2]

[2 The author, by request, made this translation many years later.]

ὁ παῖς ὁ κύκλῳ περιφορὰν πϱ γράφων[1]
1 4   1   5   9   2   6
οὐκ εὐθὺς ἠὐπόρησε διάμετρον μετροῦν.
3   5   8   9   7
ἀναλογίας γὰϱ ἦν μὲν εὔφορτον κάϱα,
9   3   2   3   8   4
ἀχηνία δὲ μνῆσις· ἀλλὰ νῦν ἔφη,
6   2   6   4   3   3
'σκέψασθε πῶς με Κνόξιος παρηγοϱεῖ.'
8   3   2   7   9

—The *Salopian, November* 1917

—RONALD A. KNOX

[1] ἰοῦ· διέλιπον πέντε γραμμάτων ἔπος.

A Group of Limericks

THE YOUNG LADY NAMED BRIGHT

In Fantasia Mathematica *I quoted this well-known limerick as follows:*

> There was a young lady named Bright,
> Who traveled much faster than light.
>   She started one day
>   In the relative way,
> And returned on the previous night.

I credited this, in the phrase of Walter de la Mare, to that "most modest of all men of genius, Mr. Anon." In David McCord's classic anthology What Cheer *I find the author given as one Helen Barton Tuttle. Since then, however, I have received an interesting communication from a citizen or citizeness of Winnipeg whose name is either Mel Stover or Mae Stover—the handwriting is entirely clear except for the signature. Mr. or Mrs. or Miss Stover informs me that the famous limerick was written by neither Anon. nor Helen Barton Tuttle, but by Professor A. H. Reginald Buller, F.R.S. Professor Buller was an eminent botanist at the University of Manitoba, one of the biggest mushroom men in the world. He published the limerick in* Punch, *received £2 for it and "was more excited at the check than he was later when his book on fungi was published." Later on, writes my courteous correspondent, after Einstein had extended his theory, Professor Buller wrote a sequel to the adventures of Miss Bright. This sequel I am happy to preserve for posterity.*

To her friends said the Bright one in chatter,
"I have learned something new about matter:
*   As my speed was so great*
*   Much increased was my weight,*
Yet I failed to become any fatter!"

THERE WAS AN OLD MAN WHO SAID, "DO . . ."

There was an old man who said, "Do
Tell me how I'm to add two and two?
*   I'm not very sure*
*   That it doesn't make four—*
But I fear that is almost too few."

—AUTHOR UNKNOWN

SNIP, SNIP

The topologist's mind came unguided
When his theories, some colleagues derided.
*   Out of Moebius strips*
*   Paper dolls he now snips,*
Non-Euclidean, closed, and one-sided.

—HILBERT SCHENCK, JR.

"WELL!—BACK TO THE OLD DRAWING BOARD."

The Young Man of Sid. Sussex

There was a young man of Sid. Sussex,
Who insisted that w + x
Was the same as xw;
So they said, "Sir, we'll trouble you
To confine that idea to Sid. Sussex."

—ARTHUR C. HILTON

Note: I learn from Mr. David McCord's fine anthology, What
Cheer, *where I originally found this, that the "Sid." in "Sid.*
Sussex" *is short for Sidney in Sidney Sussex, a Cambridge*
college.

Pun in Orbit

Said a rocket man, winking an eye,
"Into orbits computers must fly.
Now it might be more sound,
If they stayed on the ground,
But the people want π in the sky."

—HILBERT SCHENCK, JR.

A Mathematician Confided

A mathematician confided
That a Moebius band is one-sided.
And you'll get quite a laugh
If you cut one in half,
For it stays in one piece when divided.

—AUTHOR UNKNOWN

A Mathematician Named Klein

A mathematician named Klein
Thought the Moebius band was divine.
Said he, "If you glue
The edges of two,
You'll get a weird bottle like mine."

—Author Unknown

Three Random Points

❧

The first of these, Santayana's delightful ribbing of Josiah Royce and the school of absolute idealism, is to be found in his Character and Opinion in the United States. *It was pointed out to me by the late Gail Kennedy, Professor of Philosophy at Amherst College. If I grasp it properly, it is an example of reflexive paradox, of which amusing examples abound. One of the prettiest of these I came across in J. E. Littlewood's* A Mathematician's Miscellany. *Professor Littlewood mentions a* Spectator *competition, the assigned subject being: "What Would You Like Most to Read on Opening the Morning Paper?" The first prize was won by the following:*

Our Second Competition

The first prize in the second of this year's competitions goes to Mr. Arthur Robinson, whose witty entry was easily the best of those we received. His choice of what he would like to read on opening his paper was headed, "Our Second Competition," and was as follows: "The first prize in the second of this year's competitions goes to Mr. Arthur Robinson, whose witty entry was easily the best of those we received. His choice of what he would like to read on opening his paper was headed 'Our Second Competition,' but owing to paper restrictions we cannot print all of it."

THE MAP OF ENGLAND AND THE ABSOLUTE

ROYCE, however, in saying all this, also wished not to say it, and his two thick volumes on "The World and the Individual" leave their subject wrapped in utter obscurity. Perceiving the fact when he had finished, he very characteristically added a "Supplementary Essay" of a hundred more pages, in finer print, in which to come to the point. Imagine, he said, an absolutely exhaustive map of England spread out upon English soil. The map would be a part of England, yet it would reproduce every feature of England, including itself; so that the map would reappear on a smaller scale within itself an infinite number of times, like a mirror reflected in a mirror. In this way we might be individuals within a larger individual and no less actual and complete than he. Does this solve the problem? If we take the illustration as it stands, there is still only one individual in existence, the material England, all the maps being parts of its single surface; nor will it at all resemble the maps, since it will be washed by the sea and surrounded by foreign nations and not, like the maps, by other Englands enveloping it. If, on the contrary, we equalize the status of all the members of the series, by making it infinite in both directions, then there would be no England at all, but only map within map of England. There would be no absolute mind inclusive but not included, and the Absolute would be the series as a whole, utterly different from any of its members. It would be a series while they were maps, a truth while they were minds; and if the Absolute from the beginning had been regarded as a truth only, there never would have been any difficulty in the existence of individuals under it. Moreover, if the individuals are all exactly alike, does not their exact similarity defeat the whole purpose of the speculation, which was to vindicate the equal reality of the whole and of its *limited* parts? And if each of us, living through infinite time, goes through precisely the same experiences as everyone else, why this vain repetition? Is it not enough for this insatiable world to live its life once? Why not admit solipsism and be true to the transcendental method? Because of conscience and good sense? But then the infinite series of maps is useless, England is herself again, and the prospect opens before us of an infinite number of supplementary essays.

—GEORGE SANTAYANA

CUPID WITH AN ADDING MACHINE

MOST PEOPLE, particularly women, would say that statistics have very little to do with romance. But they would be wrong. Statistical chance enters into almost every phase of a person's love life, and often to a rather frightening degree.

Let's start from Boy Meets Girl and consider especially that fascinating custom known as the Blind Date. Now, you would expect that blind dates would have at least a fifty-fifty chance of working out well. So why is it that they so often fizzle? The statistician can tell you why. Statistically speaking, the average blind date has only one chance in four of success. Here are the four possible chances:

1. *Boy likes girl;*
girl does not like boy.

2. *Girl likes boy;*
boy does not like girl.

3. *Girl does not like boy*
boy does not like girl. (

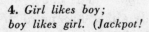

4. *Girl likes boy;*
boy likes girl. (Jackpot!

This table of chances should be a warning to inveterate match-makers (such as this writer's wife): think twice before trying to marry off your friends! Remember, it takes *more* than two to make a match—it takes two who happen to have the same favorable reaction. And that's a four-to-one bet!

But let us suppose that the blind date is a jackpot. What are the chances that it will produce wedding bells? Not as good as Cupid might wish—not right away, anyhow. A leading marriage survey shows that people who marry have generally known each other for at least two years.

Such a finding, coupled with the known fact that the average American female marries at about the age of twenty, suggests an interesting statistical theory:

The average American girl of eighteen already knows the boy she will marry!

If this theory seems to make romance too cut and dried, don't worry. Though statistics may suggest that she knows the boy she'll marry, statistics cannot suggest *which* boy! Only the statistics of her own celebrated intuition can decide this question, and even Einstein would never have dared contemplate the mathematics of a pretty young lady's mind.

But let us say that our average young lady reaches the age of twenty and marries. What are the chances of her presenting her average young husband with a boy? Exactly fifty-fifty. With a girl? Exactly fifty-fifty. *However, once a wife has produced a child, the laws of chance get cranky. If she has a girl first, there is no special chance that she'll balance up with a boy next time.* The laws of chance say that she has to start all over again, and her chance of producing a boy is still the same old fifty-fifty. This is one reason why parents should be thankful for whatever kind of brood statistics see fit to deal out.

What do all these facts and figures mean to a young couple in love? Probably very little. Go ahead and sign the license and drink a toast:

"Here's to Love and Mathematics!"

—CHARLES D. RICE

THE MINIVER PROBLEM

In that once famous wartime best-seller, Mrs. Miniver, *by Jan Struther, there is an interesting paragraph illustrating the way in which the language of mathematics may be used to illuminate life:*

She saw every relationship as a pair of intersecting circles. It would seem at first glance that the more they overlapped the better the relationship; but this is not so. Beyond a certain point the law of diminishing returns sets in, and there are not enough private resources left on either side to enrich the life that is shared. Probably perfection is reached when the area of the two outer crescents, added together, is exactly equal to that of the leaf-shaped piece in the middle. On paper there must be some neat mathematical formula for arriving at this; in life, none.

In L. A. Graham's Ingenious Mathematical Problems and Methods *there may be found a solution to the Miniver problem. Mr. Graham writes:*

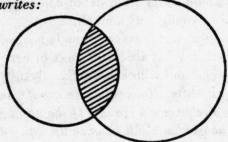

REMEMBERING THAT the two circles are rarely equal, what is the mathematical answer to Mrs. Miniver's enigma?

Mrs. Miniver's enigma of the life shared in the overlapping circles presented a transcendent problem, both social and mathematical. Miss Struther, author of *Mrs. Miniver*, had no idea that she was stirring up a mathematical hornets' nest when she wrote the lines quoted in the problem. Actually this turned out to be quite an interesting application of the geometry of sectors of circles and transcendental equations, expressing their relationships, as will be seen in the solution that follows by Mr. Wm. W. Johnson, of Cleveland:

"Let the areas of the circles of radii a and b be A_1 and A_2 $(a \leqq b)$, the area of the leaf be L, the area of the crescent of the smaller circle be C_1 and the area of the crescent of the larger circle be C_2. Then $L + C_1 = A_1$ and $L + C_2 = A_2$ whence $2L + C_1 + C_2 = A_1 + A_2$. For the perfection Mrs. Miniver envisions $L = C_1 + C_2$ whence $3L = A_1 + A_2$ and $L = (A_1 + A_2)/3$. As seen in Fig. 55B, the limit of L is A_1, whence $A_1 \geqq (A_1 + A_2)/3$ and therefore $A_2 \leqq 2A_1$. Thus it is seen that if the capacity of the

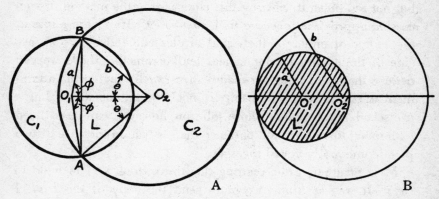

A   B

more capable of the two individuals concerned is more than twice that of the less capable, no ideal relationship can be realized. In case it is exactly twice, the less capable will be completely immersed in the other and no private resources will be left to that member of the pair. In the general case let the ratio of the larger to the smaller radius be $r = b/a$; then $r \leqq \sqrt{2}$ for the ideal condition to exist. If one arc side of the leaf subtends an angle 2θ at the center O_2 (Fig. 55A) of the larger circle and the other arc side of the leaf subtends an angle 2Φ at the center O_1 of the other circle, then it is seen from the figure that L = sector O_2AB — triangle O_2AB + sector O_1AB — triangle O_1AB, so that for ideal conditions when $3L = A_1 + A_2$, $L = b^2\theta + a^2\Phi - b$ $\sin \theta$ (a $\cos\Phi$ + b $\cos\theta$) = π ($a^2 + b^2$)/3. But b $\sin \theta$ = a $\sin\Phi$, whence a $\cos \Phi = \sqrt{a^2 - b^2\sin^2\theta}$, so that $b^2\theta + a^2$ *arcsin* (b $\sin \theta$)/a -- b $\sin \theta$ (b $\cos \theta + \sqrt{a^2 - b^2\sin^2\theta}$) = π ($a^2 + b^2$)/3; or since b/a = r, the equation in terms of the unknown angle θ is $r^2\theta$ + arcsin (r sin θ) -- r $\sin\theta$ (r $\cos\theta + \sqrt{1 - r^2\sin^2\theta}$) = π $(1 + r^2)$/3. This is the equation that must be solved for θ when the ratio r is given. In a given case this transcendental equation could only be solved by trial involving much time and patience. Thus instead of a neat mathematical formula for the solution, mathematics remains true to the social problem by presenting a situation of transcendent difficulty for an ideal solution. In the special case of a perfect mating, r = 1 and our equation becomes $2\theta - \sin 2\theta = 2\pi/3$. Even this equation is transcendental but not too difficult. Solving this equation by the method of successive approximations, we find $2\theta = 149° 16.3'$, the angle at the center of either of the equal circles subtended by one arc side of the common symmetrical leaf. From the above we can deduce that even when two people are exactly mated the attainment of an ideal relationship is not a mundane affair but a transcendental problem whose solution, however, can be realized with much less effort and patience than is true in the case of two people unequally yoked together."

Miss Struther, after reading the above, took pen in hand to say: "It was so kind of you to send the copy of the *Dial*. I enjoyed looking at it, and I was interested to see the solution of Mrs. Miniver's problem. I'm afraid the mathematics are a bit highbrow for me, but I'll take your word for them."

—JAN STRUTHER AND L. A. GRAHAM

About the Author

Clifton Fadiman's reputation as essayist, editor, critic, anthologist and radio and television personality has long been established. He is one of the judges of the Book-of-the-Month Club. His anthologies, Reading I've Liked, The American Treasury, *and* Fantasia Mathematica *are known to many readers, as are his books of essays,* Party of One, Any Number Can Play *and* Enter Conversing. *One of his outstanding recent successes is his guide to the great books of the Western world,* The Lifetime Reading Plan.

Mr. Fadiman is on the board of editors of the Encyclopaedia Britannica *and is a member of the board of directors of the* Council for Basic Education.